Public Administration Illuminated and Inspired by the Arts

REGNO

REGNABO

REGNAVI

SUM SINE REGNO

ADAPTATION OF
THE WHEEL OF FORTUNE

The ink drawing, "Adaptation of the Wheel of Fortune," was created by Joanne Kontopirakis.

PUBLIC ADMINISTRATION ILLUMINATED AND INSPIRED BY THE ARTS

Edited by
Charles T. Goodsell
and
Nancy Murray

Westport, Connecticut
London

Library of Congress Cataloging-in-Publication Data

Public administration illuminated and inspired by the arts / edited by
    Charles T. Goodsell and Nancy Murray.
        p. cm.
    Includes bibliographical references and index.
    ISBN 0–275–94806–4 (alk. paper)
    1. Public administration. 2. Bureaucracy. 3. Arts. 4. Arts and
society. I. Goodsell, Charles T. II. Murray, Nancy.
JF1411.P778 1995
350—dc20   94–36666

British Library Cataloguing in Publication Data is available.

Library of Congress Catalog Card Number: 94–36666
ISBN: 0–275–94806–4

First published in 1995

Praeger Publishers, 88 Post Road West, Westport, CT 06881
An imprint of Greenwood Publishing Group, Inc.

Printed in the United States of America

The paper used in this book complies with the
Permanent Paper Standard issued by the National
Information Standards Organization (Z39.48–1984).

10 9 8 7 6 5 4 3 2

Copyright Acknowledgments

Excerpt from *John Brown's Body* by Stephen Vincent Benét. Copyright 1927, 1928 by
Stephen Vincent Benét. Copyright © 1954, 1955 by Rosemary Carr Benét. Reprinted by
permission of Henry Holt and Company, Inc.

Seven lines from "Young Lincoln" from *Poems of Edwin Markham*, selected and arranged
by Charles L. Wallis. Copyright 1950 by Virgil Markham. Copyright renewed. Reprinted by
permission of HarperCollins Publishers, Inc.

Excerpt from *The People, Yes* by Carl Sandburg, copyright 1936 by Harcourt Brace &
Company and renewed 1964 by Carl Sandburg, reprinted by permission of the publisher.

Quotations from *One Flew Over the Cuckoo's Nest* by Ken Kesey. Copyright © 1962, 1990
by Ken Kesey. Used by permission of Viking Penguin, a division of Penguin Books USA
Inc. Reprinted by permission of Sterling Lord Literistic, Inc. Copyright © 1962 by Ken
Kesey.

For my sister, Jo Goodsell

For my husband, Bob Bott

Contents

Preface

A few years ago the field of American public administration celebrated a centennial, if we think of Woodrow Wilson as its founder—or a bicentennial, if we see Alexander Hamilton in that capacity. In any case, the field has changed radically over these stretches of time. Whereas two centuries ago it began as a form of political economy and one century ago it turned inward toward public management, at the end of our tumultuous current century the field is exploding in a dozen different substantive, normative, and epistemological directions.

The great diversity and vitality being shown in what was once considered a dull subject is indeed encouraging. When future historians of the field attempt to unravel the proliferation of ideas and approaches, they may run across one particularly interesting development, occurring almost exactly fifty years ago. This was the appearance, in the field's brand new journal *Public Administration Review*, of commentary on the potential importance of fiction—particularly novels—for a deeper understanding of the practice of public administration. Since that time a relatively small but highly provocative literature has developed on what became known as "administrative fiction."

The purpose of this volume is to carry this line of literature to a new level. This is done by making four advances. First, we see novels and short fiction as only one avenue toward the greater comprehension of the intricate and subtle nature of administrative work. Additional enrichment can be found in film, drama, poetry, classical literature, visual art, and aesthetic theory. In other words, we see all of the applied and fine arts in the Western tradition as potential contributors to understanding and practicing public administration.

Second, we believe that, due to the increasingly diverse nature of contemporary society, government is becoming socially complex to an unprecedented degree. This situation requires scholars writing in public administration to broaden their knowledge base by delving into conceptual territory that is not traditional to Western thought. Hence scholarly research is needed that applies to administration the arts of cultures other than those of the West. The potential contribution of Eastern cultures to Western public administration is but one example of how other bodies of knowledge can enrich our own.

Third, we believe that the time has come to approach contributions of the arts to administration in a more systematic way. In this book we lay out a simple framework for thinking about relationships between these two apparently disparate spheres. One assumption we make is that art's contribution to administration is quite different from administration's contribution to art. The latter entails what is known as "arts management," a subfield already well established, with several graduate programs operating around the country. As for the converse direction of influence, the one about which this book is concerned, we suggest five connecting points as a way to frame the influx of potentially enriching contributions. These connectors are called "bridges" for the sake of a concrete metaphor familiar to us all.

The fourth way in which the book seeks to carry the subject to a new plane is its methodology. In the past, almost all commentaries on the contributions of liberal learning to public administration have come from scholars within the field of public administration itself. While we believe that the perspectives of public administration scholars are essential to the enterprise, we also think that the insights of scholars from the arts have something to offer. In other words, a broadening and strengthening of this interdisciplinary work is best accomplished by all those who perceive new connections, regardless of their academic orientation.

Hence the editors designed this book in a way that seeks, quite consciously, to integrate administrative and artistic knowledge in different ways. Exactly half of its fourteen chapters (1–3, 5, 6, 12, 14) are written by public administration scholars or practitioners seeking to relate their field to the arts. The writers of these chapters have used our "bridges" to import ideas from outside the field's traditional academic purview, so to speak. By contrast, five other chapters (7–11) are by individuals who are writing primarily as scholars of the arts. Their function is to utilize the bridges to export into the field of public administration a flow of ideas from their distinctly different perspectives. Finally, two chapters (4 and 13) provide disciplinary intermingling in yet another way: they have been coauthored by administration and literature scholars working together. These chapters might be said to have been prepared at the bridges themselves.

As the field of public administration continues to explode in the coming century, then, it is our hope that this book will help boost into orbit a rich set of fresh insights from the world of the arts for those who do the public's work.

We wish to make several acknowledgments for help in preparing this volume. For general intellectual inspiration in the endeavor, we must thank Dwight Waldo. Dr. Waldo began the first serious inquiry into this subject nearly forty years ago. As all students of public administration know, his influence on the development of the field has been of epic proportions, with his work on administrative fiction but a small segment of the pioneering work he has done all across the discipline.

The event that precipitated this volume was a conference conducted at Pace University in White Plains, New York, in April, 1991. Its theme was "Administrative Leadership: Lessons from Liberal Learning." The conference was organized by Nancy Murray and attended by Charles Goodsell, their joint presence thus laying the basis, in retrospect, for an eventual publishing partnership. Several other contributors to this book also attended, and the chapters in Part IV originated as papers delivered at the conference. The event was initially suggested by Ernestine S. Pantel, chair of the department of public administration at Pace from 1989 to 1991. Joseph Houle, director of the Center for Applied Ethics at Pace in 1991, supported it financially. Drs. Pantel and Houle are hereby warmly thanked for their indirect but highly important contributions to this book.

Each of the editors has individuals to thank in addition. Charles Goodsell wishes to thank Edward Artinian for his professional advice with respect to appropriate publishing outlets. He also thanks Holly Fechtmeyer, assistant vice president of Christie's, New York, and Dee Ann Mims, instructor, Center for Programs in the Humanities, Virginia Tech, for their guidance on specific arts matters. Martha Dede, a doctoral candidate at the Center for Public Administration and Policy of Virginia Tech and experienced editor, provided invaluable editing assistance at both the beginning and the concluding stages of the project. Under her skillful direction a number of word-processing problems were solved at the last minute and final logistical details worked out.

Charles Goodsell also wishes to acknowledge the office support received for the project in the 1991–92 academic year from the Levin College of Urban Affairs of Cleveland State University, and in the 1992–93 and 1993–94 years from the Center for Public Administration and Policy of Virginia Tech. Thanks are also due Tracey J. Bennett for some special final typing of the manuscript. Finally, thanks are expressed to Liz Goodsell for reading the manuscript for errors and for being the human being she is.

Nancy Murray is grateful to Charles Masiello, dean of the Dyson College of Arts and Sciences of Pace University, for his support of her scholarly endeavors, including a course reduction for a key semester. She expresses appreciation to Joseph Morreale, chair of Pace's department of public administration, for consistent encouragement as well. Anthony Cupaiuolo, director of the Edwin G. Michaelian Institute for Public Policy and Management at Pace, has provided opportunity for increased understanding of Eastern approaches to administration via interaction with local Japanese officials.

Others whose help is acknowledged by Nancy Murray include Heriberto Dixon of the New School for Social Research, who brought the Wheel of Fortune to her attention; staff of the School of Visual Arts in New York City, for bringing her into contact with the artist Joanne Kontopirakis; Iason Iasonides, her research assistant; the staff of Pace's department of public administration and Michaelian Institute, especially Susan Sebring, Lorraine Monaco, Kathleen DuPerrousel, Clara Swee, and Chris Thorne; and finally her husband, Bob Bott, for always being there, and her children, Roberta and Jonathan Bott, for listening patiently to discourses on Eastern metaphysics.

Part I
Making Connections Between the Spheres

Prologue: Building New Bridges

Charles T. Goodsell and Nancy Murray

A PAINTED VISION

Imagine yourself in an art gallery, looking at a grouping of four large, allegorical landscape paintings. They are executed in the literal style of the Hudson River School landscape painters of the early nineteenth century, full of detail as well as scope. As in Thomas Cole's great series paintings, each landscape represents a different point in time.

The first painting shows a swift river dividing two pieces of land. Spanning the river between them is a narrow, swinging bridge. In this daytime view, one can see that the land on each side of the river has been put to simple, agrarian use. On one side of the river the flat plains between the hillsides are plowed with perfectly straight furrows. Orchards and vegetable plots are divided into neat, isolated squares. Pathways between them are straight and direct, and along them peasants move back and forth to their labors.

The land on the other side of the river presents a quite different scene. Cleverly terraced furrows curve around the hillsides. Vegetables grow in gracefully placed beds, with clumps of fruit trees interspersed. Workers walk along meandering pathways, at whose intersections benches are placed for rest and a pleasant view. Common areas with fire pits at their centers border the riverbank.

We turn now to the second painting of the group. It is the same scene, at evening. On the side of the river with the more linear and regularized arrangements, the workers and their families are resting from their labors or doing chores prior to retiring to their huts. On the river's other side, the villagers are gathered about their communal areas, singing, playing lutes, and dancing in the firelight. Group storytelling appears to be taking place around the campfires.

The third landscape of the set provides another daytime scene. It is similar to the first, except that several sturdy bridges have been built across the river. Now it is possible for those living on both banks to cross the river safely and in large numbers. They are doing so, conversing and gesturing with individuals from the other side. Within small gatherings demonstrations are being given of lute playing and wood carving, and there is more storytelling.

In the fourth and final allegorical landscape of the series, at twilight, one can see in the glowing light of the setting sun that the land whose features were linear and divided is now transformed. Like its counterpart across the river, it has terraced farming, interspersed plantings, and curvilinear beds and paths, albeit arranged in new forms. Villagers on the altered side are preparing for craft and musical events around campfires. They appear to be preparing for a festival, to which their friends across the river must be invited.

This painted vision represents the plan for this book. It also reveals the book's hope for the field of public administration. To us, public administration, as a field of academic study and realm of management and policy practice, has since its origins been cut off, for the most part, from a rich source of cultural nourishment. This source is the humane, provocative, imagination-firing qualities of the arts, both fine and applied. While some meager connections and limited crossover points have long existed between public administration and the arts, these have not been sufficient to allow liberated movement between the two spheres.

The intention of this book is to build conceptual bridges between these spheres and provide concrete examples that will encourage a more heavily traversed set of connecting points between administration and the arts. Its purpose in so doing is not merely to create stimulation and enjoyment, as worthy as such motivation may be, but to infuse the theory and practice of public administration with what we believe are substantial, long-term benefits. The strong technocratic and managerial emphases that tend to mark the field can be meaningfully supplemented. Administrators can learn more deeply about themselves and their organizations. Theorists of administration can receive stimulation from new ideas, new language, new symbols.

In the final scene of our painted vision, the formerly linear land with its utilitarian society was, as a result of becoming well connected to the opposite shore, enriched. The title of the book alludes to two ways in which the arts can enrich public administration. First, using the metaphor of light, the arts can illuminate the study and practice of public administration. This illumination allows its greater possibilities to be "seen" and thereby pursued. Second, alluding to the potentialities of the human spirit, the study and practice of public administration can be inspired by the arts.

The illuminating and inspiring capacities of the arts lie both in how people think about art, which is the study of aesthetics, and in the content of art itself, that is, concrete works that we see, hear, read, and feel. These contributions come in part from "high" or classic art, for example, learned discussions of aesthetic philosophy and the great novels, plays, poems, and edifices. They can also derive from the artistic content of popular culture, such as the best of motion pictures, television programs, and entertainment fiction. Even an everyday ritual like the Japanese tea ceremony is, we believe, capable of illuminating and inspiring administration.

This idea may jar those accustomed to orthodox approaches to public administration. The book departs from the general norms of the field in rejecting a purely instrumental or utilitarian view of the field. It looks beyond the social and natural sciences—the field's customary sources for interdisciplinary stimulation—to the arts and humanities. While such an approach to the field is by no means confined to this book, as will be pointed out below, we hope to explore the interplay of art and administration with added rigor, more elaboration, wider scope, and greater imagination than has been done in the past.

The proposition that we draw seriously and in a sustained way on the arts to enhance the study and practice of public administration will be considered idealistic or "far out" by many. The tendency of most students and doers of the field, as well as those of other practical and applied fields, is to regard the arts as belonging to a self-contained and rather elitist cultural world that is quite apart from the hurly-burly of conducting the public's business. Professional attention to painting, classical music, stage drama, opera, and the ballet is seen primarily as the province of artists and their associates, with the public bureaucrat limited to an occasional visit to the concert hall or museum.

These doubts notwithstanding, this book seeks to make the case that conceptual bridges can be built over the perceived gulfs and incongruities separating the two spheres; valuable contributions to the individual and collective levels of public administration can be transported across these bridges; and that the applied, practical, and instrumental processes and products of administration can be infused with insight and inspiration from the processes and products of artistic achievement.

THE BRIDGES TO BE BUILT

We propose that five conceptual bridges be built across the chasm that is usually seen as separating public administration and the arts. It is across these bridges that the opportunities for the enrichment of administration can be carried, in our view, just as occurred across the allegorical river of our imagined landscapes.

The first bridge relates to public administration theory. It is our view that the theoretical development of our field can benefit substantially from exposure to the theory and philosophy of aesthetics, broadly defined. While aesthetic inquiry is manifestly intended to comprehend beauty and to consider the individual's place in that abstraction, it can have application to the practical affairs of administration, often by analogy. We refer to this connecting point between the arts and public administration as the Theory Bridge.

A second bridge pertains to the values that infuse public bureaucracies. The foundations of this Values Bridge have already been laid by others. For several decades, a number of commentators in the field have made the point that the study of administration benefits from reading fiction. As will be spelled out below, they argue that novels and other forms of fiction on administrative subjects can teach us insights not normally attainable in texts or classrooms. We agree fully, and stress that one of fiction's most important contributions is to translate into concrete form such norm-laden abstractions as power, ambition, survival, caring, and vision. Expressed differently, such literature has the capacity to animate identified values in administration, whether they be stated derogatorily (e.g., "empire building") or approvingly (e.g., "institution building").

A third connector, which we call the Leadership Bridge, enables us to bring alive the pathos and humanity of individual leaders depicted in the arts, particularly literature but also film and video. Great women and men, as well as greatly evil women and men, of course abound in fiction and biography. The finest of literature, as by a Shakespeare or Cervantes, makes vivid the multidimensionality, complexity, and ambiguity of human conduct. Here, then, is another contribution from administrative fiction: a deeper understanding of the ways—impressive, abhorrent, and temporizing—by which organizational leaders face the normative tensions and dilemmas of their daily work. To organizational outsiders, this can be eye-opening; to the leaders themselves, it can serve as a stimulus for reflection and self-examination.

The fourth bridge relates to the outcomes of administration, public policy. One might think that this Policy Bridge would be relatively weak, for the outcomes of democratic processes are thought of as the product of very crass and mundane influences, far removed from something as esoteric as the arts. The arts seem exceedingly distant from the strategizing of elected officials, the pleadings of pressure groups, or the conduct of rational analysis by experts. Yet all of these efforts to make policy take place in a democracy, in the arena of broader public discourse. Here, influences build not merely from attempts to control but also from the subtle and unpredictable flow of ideas. At times the trends of popular culture or even works of fine art may set the stage for emergence of "an idea whose time has come." Key novels decisively shaped public opinion on the abolition of slavery and the regulation of meatpackers, for example. Dramatic paintings of the American West stimulated settlement beyond the plains and the creation of national parks. In more recent times, the popularity of science fiction set the stage for space exploration, as we shall see.

The Teaching Bridge is the fifth and final connector between public administration and the arts. Teaching is clearly a subject of great moment to practitioners as well as to educators, because it affects who enters the public service with what capacities and aspirations. Enthusiasts of administrative fiction have argued for some years that one of the few ways we have to transmit the subtleties of administrative processes to novice students in an otherwise sterile classroom is through novels or film. We agree wholeheartedly. The vividness and concreteness of these media of learning cannot help but buttress traditional pedagogical methods. The only question is how to identify the best possible materials for this purpose and present them imaginatively.

These five bridges, then, designed to connect the ostensibly unrelated spheres of the arts and public administration, form the conceptual framework of this book. They can also be seen in the book's organizational framework. The parts of the book correspond to the bridges even though individual chapters may touch on all of them. The Theory Bridge is emphasized in the two chapters forming Part II. The Values Bridge is particularly stressed in the essays comprising Part III. The Leadership Bridge is the unifying theme of Part IV, whose chapters draw understandings for administration from powerful literary characters or historical figures. The Policy and Teaching Bridges are crossed primarily in Part V.

Part VI draws on the connections made across all five bridges to synthesize the book's content regarding enrichment of public administration by means of ideas and works from the arts.

ADMINISTRATIVE FICTION

The existing literature on administrative fiction as a tool for understanding public administration has been mentioned. It helps to lay the foundations for our Values, Leadership, and Teaching bridges. We now briefly review and comment on this literature, constituting as it does the predecessor work for this book. A somewhat comparable literature exists in the field of business management.[1]

Academic discussion of administrative fiction related to the public sector is often traced to a 1924 article by Humbert Wolfe. In this pioneering essay, "Some Public Servants in Fiction," Wolfe examines how public servants are portrayed in English novels. He concludes that two quite unflattering types can be found: the "mandarin-cum-parasite" who wields power for its own sake, and the victim of the bureaucratic system who is "relegated to penal servitude for life."[2]

Discussion in the United States of public-sector administrative fiction started with a series of reviews of novels, published in the 1940s in *Public Administration Review (PAR)*. The reviewers, who included such eminent scholars as Rowland Egger and Stephen Bailey, argued that, in a manner radical for that time, the novels actually spoke more truth about public administration than did much of the professional literature. The first such review was Rowland Egger's 1944 essay on John Hersey's *A Bell for Adano*, the World War II story of how a major in the Allied military government administered a small Italian seaport during the early days of the occupation. Egger says caustically:

In 269 pages of simple, beautiful, vivid fiction, Hersey has said more that is valid for all sincere and humble men everywhere who are honestly attempting to discharge their administrative mandates than is contained in all the pompous tomes which have so far appeared on the subject of public administration.[3]

Five years later *PAR* published a review by Stephen Bailey of Pat Frank's State Department thriller, *An Affair of State*, followed by another review by Egger, of George Stewart's *Fire*, the story of a forest fire in a fictional national park. Bailey, a political scientist, began his review thus:

Whether we care to admit it or not, most cartoonists, many novelists, poets, and playwrights, some painters and musicians, and even a few literary critics have a far deeper insight into political man, or more accurately, into man in a political or administrative context, than all but a thimbleful of political scientists and public administration experts.[4]

The first systematic examination of administrative fiction as a topic of inquiry was undertaken, not surprisingly, by the field's savant, Dwight Waldo. In a chapter in his 1956 book *Perspectives on Administration*, Waldo contends that literary treatments of governmental life provide the reader with a number of valuable insights. These include a deeper understanding of the administrative world, exposure to settings not directly experienced by the reader, the benefit of outsiders' views, a cathartic release, a more rounded view of life, the psychological and moral "feel" of decision making, and "a Wisdom it is impossible to get from the professional writings." In light of these advantages, Waldo asserts that fictional literature "complements and supplements" what we can learn from scholarly sources, yet "does not replace or nullify" professional writings.[5]

A dozen years later Waldo reassessed his position on the subject. In a monograph on novelists' treatments of organization and administration, he states that although the advantages of such literary works remain, they are countered by a tendency for the fiction writer "to be increasingly negative, hostile, destructive." These words were written, it is important to note, in the turbulence of Berkeley of the 1960s. Because authors of fiction are so alienated from government and the establishment in general, Waldo felt, their treatment of administrators is one-sided and overcritical. This leads Waldo to suggest what is in effect a kind of two-worlds thesis: artists such as the novelist are instinctively "anti," as he calls them, whereas social scientists studying the world seek "to go forward." To resolve the difference between the two, Waldo proposed a "sidewise" direction of collaboration—"creative imagination combined with scientific probing and testing."[6]

To some extent the rising interest in fiction as a tool of understanding directly challenged the premises of logical positivism that undergirded social science behavioralism at this time. Egger, an outspoken opponent of attempts to study politics scientifically, praised administrative fiction as a way to preserve humanistic social inquiry in the face of a "mensurative" and philistine behavioralism. Howard McCurdy, one of this volume's contributors, argued that fiction may actually help replace a dying positivism, in that it gives us more insight into subjective reality than does the new wave of phenomenological study. Echoing McCurdy, Thomas McDaniel wrote that the administrative novel provides a useful way to derive "meaning" from the essentially subjective processes of administration.[7]

Another issue to emerge was one's general normative posture with respect to the public administrator and organized bureaucracies. As we saw, Wolfe's conceptual models of the bureaucrat were pejorative, depicting that person as either parasite or slave. H. J. Friedsam, in a 1954 article in *Social Forces*, wrote that the novelists' bureaucrat is more properly seen as a tragic hero, caught in an irreconcilable bind between organizational imperatives on the one hand and a craving for intellectual freedom on the other. Waldo, suggesting that the negative portrayals of government embody biases as well as insights, lamented that novelists seem automatically to present a hostile, destructive, and presumably unfair picture of public officials and public bureaucracy. McCurdy notes that with the exception of John Hersey in *A Bell for Adano*, most administrative novelists are attracted to government as an instrument of reform but then turn against it in its administrative manifestations.[8]

A reader of administrative writings compiled under the leadership of another of our contributors, Marc Holzer, utilizes an overtly normative framework for its analysis. Assuming that fictional treatments of bureaucracy are negative, Holzer and his associates introduced their book with a "Matrix of Concern in Fiction." By means of this, one is enabled to categorize "Pessimistic Views of Administration's Impact on Individual Values." Examples of the categories given are "stifling," "demoralizing/corrupting," "impersonal," and "unjust." The authors conclude that "if administrative fiction is, on the whole, pessimistic, then we should try to understand why. Those of us most concerned with administration should perhaps squirm more and smile less at the messages fiction contains."[9]

Each reader will come to this volume with his or her own values and images with respect to bureaucracy, and will no doubt depart from it with just as much divergence of viewpoint. Indeed, the contributors to this book vary considerably in their normative approach. The point is not whether the arts will tell us conclusively whether in reality bureaucracy is "good" or "bad," but rather that they help us look more deeply into its virtues and maladies, depending on which "reality" we choose to examine. In any case, our book assumes that the administrative system is worth illuminating for all that it may be—and that those who work within it are worth inspiring, for all that they may become.

We turn, in the remainder of this chapter, to selected examples of art that illuminate and inspire public administration. We do this to show how our five connecting bridges can be crossed. Three examples have been chosen. They are deliberately diverse, so as to demonstrate the range of pertinent kinds of art. The first is Homer's epic poem the *Odyssey*, one of the oldest narrative works in Western literature. The second is the Wheel of Fortune, a much repeated graphic image from the Middle Ages. The third, taken from popular entertainment, is the motion picture *Star Wars*, one of the more influential films of our time.

CROSSINGS: THE ODYSSEY

The era of Odysseus was before recorded history, probably in the Bronze Age. It was a time of intense chaos fueled by violence and dangerous forces vying for supremacy. Society was organized without national boundaries, and individuals were defined by the cities or the tribes to which they belonged. Odysseus was a member of a powerful tribe called the Achaeans. Like other tribes, the Achaeans were led by a king who relied upon the princes of cities and clans to carry out his dictates.

We discuss the relationships between this great literary classic and contemporary public administration in terms of four of our bridges: Theory, Values, Leadership, and Teaching.

The Theory Bridge

The *Odyssey* is a superb example of mythic exposition. The point of this for public administration theory is that the power of myth is not irrelevant to the day-to-day running of a government.

What do we mean by "myth"? In one sense, a myth is a pervasive falsehood usually not recognized as such. An example in our field is the notion that bureaucracy in America is generally incompetent. We are not employing this meaning here. Instead, "myth" is used in its larger sense, which is that of a higher truth—whose validity is greater than simple historical or factual accuracy. An illustration from our field is the politics–administration dichotomy. We all know that politics and administration completely intermingle; yet the higher truth is that the people, through their elected representatives, must ultimately control the career bureaucracy.

The *Odyssey* is a great mythic poem about a hero's quest. It tells the story of the hero, Odysseus, and the divine heroine, Pallas Athene. Being a man of his time, Odysseus believed in and fulfilled his role as prince of the city. As a good prince, his duty was to lead his men in frequent clashes with neighboring clans. Committed to the tradition of becoming a conquering hero acclaimed for his daring and supreme courage, Odysseus was ready for the challenge. When it was decided to avenge the kidnapping of the Achaean princess Helen by the Trojan prince Paris, the men of Ithaca joined forces to lay siege to the city of Troy. His legendary wiles, indomitable will, and broad shoulders served Odysseus well in the long, hard battle that ended with an Achaean victory.

Public administrators, too, engage in visionary quests, make daring choices, and—occasionally—overcome adversities in such a way as to deserve being thought of as heroines and heroes. Fred Kramer argues that there are two levels on which Odysseus's quest has meaning for modern public administration.[10] One is the metaphors it provides for organizational and policy struggles, such as capturing Troy by means of the wooden horse. The deeper meaning, says Kramer, is how the poem represents the journey a human being makes to self-understanding. Homer teaches us, by means of that epic journey, the great truth that a person must grow, develop, and learn from experience—often under conditions of great adversity. This process can be most humbling but, in the end, is potentially uplifting. The professional public administrator, if committed to fulfillment of her or his potential, must take a long personal journey, thereby identifying with an ancient mythical colleague.

The Values Bridge

Homer's great poem also animates essential values of public administration. In his many years of journey and travail between Troy and Ithaca, Odysseus had to exhibit nearly every form of steadfastness and courage. His experiences required reactions not unlike the savvy and dedication required of any good public servant of high responsibility. The good bureaucrat must ward off the seductive lure of lotus flowers in the form of postemployment conflict of interest. The decision maker must steer between the Scylla and Charybdis of competing public goods. The successful mover of a program must overwhelm and escape the cave of Cyclopsian pressure groups.

Odysseus's wife, Penelope, directed their son, Telemachus, to set sail to look for him. But the inexperienced young man was not prepared for the task. Mentor, left behind by Odysseus to look after the palace and grounds in his absence, in a way steps into the breach when Athena assumes

Mentor's appearance and accompanies Telemachus on the journey. Along the way, "Mentor" gives Telemachus the encouragement necessary to mature and function as a responsible adult. The valued process of "mentoring" is still with us in public administration.

The Leadership Bridge

Like leaders today, Odysseus was a man of immense complexity whose personality exhibited a broad range of behaviors. He was neither saint nor sinner, but immensely human. Capable of potential greatness and personal destruction, he wandered for nine years after the end of the Trojan War before being held captive on the island of Ogygia, by the nymph Calypso. Subjected to great temptations and insurmountable problems visited upon him by the inscrutable gods, Odysseus had a perilous journey indeed. For over 2,000 years, the trials of this archetypal hero have inspired leaders in many walks of life to transcend the difficulties of their situations and see the world in a different light.

The pages of the *Odyssey* are alive with ambiguity and difficult choices. Leaders in public administration often walk a narrow path between their own policy wishes and the instructions of political superiors. Like Odysseus, they possess flaws of character, and some even become tragic figures. The pathos and humanity of Odysseus are mirrored in every mature individual and, because of the public servant's obligations to serve rather than aspire, are often played out without sensationalism or fanfare.

Kramer contends that the *Odyssey* can be conceived as recounting for us quite explicit aspects of good leadership. He compares the prescriptions of Warren Bennis on the subject to lessons taught to Odysseus. These include management of attention through a sense of vision (e.g., visiting Hades as the concluding triumph before returning to Ithaca); the management of meaning through communication (persuasive and sometimes agonizing dialogues with his mother, warriors, and other heroes); management of trust through reliability and constancy (confronting the enchantress Circe to regain his lost men, whom she had turned into swine); and management of self through knowing one's skills and using them effectively (the entire metaphoric journey to self-understanding, climaxed by the visit to Hades).[11]

The Teaching Bridge

The *Odyssey* can be a valuable classroom tool because it is dramatic, universal, and wrought with tangible ambiguities with which students can wrestle. In the characters, dilemmas, and twistings of plot, students can contemplate the eternal themes embodied in this great epic poem while broadening their base of liberal knowledge and appreciation for classical literature.

A part of the poem that illustrates its teaching potential concerns Pallas Athene, goddess of wisdom and daughter of Zeus, the king of the gods. She favors Odysseus, whom she considers a godlike mortal worthy of special treatment. Appearing before a meeting of the Council of the Gods on Mount Olympus, Athene appeals directly to her father to issue an order allowing Odysseus to return home to Ithaca. She reminds Zeus of the sacrifices and offerings Odysseus has made to the gods and insists that his loyalty be rewarded. Aware that Poseidon, god of the sea and avowed enemy of Odysseus, is absent from the Council meeting, Athene wisely chooses this time to make her case. What better material is available for discussing the reasoned judgment necessary for appealing to higher authority, plus the savvy needed to know when to do so?

Not all the gods were as kindly disposed toward Odysseus as Athene. Often at odds with one another, the deities tended to wreak vengeance upon themselves and the mortals they were sworn to guide. Odysseus was subjected to the vagaries of these divine interferences, which seemed intent on leading him to his own destruction. From their lofty heights, the gods appeared to take perverse pleasure in the difficulties they visited upon the earth. Much of what happens to Odysseus stems from actions by the gods to assist or harm him.

Class discussion of this constant shifting of one's position in life vis-à-vis external interventions in human affairs can underscore the elemental idea that public administrators constantly face the vagaries of pressure groups, political enemies, hostile media, and chance decisions of "fate." In the midst of such uncertainty, judgment must nonetheless be exercised and decisions made, despite the felt presence of inscrutable forces and the realization that outcomes are unpredictable. The unclear intent of those around us must also be accepted; like Odysseus, who had to second-guess what the gods intended for him, administrators must consider the hidden agendas behind every case made before them. Successful public executives are those who can see behind the forces that create conflict, rise above the negativism inherent in such hostility, move ahead courageously to take reasoned action, and escape from the prison of their own turbulent emotions that the uncertainty creates.

Always, this great work of poetic art talks to us at the level of our individual personhood. Odysseus as an individual escaped from Ogygia and the clutches of Cyclops. This feat provided him with the confidence necessary to overcome the difficulties he faced on the way home to Ithaca. Like Odysseus, mortal men and women are able to take charge of their lives, despite the countless pitfalls known to be ahead. The choice to do so involves the willingness to transform oneself from observer to actor, a step of great commitment.

CROSSINGS: THE WHEEL OF FORTUNE

Art is able to express life in the marks of the artist's brush, as well as in the strokes of the writer's pen and the sounds of the musician's instrument. The adage "A picture is worth a thousand words" expresses the truism that the visual arts can have great meaning and impact. This is of course true for public administration as well as other realms of personal and social experience.

The visual image we consider here is the Wheel of Fortune, a graphic representation that dates back to ancient times. While many versions can be found (including one on Tarot cards), the interpretation of this image that we consider here is by the Roman philosopher and statesman Boethius, who probably lived from about 475 to about 525.

Boethius described the Wheel of Fortune as a symbol of how the proud are debased and the fallen are elevated. It represents how power-holding in human affairs follows an inevitable rhythm, with aspirants inexorably replacing the empowered from time to time. The Wheel depicts four human figures on the rim of a rotating circle. An aspiring figure is ascending the left side of the Wheel, eager to capture the crown. A crowned figure is positioned at the top, enjoying fame and fortune for the moment. To the right, descending rapidly with the Wheel's turning, is a pitiful figure dressed in tatters, falling from power. A fourth figure lies at the bottom of the Wheel, in abject defeat. A fifth is Fortune, who rotates the Wheel in its ceaseless turnings (see frontispiece; our version also contains a sixth figure, to be explained below).

This symbol, in one form or another, is seen in many tapestries, engravings, and manuscripts of the Renaissance and earlier. Sometimes it can be seen in the rose window of French Romanesque churches, with the stone surrounding the window inscribed "Regnabo" (I shall reign), "Regno" (I reign), "Regnavi" (I have reigned), and "Sum Sine Regno" (I am without a reign).[12]

In a word, the Wheel of Fortune represents the transitory nature of power. Those who crave it scramble incessantly for the crown, only to be eventually dethroned and disgraced. Boethius's interest in the Wheel may have arisen from his personal life experiences. He entered public service as a young man, rising to the post of prime minister by 522. Surely, in his own ascent to power, he personally witnessed the fleeting and pathetic nature of unrestrained power-seeking, and perhaps experienced it himself. But his training as a philosopher held him in good stead; rather than being discarded to powerless obscurity at the bottom of the Wheel, Boethius acquired a lasting reputation rivaling that of Demosthenes and Cicero. Hence, in a sense, he escaped the Wheel's merciless rotation, an option we now consider.13

The Theory Bridge

In antiquity and the Middle Ages the masses could not read, so graphic symbols, paintings, and architecture took on great significance as communicators. Yet even in today's information-soaked, literate society, graphic representation continues to possess great power. The pervasive influence of television makes the point unmistakably.

Graphic images are also important to public administration. Consider, for example, the influence of the pyramidal organization chart on how we think about authority in the field. Indeed, such charts become, for many organizations, the literal image by which members visualize the unit's structure and functions. It suggests unified control, functional specialty, and integrated coordination, all hallmarks of classic administrative theory.

Another ubiquitous graphic form in administration is the input–output flow chart, which by the configuration of its design suggests a view of the world that embraces linearity, closure, comprehensibility, and opportunity for intervention. A third illustration of graphic power in our field is the line graph. The slope of the line, whether up, down, or flat, tells us whether conditions are improving, deteriorating, or staying the same. This imagery implicitly assumes, without giving us a chance to weigh these premises, that we actually know this to be the case. That is, it is tacitly agreed that some specific aspect of our world is objectively definable, measurable, and evaluable. In effect, this simple picture transmits an entire epistemology. It is, indeed, worth a thousand words.

Innovators in the field recognize the power of graphic symbols and develop their own as a means of creating new imagery. A famous example is the matrix diagram, utilized to support organizational decentralization within the National Aeronautics and Space Administration in the 1960s. The diagram's intent was to suggest that authority flowed simultaneously from both headquarters program offices and field space centers, not just a vertical hierarchy. In another graphic form that departs from the pyramid, circles are connected with arrows. These often depict interorganizational networks, seen by some as the key form of institutional relationship required for today's world. Theorist Ralph Hummel has proposed the circle, as opposed to the pyramid, as the icon needed to inspire appropriate ways of management in postmodern society.[14]

The Values Bridge

Like all condensed symbols, the value implications of the Wheel of Fortune can be interpreted on many levels. One aspect on which we can reflect is the contrasting meaning of the rotating figures at the rim of the Wheel versus those at its center. Our illustration shows two still figures, Fortune and a sixth figure standing next to her. One hand of that additional person rests on the Wheel, the other on Fortune's shoulder.

To us, taking this liberty with the traditional image suggests how it is possible to conceive of two quite different value systems in government. One is directed to satisfaction of personal ambition and the attainment of power for its own sake. The other is centered not on ego gratification but on quiet influence over the process of rule. The sixth figure, while not in the public eye, nonetheless exercises depersonalized power through being directly connected with both the rotations of fame and the turnings of fate.

Surely, depiction of the electoral officeholder as riding the Wheel and the career civil servant as standing by it vastly oversimplifies and grossly stereotypes those who govern. Yet the image of the sixth figure suggests an attractive ideal for the public administrator—one who is totally engaged with power and yet removed from its private temptations.

Boethius was not the only interpreter of the Wheel of Fortune. Another traditional meaning of the symbol has to do with light. Some have likened the wheel to the sun, the symbol of intelligence and spiritual illumination. In ancient times, it was believed that a fiery wheel would "stimulate the sun in its activity and . . . ward off winter and death." To this end, the summer solstice was celebrated as a "wheel of fire" rolling down a hill.[15]

This metaphor can also animate administrative values. The word "illumination" in our book's title suggests the capacity to know and learn. In some ways, the task of modern public administration is to bring "the Enlightenment" of research, expertise, analysis, and a knowledge of past programs to public problems. The light metaphor can also be used to underscore the need to "focus" our precious tax-based public resources wisely. In the realm of organizational development, open dialogue and revelation of underlying tensions allow intraorganizational stresses to be exposed to "the light of day." Fred Riggs, in a brilliant use of the light metaphor, described the value ambiguity within public administration in developing countries as "prismatic," as in decomposed sunlight.[16]

CROSSINGS: STAR WARS

Our final illustration of crossing the conceptual bridges between art and public administration is in the realm of popular art, not great literature or ancient symbolism. But the motion picture *Star Wars* is not simply entertainment, even if it is entertaining. The film is a modern fairy tale, replete with the adventures of heroes and antiheroes. Like all fairy tales, it plays to our fantasies and fears.

The background of this tale is that the once thriving Old Republic, part of a far-flung galactic Empire, was strong and good. Now, it is dominated by the powers of evil that have laid claim to the galaxy. Under the rule of a new and unscrupulous Emperor, the protectors of the people—the Jedi knights—were annihilated.

As the story opens, the many worlds of the galaxy are subjected to the cruel power of the conquering Imperial forces. In the midst of the shadow cast by this oppression, however, a few lights of hope flicker. Luke Skywalker lives on Tatooine, a desertlike world in the galaxy. The dryness and heat of Tatooine's climate and the brightness of its light seem to radiate from the screen as the viewer watches Luke perform his daily routine. The radiance of the place is reminiscent of the sun, and its brightness provides a fitting background for the soon-to-be-illustrious Luke.

Convinced that a growing rebellion of the recalcitrant systems against the evil Empire is about to reach Tatooine, Luke is on the cusp of change. Like the young men of any generation, he is eager to make his way in the world and discover the true measure of himself.

Many surprises lie in store for Luke when he makes the acquaintance of an old man named Ben Kenobi. Ben is actually General Obi-Wan Kenobi, a famous Jedi knight of the Old Republic who mentored Luke's dead father. As Jedi knights, both men recognized the power within themselves and used this Force to protect the Empire against the evil intentions of dangerous marauders.

General Kenobi trained many knights, but only one used the power of the Force within himself for evil purposes. This is Darth Vader, the epics's memorable antagonist who helped bring about the fall of the Jedi. When

Ben presents Luke with the Lightsaber that belonged to his father, his transformation from a typical teenager to a budding hero is assured. This symbolic weapon inspires Luke to use the power of the Force to restore the Empire to its former glory. But he does not act alone. Princess Leia, a powerful senator, appears to Ben through electromagnetic waves and appeals to him to journey to Alderaan and help regain the Empire. Her beauty and intensity spur Luke to action, and his transformation is complete.

The Values Bridge

The imagery of this story, as vivid in the minds of theatergoers as are the stories of Hans Christian Andersen to readers, animates values in the stark and dramatic way that only a fairy tale can accomplish. The overriding dramatic device of the tale is the stark contrast between Good and Evil. The presence of Darth Vader on the screen leaves no doubt concerning his intentions. This fascinating personification of evil hides his face behind a metallic mask and speaks with an echoing, inhuman voice. His walk is characterized by the heavy pounding of steel. Arrogant and self-serving, Vader attempts to control and subdue all who stand in his way. Fear and oppression are the means by which he intimidates others and achieves his own purposes.

By contrast, Ben Kenobi appears as a white-bearded gentleman clad in a belted robe not unlike the garb of a monk. His kind, grandfatherly demeanor is diametrically opposed to that of Vader. Kenobi is quietly self-assured and detached, with gentle speech and manner. We regard him not with horrified fascination but with acceptance and trust. Luke Skywalker is the impish but essentially innocent teenager, awaiting the transformation to heroic glory; meanwhile, Princess Leia—as usual more mature than her male counterpart—already personifies wise power.

Like Vader, some public administrators are dedicated to intimidating their rivals and ruling their empires with an iron mask, artificial voice, and pounding walk. Like Ben, other public administrators are dedicated to helping people discover their own power so that they may improve the part of the world affected by their work. While the Darth Vaders of government use power to gratify their egos through oppression, the General Kenobis of government command programs to serve the public, stepping and speaking more quietly and gently. True, we are more fascinated dramatically with the Darth Vaders of this world, but we trust the General Kenobis—the relationship that in the long run really counts in the processes of cooperative action. Moreover, sometimes self-effacing generals in real life—such as George C. Marshall—actually do save empires.

The Leadership Bridge

Most public administrators are not heroes or heroines but ordinary people. This means that frailty, ambivalence, and indecision are in their being, as well as the potential to soar. Hence the character in *Star Wars* most relevant to administrative leaders may not be Ben, Luke, or Leia, but Han Solo.

Solo is captain of the *Millennium Falcon*, the spaceship that took Luke and Ben to the Alderaan system. He is a handsome young man, somewhat older than Luke and more worldly. Possessing a survivor mentality, he is deeply rooted in the here and now. While honest and brave, he is not interested in becoming a hero and does not aspire to greatness. Yet when Luke becomes desperate for help in the war against the enemy battleship, Solo joins him in the struggle.

Many public administrators will identify with Han Solo. They have no pretense to glory and are content to carry out their daily tasks to the best of their abilities. There are times, however, when the exigencies of administrative life require them to go beyond the ordinary range of expectations. These demands may be as mundane as helping a colleague in trouble or as lofty as objecting to policy on principle. In such situations, ordinary men and women feel uncertain about what to do. Fantasy figures like Captain Solo can give them food for thought.

The Policy Bridge

Star Wars continued a series of futuristic science fiction films that began in the 1920s and became particularly prominent in the 1960s. These films helped to fuel the public's imagination with respect to space travel. This was particularly so with *2001: A Space Odyssey*. The film analyzed here contains more military action than *2001*, with plenty of firing weapons, massive space battleships, walking armored vehicles, and rocket fighters moving at incredible speeds. Hence it may have fired the imagination of military planners with respect to war beyond our atmosphere. In any case, the film's title became the informal name of the Reagan administration's highly controversial missile defense system, a remarkable form of recognition in its own right.

The Teaching Bridge

Because of the medium of video, the use of films in the classroom is today logistically easy and culturally natural. The dramatic nature of this particular modern-day fairy tale, as well as its impressive display of technological imagination, is capable of provoking students to a stirring discussion. Among the potential themes for discourse are the stark contrasts of good and evil, the ways in which both are revealed in public bureaucracy, the potentialities for inspirational guidance, the transformation of teenagers into adults, and the ambivalence inherent in leadership. Also provocative would be the question of whether the picture's policy namesake was in fact true to the values underlying the Force and Lightsaber, in our peculiarly democratic Empire.

Now that we have studied four allegorical paintings, crossed five conceptual bridges, reviewed seven decades of discussion on administrative fiction, and considered the relevance to public administration of three works of popular or classic art, we are now ready for the unorthodox essays that follow.

These fall into five parts. The first offers a set of approaches to administrative theory based on ideas from the field of aesthetics. The next considers the commentaries that particular works of fiction and film make on the values that imbue public bureaucracy. The third part draws implications from classical and popular literature for public administrators as leaders. The fourth examines contributions by the arts to public policy-making and the teaching of public administration. The final part of the book synthesizes the contributions that seem possible by crossing the bridges that span our two spheres. We hope these ideas will challenge your intellect and stimulate your passions, standards by which both great art and great administration should be judged.

NOTES

1. Kenneth S. Lynn, "Authors in Search of the Businessman," *Harvard Business Review* 34 (September–October 1956): 116–24; William G. Scott, "The Novelists' Picture of Management and Managers," *Personnel Administration* 22 (January–February 1959): 9–19; American Management Association, "The Executive in Fiction: A Symposium," in *People at Work: The Human Element in Modern Business*, Management Report no. 1 (New York: AMA, 1957): 178–95.

2. Humbert Wolfe, "Some Public Servants in Fiction," *Public Administration* 2 (January 1924): 39–57.

3. Rowland Egger, "Fable for Wise Men," *Public Administration Review* 4 (Autumn 1944): 371–76, quote at 371.

4. Stephen K. Bailey, "A Frank Statement of Affairs," *Public Administration Review* 9 (Winter 1949): 51–53, quote at 51. Egger's review of *Fire* is "Saga of a Lost Shoe," *Public Administration Review* 9 (Summer 1949): 221–34. During 1957 and 1958, *PAR* ran a regular department of such book reviews, called "P.I.& E.," which stands for "provocative, informative, and enjoyable."

5. Dwight Waldo, *Perspectives on Administration* (University: University of Alabama Press, 1956), 79–88.

6. Dwight Waldo, *The Novelist on Organization and Administration: An Inquiry into the Relationship Between Two Worlds* (Berkeley: University of California Press, 1968), 56, 58, 68, 71, 74.

7. Rowland Egger, "The Administrative Novel," *American Political Science Review* 53 (June 1959): 448–55; Howard E. McCurdy, "Fiction, Phenomenology, and Public Administration," *Public Administration Review* 33 (January–February 1973): 52–60; Thomas R. McDaniel, "The Search for the 'Administrative Novel,'" *Public Administration Review* 38 (November–December 1978): 545–49.

8. H. J. Friedsam, "Bureaucrats as Heroes," *Social Forces* 32 (March 1954): 269–74; Waldo, *The Novelist on Organization and Administration*, 56. Howard E. McCurdy, "How Novelists View Public Administration," in *A Centennial History of the American Administrative State*, ed. Ralph C. Chandler (New York: Free Press, 1987).

9. Marc Holzer, Kenneth Morris, and William Ludwin, eds., *Literature in Bureaucracy: Readings in Administrative Fiction* (Wayne, N.J.: Avery Publishing Group, 1979), ix–x.

10. Fred A. Kramer, "Myth and Metaphor as a Means to Expand Public Administrative Thought," paper presented at panel on "Aesthetic Perspectives in Public Administration," annual meeting of American Political Science Association, Washington, D.C., August 29, 1991.

11. Ibid.

12. James Hall, *Dictionary of Subjects and Symbols in Art* (New York: Harper & Row, 1974), 127–28.

13. Will Durant, *The Age of Faith* (New York: Simon and Schuster, 1950), 100.

14. Ralph P. Hummel, "Circle Managers and Pyramid Managers: Icons for the Post-Modern Public Administrator," in *Images and Identities in Public Administration* ed. Henry D. Kass and Bayard L. Catron (Newbury Park, Calif.: Sage, 1990), 202–18.

15. J. E. Cirlot, *A Dictionary of Symbols*, trans. Jack Sage, 2nd ed. (London: Routledge and Kegan Paul, 1971), 370–71.

16. Fred W. Riggs, *Administration in Developing Societies: The Theory of Prismatic Society* (Boston: Houghton Mifflin, 1964). In a prior incarnation as an

academic administrator, one of the present authors once defended the organizational autonomy of his unit by depicting it graphically as the sun at the center of a miniature solar system. Although colleagues referred to the image jokingly as the "King Ra" diagram, reorganization was staved off for a year.

Part II

Ideas for Administrative Theory from the Arts

2

The Public Administrator as Artisan

Charles T. Goodsell

THE NEED FOR WORKADAY VALUES

The preceding essay contends that while we have often paid formal obeisance to the idea of public administration being an "art," we have not taken the notion seriously enough to develop an explicit theory for the concept. The motivation for theorizing in this somewhat unaccustomed manner about public administration is to give normative guidance and moral support to the individual public administrator at the microcosmic level of daily work life.

Because of the very nature of large, complex organizations, executive or managerial work within them consists of being immersed in a disconnected, harried stream of incomplete actions and fragmentary occurrences whose overall reason for being is difficult to keep in mind. Unlike other political arts, such as legislating and policy-making, in administration one deals not with the "forest" but with the "trees"—plus the bushes, shrubs, thorns, rocks, and blades of grass. Concrete, discrete, disordered, and unpredictable "minievents" crowd out, in the immediate social-psychological reality of the typical workday, the higher purposes of the program or agency. Normally one does not have the pleasure of consciously making "big" decisions or even "shaping events" discernibly. At the end of a typical day the administrator usually cannot cite dramatic results emanating from that day's work. More likely is an inability to enumerate any clear outcomes or accomplishments. This makes daily work for many administrators inherently frustrating—as is raising young children for parents who tend them on a constant basis. Yet rendering public service in the public interest, like raising children, is one of humankind's most noble pursuits. Those who perform such labor should never lose sight of this central point. Thus the importance of providing the public administrator with a satisfactory and supportive value system is of concern to all of us.

Several normative ideas and supportive systems already exist for the public administrator. I am going to make the rather bold argument that they tend, however, to operate at the macrocosmic rather than the microcosmic level. Generalized norms of legality, constitutionality, and personal ethics are examples. These great beacons of administrative conduct are essential to democratic and honest administration and should in no way be disparaged. But, rather than guiding the administrator routinely in handling the workday's hundreds of minievents, they come to bear in relatively infrequent borderline situations. In fact, the potentially illegal or unethical act looms large in our minds precisely because of its comparative rarity.

Another indispensable set of administrative values derives from the notion of faithful and efficient enforcement of statutes and orders. Yet while such written mandates give essential overall guidance to the program or organization, their content is often a background charter for performance rather than a guidebook for minute-by-minute conduct. Similarly, the traditional "triple E" values of economy, efficiency, and effectiveness are salutary in the abstract. Yet the practitioners of total quality management (TQM) tell us that they apply primarily at the system level and have relatively little relevance at the individual case or worker level. As for the "newer" administrative values of equity, justice, fairness, citizen involvement, organization development, and communitarian dialogue, they are essentially bedrock, philosophical underpinnings of our work. Many of the administrator's daily "in box" items and "fires" to fight can be related to these values, but usually only after mature reflection. At the moment of action, I would submit, they are not the source of explicit guidance or a sense of deeper satisfaction.

The value system being proposed here, in contrast, is intended to operate precisely at the workaday, individual, and concrete level. It does so, quite simply, by asking the public administrator to perform each individual task—no matter how "small"—*well*, in the deepest sense of that word. With respect to *that* action, handled *that* moment, by *that* individual: Was it performed with a sense of sure execution and mastery? Was it carried out with flair and distinctiveness? Was it articulated in a form appropriate to its own purposes? Did the act respect the potentialities of the human and material resources thereby committed? Did it involve an ability to be creative in restating confused situations? If these questions can be answered affirmatively, I believe, the administrator's daily work *is* capable of becoming recognizably well done—and thereby intrinsically meaningful and gratifying—even when at the end of the day it is difficult to answer, along with the harried parent, "Just what did I get done today?"

AESTHETICS AND ADMINISTRATION

In constructing this normative model for public administration, I draw on the field of aesthetics. Aesthetic philosophy and the theory of art are usually not seen by public administrators as pertaining to their utilitarian and down-to-earth work. Likewise, most aestheticians regard their realm as pertaining to beautiful objects such as paintings and pieces of sculpture—or, perhaps, elevated activities such as writing great literature or performing great music. Certainly, administration is not a "fine" art like painting, sculpture, literature, music, and the dance. Whereas these arts produce things that are valued in themselves and need no external reason for being beyond their innate beauty or "fineness," public administration exists not to produce beauty but to achieve the ends of government. This is a truism of which we must never lose sight. Indeed, the very juxtaposition of the words "beauty" and "administration" induces a certain repugnance in our democratic minds, and properly so. The meticulous bureaucrat who finds innate "beauty" in perfectly phrased regulations or exquisitely kept records is, and properly so, an object of contempt in the literature that satirizes bureaucracy.

The point, however, is not to hold up an ideal of "beautiful" administration. It is, rather, to argue that the carrying out of common professional duties by public administrators can, with considerable payoff for both administrator and citizen, be viewed as the execution of an applied or practical art. In this sense public administration is parallel to architecture, medicine, cabinetmaking, bookbinding, potting, weaving, and even teaching. It is an "art" in the ancient sense of that word, that is, it embodies a specialized skill that is capable of creating results that are both usable and pleasing to behold. Specific objects are created and tasks performed, in ways and with consequences that establish in the minds of both creator and audience a sense of intrinsic satisfaction, above and beyond the utilitarian purpose at hand. In short, the value system I am proposing is not that of the pure artist but that of the artisan—an ideal to which the public administrator can and should, I submit, aspire.

Others have posited the notion of administration as an art. In 1951 Ordway Tead declared that public administration is not merely an art but a "fine art."[1] It is so, he said, because of the great skill, discernment, and moral fortitude required of the administrator, as well as the high purpose served—which Tead described as induced collaborative action between individuals on an organized basis. Kenneth Eble, who was inspired by Tead when writing on leadership in higher education, termed administration an art because of the "complexities and subtleties of working with people, the skill and sensitivity necessary to doing it well, and the fulfillment of one's vision largely through other people."[2]

Interestingly enough, policy analysis, a subfield of public administration we usually suspect of harboring technocratic tendencies, also employs the artistic metaphor. It is found, for example, in the titles of Aaron Wildavsky's *Speaking Truth to Power: The Art and Craft of Policy Analysis* and Peter House's *The Art of Public Policy Analysis*. Wildavsky's "art" refers to discovering problems that decision makers can profitably tackle, using the techniques and resources available. House's use of "art" points to the human-oriented and political skills that the analyst needs, beyond computer technology and quantitative method.[3] While the comments of these writers all express important truths, they do not constitute the argument being made here. To me, the "artisan" public administrator is not merely a discerning, moral, visionary "people person" or, for that matter, a savvy discoverer of doable problems. Rather, he or she—if doing the job well— subscribes to certain specific normative ideas derived from aesthetic theory. We turn now to these ideas: craft, style, form, respect for materials, and creativity.

CRAFT

The word "craft," like "art," has also been used in textbook titles. George Berkley, in *The Craft of Public Administration*, argues that administration is unpredictable and nonrigorous, and hence cannot be viewed as a science. But, he continues, it is not an art either, since it can and should be judged by objective standards. As a consequence he regards administration as occupying the intermediate ground of craft. Wildavsky's use of the word "craft" in the title of his policy text conveys the point that analysis must be technically well done in order to make it persuasive to others. In a more recent characterization of policy analysis, Giandomenico Majone argues that the "craft" of analysis lies in the careful making of arguments based on logic and evidence that are stated with cogency and clarity.[4]

I shall propose a somewhat broader application of the concept of craft to public administration, based on four elements: mastery, identity, responsibility, and practical learning.

Mastery of a difficult and specialized task is at the core of craftsmanship. It stands on its own as a tangible sign of achievement. Mastery of something is a clear way of telling ourselves and others that we "count," that we have meaning. This is perhaps the origin of the phrase "the thrill of mastery." A psychic boost derives both from doing the complex act in a seemingly effortless way and from producing an outcome that can be admired by others. The master demonstrates, unmistakably and repeatedly, that rare ability of being able to do something to its fullest potential. Mastery's appeal is, moreover, situated in a time dimension: it clearly has not been attained overnight, but only over a long period of hard effort and steady growth, leading up to the present level of competence. In this sense, current mastery stands as a monument to past laborious efforts that, in effect, legitimize the master's status as earned rather than bestowed.

This simple yet profound idea of mastery, I suggest, is capable of infecting the daily tasks of administration. If recognized and articulated (at least to oneself) in relation to each task, it can impart to the administrator a degree of commitment and pride that does not emanate from any other source. Moreover, it can operate at the microcosmic level. Individual tasks, no matter how mundane or brief, can be performed in a "masterly" way— within their own terms of reference.

In part I am referring to mechanical matters such as writing the clear and succinct memo, placing the smooth telephone call, conducting the effective meeting, or making the powerful speech. But what really counts, of course, is not the words or format of the act of communication itself. Rather, it is the ability to sense the requirements of the situation and to draw consciously from one's repertoire of communication and emotional skills to put together the "right" combination. Especially hard are the "tough" memos, calls, and confrontations, for these are the ones involving tension, conflict, and the exercise of power. Here the craft of day-to-day administration reaches its highest challenge. Disciplining the problem employee, defusing the angry complaint, and taking the unpopular but necessary decision are constant and often unexpected challenges for every administrator. In them, one can fall grievously short with a single misstatement or even a nonverbal cue. Required are a subtle and tailored combination of wits, toughness, and sensitivity, plus ability to control oneself under pressure. Exercising this craft is not always easy to appreciate, for when it is done well, the tasks look transparently easy. But the craft's masters know what is involved and can make a point of taking personal pride in what they do.

The idea of craft has other normative contributions to make to administration as well. It can impart a sense of personal identity to the craftsperson. Administrators can be known by more than their rank, job, position, or employer. They can also be known as members of that select company, masters of the administrative craft. As sociologists of craft point out, the very difficulty of achieving master status creates a sense of group distinctiveness. Craftspersons can and do admire each other's work and are naturally drawn into relationships of mutual interest and colleagueship. This combination of hard-earned distinctiveness and colleagueship constitutes a kind of natural binding glue between craftspersons working in widely separated places and organizations. The guilds of the Middle Ages, whose members' faces were carved on public display boards along with the symbols of their trade, were among the most powerful organizations of their time.[5]

Could we draw on this natural comradeship to anchor artisan administrators more firmly in association with their brothers and sisters? This is a claimed goal for many professional associations, but unfortunately they tend to become entrepreneurial entities concerned more with "marketing" themselves (i.e., expanding membership and income) than with providing meaning and support for members in their work lives. A "public administration guild," properly speaking, would emphasize not membership growth but membership exclusiveness—with only journeymen or full masters admitted. Perhaps this kind of organization should be explored for our field, since we clearly do not have it now.

Art historian Alison Burford, studying craftsmanship in ancient Greece and Rome, sought to put his finger on the common attribute of craft in this age of artistic flowering. His conclusion was that this commonality is the craftperson's sense of identification with his or her work.[6] Whether ancient artisans did or did not actually sign their pots, tiles, statues, and manuscripts, they did take personal pride in what they had created and accepted responsibility for their work. The idea is epitomized by the red stamp or "chop" found at the bottom of Chinese paintings and scrolls.

Administrators often do sign their work, such as letters, memoranda, and similar communications. Bureaucrats initial "buck" slips, and E-mail is sent from a user ID. The greatest problem with personal identification with one's work lies not in registering the source but in the hierarchical form of administrative organization. The upward "clearance" process for important communications and proposals causes the end "product" to appear organizational, not individual. The originator's work is almost always altered, and that person's name is often treated rather cavalierly.

For external consumption this must be the case, for all acts are in the name of the agency's legal head. Within the organization, however, a norm suggested by the craft notion is to give adequate, explicit credit to the person who actually "did the work." Acknowledgment by superiors of the right to a "chop" can be a simple but rewarding act. It is important for all insiders—and as many informed outsiders as possible, for that matter—to keep in mind that good administration is individually handcrafted, not anonymously mass-produced.

A final attribute of craft has to do with training. Traditional craft knowledge is not systematically codified and written down. It is known informally, passed on verbally to apprentices and journeymen over time. It also derives from concrete situations rather than general principles. Much to his disgust, Frederick Winslow Taylor discovered such craft knowledge to be guiding the lathe operators at the Midvale plant; his attempts to rectify the situation resulted, in a sense, in what we know as modern management. Perhaps much good was lost in the process.

Reinstilling a sense of craft in today's administrative world would not do away with written instructions, generalized prescriptions, and assembled training sessions, of course. Yet this aspect of the artistry of administration gives us added respect for the great importance of such individualized devices as the internship, shadowing, and the "mentoring" named after Odysseus's servant. We often advocate these things because they "seem right," without really understanding why they are essential. But they *are* essential, simply because artisanship cannot be reduced to abstractions and sociotechnical systems. To be taught, the subtleties of administration require direct demonstration; to be learned, they require firsthand experience.

STYLE

The word "style" has multiple meanings. One is the possession of flair or finesse. We say that a person "has style" if she or he is poised, civil, sophisticated, exhibits grace and dignity, and operates with agility.

Surely these qualities have applicability to doing the public's business. In fact they can be used as significant criteria in judging everyday acts of administration, for departures from them can cause much mischief. In the continuous interpersonal interaction of the office, a posture of graceful civility is important. Beyond that obvious point, when negotiating with powerful members of external constituencies, a clumsy awkwardness or painful self-consciousness will put the administrator at a distinct disadvantage; a confident spokesperson for the public interest is a good thing for us all. Thus we are talking here about more than pleasant manners. While adoption of the proverbial British "knife and fork" civil service test would clearly be inappropriate to this time and place, let us not belittle the value of "having style" in this sense of the word.

In aesthetic theory the concept of style is more complex. Much ink has been spilled on the development and integrity of the term. Some contend it is an elusive concept that dissolves when scrutinized too closely. Others argue that the notion has its value if not pushed too hard.

The central idea of style in art is one of meaningful classification. Painters, sculptors, writers, and composers are said to develop distinctive orientations, methods, and outlooks. When these attributes are held in common by a number of creative persons, a perceived "style" or school is established. This phenomenon can be a result of working together in a given era or place, or of expressing parallel inner proclivities, or both. Retrospectively identified styles, such as the classic, the baroque, the expressist, and the like serve several purposes. They make ordered sense, historically, of a variety of artistic outputs, usually after the fact. By such means we can trace the evolution of successive artistic outputs, for instance, from Romanesque to Gothic. For individual artists, being associated with a labeled style provides a sense of identity and hence validity. For the creative leaders within a given school, the concept offers the motivation to develop a style further or even break out of it.

Are there "styles" of administration? Certainly we have been bombarded in the management and public administration literature by various typologies of behavior. To cite just a few examples, Douglas McGregor postulates about administrators who follow Theory X and those who accept Theory Y. Anthony Downs talks of Climbers, Conservers, Advocates, and Zealots.[7] By the Myers-Briggs Type Indicator (MBTI) we assume Jungian dichotomies of extroversion vs. introversion, sensing vs. intuition, thinking vs. feeling, and judgment vs. perception, with a resultant sixteen different combinations of psychological predisposition. One is tempted to equate the ESTJ with classicism and the INFP with Romanticism, although such speculation would surely make art critics cringe.

The assumption that types of administrative behavior can, in fact, be looked upon as distinctive styles does contribute to a workaday value system for administration in three ways. First, it allows us to accept many different varieties of administrative behavior as possessing individual validity. "Being different" is not the same as being wrong (this, in fact, is a major proposition of the Myers-Briggs approach). Acceptance of individual differences is an important point to press upon organizations, for they tend to expect homogeneous behavior in accord with their corporate culture. Also, the point should be continuously brought to the attention of management theorists, for they tend to demand conformity to their own doctrine of leadership at the expense of all others. By contrast, the notion of style calls upon us to evaluate each administrator on his or her own terms, whether or not that person's style is like our own. What is important is whether the individual performs in accord with an integrated and mature version of the style that has been adopted or developed.

Second, the artistic notion of style reminds us that behavioral differences may be due not only to internal psychological predispositions, as is assumed by the MBTI, but also to such variables as cultural origins, era and institution of higher education, and programmatic bias. That Beethoven was a German, that Delacroix was trained at the Ecole des Beaux Arts, and that both lived in the Napoleonic era cannot be ignored. Likewise, we should expect different styles from administrators socialized to the rationalist mores of public management, trained in the analytical techniques of a policy program, or dedicated to the latest organization development methodologies. Likewise, the police chief will behave differently from the head of the welfare department, and rightfully so. The minority executive who came to maturity on the streets of the inner city will likely exhibit a different style than the white Ivy League law school graduate.

Finally, the notion of style as applied to administration helps us resist the shackles of implicit orthodoxy. As art historian James S. Ackerman has said, we should reject the notion that the stylist must seek equivalence with the foremost exponent of a school or work toward some imaginary, unattained ideal.[8] Instead, stylistic development must be regarded not as predetermined but as openly evolutionary, moving toward ever new and fresh manifestations. Hence young administrators should not attempt to emulate, literally, either the academic models of leadership they find in their textbooks or the personal heroes they encounter in the classroom or internship.

Parallel to this idea is the expectation that each established stylistic school, no matter how elaborated and dazzling, must always decline—if for no other reason than the need for the upcoming young to rebel and make their own mark. In short, the fashionable must, and always should, go out of fashion, in public administration as well as in art. We should keep this in mind as we witness the continuous parade of rising and falling paradigmatic orthodoxies in our own field; aesthetic theory suggests this as a natural and healthy sequence, not a sign of disintegration or disorderliness within the discipline.

FORM

Artistic form is a paradox. It calls for creativity within convention. The standard three movements of the sonata, the fourteen lines of the sonnet, and the three panels of the triptych illustrate the use of established rules as a basis for endless artistic creativity.

There are at least three reasons for this paradox of artistic form. First, the conventions discipline and thereby liberate. By limiting the painter to a given medium with known properties and to a canvas of set dimensions, an opportunity for focused creative effort is provided. Second, conventions help the beholder of artwork digest and appreciate what is being experienced. Even though the work is being witnessed for the first time, it is presented in a form that is recognizable. Third, form constitutes the means by which an impulse of artistic expression achieves organic unity. An abstract idea, a slice of human experience, or a time–space fragment of nature is reduced to encapsulated form. Pieces are assembled into wholes and the confusion of life becomes clarified in one unified entity. A good illustration is the artful biography that gives overall meaning to the life portrayed—even though, on a day-to-day basis, that life was, like our own, particularized and disparate.

Although public administration's purpose in human affairs is very different from that of art, the idea of form is not alien to it. Viewing management as a "performing art," consultant Peter Vaill has warned that if corporate managers ride roughshod over accepted forms of the organization while pursuing their objectives, they will unbalance it to the detriment of all. Vaill also argues that the idea of form allows us to take cognizance of the pleasure that can be derived from the process of doing the work.[9]

What might "good" form be in public administration? One answer is to do things in ways that are appropriate to the purposes of the action. We should conduct a briefing, for example, quite differently from conducting a retreat. The briefing's concise exposition, visual aids, and question-and-answer format are appropriate for presenting a preconceived "case" to superiors or press. By contrast, the long duration, removed setting, and relaxed atmosphere of the retreat are appropriate for inducing people to lower their defenses and engage in relatively unstructured discourse. Each form offers a discipline within which creativity can occur. Each form is familiar to participants and thus acceptable in its own place. Also, each form reduces reality to an encapsulated, and hence understandable, version—an enumerated and confidently known depiction of the situation in the briefing and an emerging consensus or definition of the problem in the retreat. Each administrative tool is powerful, but only if it employs its appropriate form: if reality were allowed to emerge gradually in the briefing, or if leaders were portrayed as all-knowing in the retreat, nothing would be achieved.

MATERIALS

Aesthetic theory gives considerable attention to the importance and role of the materials of art—the clay, marble, oils, tempera, wood, metal, concrete, ballet movements, musical notes and sounds, and words and phrases of the literary heritage. The subject has been addressed at least since Aristotle, for whom material was one of the four "causes" of art.

In a classic essay of the eighteenth century, German playwright Gotthold Lessing enunciated the principle of *Materialgerechtigkeit*, or doing justice to the nature of the material.[10] This principle calls upon the artist to treat the unique qualities of each medium with respect and to employ the medium in such a manner as to bring out its full potential. Not merely dead matter or passive resource to be exploited at will, the material possesses unique properties that must be understood and obeyed. Hence the material itself contributes to and becomes part of the end product. In a famous illustration, Michelangelo would alter his sculpting in midcourse upon discovery of an unexpected vein in the marble that could be used to advantage. Accordingly, in the words of D. W. Gotshalk, the material itself possesses a "quasi-creative fecundity."[11]

What are the materials of the administrative artisan? Ordway Tead, in his treatment of the art of administration, said that it utilizes three media: organization, people, and the democratic cultural setting.[12] Other possibilities that come to mind are legal authority, funding, technology, and action repertoires. Several such lists could be proposed and defended; the interesting point, however, is what the principle of doing justice to the nature of one's materials means for public administration.

The key lesson is that the norm of "efficient use of resources" falls short as a value precept for the public administrator. The managerialist notion of strict and optimal control of everything within one's sway is not enough. The materials at hand are not mere "inputs" but items of substantial and sometimes precious value, the use of which is a privilege as much as it is a right.

I make this point not to underscore the public administrator's responsibility as a fiduciary for the public trust, although that value, too, is of central importance. The relevance of the *Materialgerechtigkeit* principle for administration is that it demands that imperatives inherent in the unique nature of the materials at hand be obeyed: that, for example, the legitimacy of legal authority is not eroded by taking unexplained actions not linked directly to that authority; that the sustaining values of the organization's culture are not trampled upon needlessly in an effort to "shake up" the agency; that the renewing potential of new technology is not lost through a Luddite attitude; and, most important of all, that the precious uniqueness of each employee and coworker is not lost sight of, in our eagerness to guide the institution and increase its productivity. In short, the artisan administrator does not really "manage"—he or she joins with the materials involved for a common act of creation.

CREATIVITY

The concept of creativity infuses and transcends all we have said about the values and lessons of artisanship for the everyday tasks of administration. By definition the artist is creative. This is not the case with the administrator. Hence we are asking for something that is not, unfortunately, "natural" in the administrative world. Let us conclude this chapter by capturing more pointedly the notion of artistic creativity as applied to administration.

Not all concepts of artistic creativity will apply. Plato's view of art was that, as a mere imitation of earthly forms—which are themselves imitations of the ideal—art bears only the remotest relation to reality. Hence artistic creativity in a Platonic sense would be an exercise in irrelevance—much as seeking new ways of doing things is seen by the cynical, status quo-oriented bureaucrat as ignoring "realities." Also inapplicable is the view of the Italian philosopher Benedetto Croce, who contends that art is a mere subjective outpouring of the personal feelings of the artist. If that is so, artistic conduct in administration becomes the public display of the administrator's personal ego and not much else. The administrator as genius who alone knows what is beautiful and right is not the model we wish to follow.

Art theorist D. W. Gotshalk propounds another view of artistic creativity that might be seen as advancing a "social" theory of art. To him, the creative act consists of interaction between the artist and the material in such a manner that an imaginative reintegration of symbolic elements is achieved. The resulting new synthesis integrates those elements in a wholly new and arresting manner. The consequence is a product that is spiritually self-rewarding to the artist and yet, in order to complete the artistic experience, must also be apprehended by critics and audiences. Moreover, this imaginative reintegration does not occur in isolation but is immersed in, and penetrated by, the larger environment. In addition to being the product of a single mind, then, art calls for reciprocation with others and a reflection of the contemporary world. The overall result, says Gotshalk, is a heightened capacity for human experience and an elevated sense of human worth.[13]

Art theorists, in discussing the unity and diversity present in the fine arts, often make the distinction between arts that produce objects that exist in space, such as paintings and statues, and those whose product unfolds over time to the audience, as in literature and music. In the first case the creative reintegration is "synoptic," taking place instantaneously in its entirety; in the second, the creative statement possesses an innate temporal dimension.[14]

In relating these ideas to creative administration we must, of course, add the caveat that the artisan, unlike the pure artist, must also be concerned with practical use. Nonetheless, the creative process of reintegrating symbols before an audience and within an environment is precisely what administrators do when they are "creative." They take a confused and muddied situation, determine those elements to which they wish to draw attention and how, and then fashion these into a fabricated whole that is freshly new and coherent. The consequence is "fiction," if you will, in that although the reintegration must recognize "the facts," it could be accomplished a thousand different ways. The way chosen, however, is the way the administrator wishes to represent the situation and have it accepted. This is what goes on when a problem is analyzed, a decision is defended, a report is written, a consensus is articulated. Each action, if the reintegration seems "obviously true" or "clearly the thing we must do," is a work of applied art. The actual pieces of paper or spoken words that state or trigger the action are creations in the synoptic sense; the processes by which the actions are first derived (often participatively) and later presented (often persuasively) are creative in the temporal sense.

RECAPITULATION

I have proposed an explicit theory of "artful" public admininistration, drawing on ideas from aesthetic philosophy. My purpose is not to make public administration more esoteric. Quite the opposite. My purpose is to assist practicing administrators in their everyday work lives who, like practicing parents, in the harried and fragmented nature of their work, find it difficult to retain a sense of self-worth and achievement. The artisan administrator, by doing the job well in the deepest sense of that word, can achieve support and satisfaction by consciously doing even the smallest tasks with mastery, flair, and distinctiveness; employing appropriate forms in their execution; respecting the inherent importance of the human and material elements involved; and reintegrating confused situations so that all concerned can agree and cooperate.

This value system does not envision an unaccountable or isolated public administrator. First of all, those who work with the administrator will be in a position to evaluate his or her work and praise or condemn its quality and usefulness. Administration remains a wholly social enterprise, as well as a utilitarian one. Moreover, this value system does not contemplate relaxation of other sources of guidance and constraint external to the work itself, such as the law, ethical principles, requirements for efficiency and economy, and accountability to elected officials. The microcosmic nature of the artisan orientation supplements, rather than substitutes for, these more macrocosmic influences. The resulting combination of value systems, rather than undercutting the external obligations of public administrators in a democratic society, gives them the means for more inspired service within their personal work domains.

NOTES

This article is reprinted, with slight revision, with permission from *Public Administration Review* © by the American Society for Public Administration (ASPA), 1120 G. Street NW, Suite 700, Washington D.C. 2005. All rights reserved. From *Public Administration Review*, 52 4 (May–June 1992): 246–53.

1. Ordway Tead, *The Art of Administration* (New York: McGraw-Hill, 1951), 1–6.

2. Kenneth E. Eble, *The Art of Administration* (San Francisco: Jossey-Bass, 1978), xi.

3. Aaron Wildavsky, *Speaking Truth to Power* (Boston: Little, Brown, 1979), 15–16; Peter W. House, *The Art of Public Policy Analysis* (Beverly Hills; Calif.: Sage, 1982), 11.

4. George E. Berkley, *The Craft of Public Administration* (Boston: Allyn and Bacon, 1975), 3–8; Wildavsky, *Speaking Truth to Power*, 387–89; Giandomenico Majone, *Evidence, Argument, and Persuasion in the Policy Process* (New Haven: Yale University Press, 1989), 42–68.

5. Joseph Bensman and Robert Lilienfeld, *Craft and Consciousness* (New York: Wiley, 1973); Howard S. Becker, "Arts and Crafts," *American Journal of Sociology* 83, no. 4 (1978): 862–89.

6. Alison Burford, *Craftsmen in Greek and Roman Society* (Ithaca, N.Y.: Cornell University Press, 1972), 207–18.

7. Douglas McGregor, *The Human Side of Enterprise* (New York: McGraw-Hill, 1960); Anthony Downs, *Inside Bureaucracy* (Boston: Little, Brown, 1967).

8. James S. Ackerman, "Style," in James S. Ackerman and Rys Carpenter, *Art and Archeology* (Englewood Cliffs, N.J.: Prentice-Hall, 1963), 174–86.

9. Peter B. Vaill, *Managing as a Performing Art* (San Francisco: Jossey-Bass, 1989), 118–19.

10. Morris Weitz, *Problems in Aesthetics*, 2nd ed. (New York: Macmillan, 1970), 292–94.

11. D. W. Gotshalk, *Art and the Social Order* (New York: Dover, 1962), 74.

12. *The Art of Administration*, 5.

13. *Art and the Social Order*, 54–55, 77–78, 202–14.

14. Rudolf Arnheim, *New Essays on the Psychology of Art* (Berkeley: University of California Press, 1986), 65–77; Moshe Barash, *Modern Theories of Art* (New York: New York University Press, 1990), 146–61.

3

The Eastern Aesthetic in Administration

Nancy Murray

APPLYING THE AESTHETIC TO ADMINISTRATION

The word "aesthetic" is used more often to refer to the beauty of an object, such as a work of art, than it is to refer to daily tasks such as those carried out in the practice of public administration. If we are to apply notions of beauty to what are generally considered mundane activities, then we must reexamine the meaning of beauty and the practice of public administration. This will help us decide whether the juxtaposition of beauty as a transcendental value and public administration as a practical value is appropriate. In other words, must the idea of beauty be limited to an appreciation of objects whose essence is such that we are attracted to them and inspired in their presence? Or can we take the idea of beauty and incorporate it into a value system that provides a benchmark for administrators to use in determining if a job is well done? If we can accomplish the latter, there is a place for aesthetic philosophy in public administration.

This chapter builds upon the thesis proposed by Charles Goodsell in Chapter 2 that aesthetic philosophy has a place in modern public administration. It does so by addressing two principles of artistic form, harmony and balance. These principles are discussed initially by referring to the aesthetic tradition, passed down to Western culture from ancient Greece, in which our perceptions of harmony and balance are rooted. Later, certain aspects of Oriental aestheticism are examined with suggestions as to ways in which they may be applied to Western administrative practice. The reason for looking to the Eastern tradition is based upon a belief that we need to respond to those who are calling for a reevaluation of the theoretical foundations of our field and upon my sense that the world is changing in significant ways. The increasing influence of Eastern philosophy upon this change is evident in the "cutting edge" literature of both the hard sciences and the social sciences. The broad scope of this chapter is intended to spark interest in ideas that I hope will stimulate thinking and dialogue in the field of public administration.

BEAUTY AND TRUTH IN THE WESTERN TRADITION

A considerable body of literature spanning a variety of philosophical perspectives has been written about the nature of beauty. Review of this literature is beyond the scope of this chapter. My intention is to adapt certain values so that they can be put to use in the daily lives of men and women who are not necessarily members of artistic or philosophical communities.

The men and women in whom we are particularly interested are those who do the work of the public, our public administrators. They practice at either of two levels of the field. At the broader, more comprehensive (macro) level, public policy is developed. At the narrower, more focused (micro) level, public policy is implemented. Many public administrators have responsibilities that involve both the development and the implementation of policy. All administrators must carry out prescribed tasks whether they are influencing policy decisions or managing a government program. If they see beauty in their daily activities, their lives will be enriched.

A definition of beauty as a value to be applied to the conduct of daily life must include the value of truth. Beauty and truth have been used interchangeably by philosophers and poets through the centuries. In "Ode on A Grecian Urn" Keats tells us that "Beauty is truth, truth beauty,—that is all ye know on earth and all ye need to know."

Some assume that truth and beauty reside in every activity, however menial it may appear. George Santayana's view of aesthetic philosophy is grounded in notions of utility. Given the utilitarian nature of public administration, his interpretation is a good place to begin. Beauty has been used by philosophers to describe the essence of something that embodies all that is good. Goodness unites beauty and truth.[1]

A musical score, for example, is said to be beautiful when it appeals to our senses and our imagination. We respond positively to a painting or a literary work when they mirror our experience and reflect our perception of reality. Works of art are considered beautiful when they impart a truth we have always known, but in a new and significant way. Goodness is the flame that ignites the spark of truth in an object and inspires us to see its beauty. In this manner, goodness achieves its purposes.

An analogy can be made to public administration at the macro level if we consider a public policy that is consistent with the mission of an agency and is implemented in a way that mirrors the intent of the legislation that produced it. This exemplifies an ideal situation in which policy is defined and executed so that intended outcomes are achieved. Whenever legislative intent has been fulfilled, the resultant consummation of democratic norms embodies a civic trueness beautiful to behold.

George Santayana reminds us that the notion of art calls for that which is beautiful to be aesthetically pleasing. This will happen if the object of our attention satisfies our senses and imagination. Science, on the other hand, requires that which is beautiful to be objectively pleasing.[2] This will happen if the object of our attention satisfies our need for careful methodological study so that errors are minimized and biases are removed. For example, a well-designed scientific inquiry may be considered beautiful because it is based upon objective facts that allow us to maintain our belief in rational investigation as the cornerstone of truth. In its reliance upon facts, science conforms to the exigencies of practical existence. Facts, being apparent to most observers, are not easily denied. Since the conclusions reached by examining them are perceived as truth, that which is good has been found.

Much of what is done at both the macro and the micro levels of public administration is based upon our appreciation of scientific analysis. At the policy level, analysts gather data relevant to the issues they are studying. They then use a modified version of the scientific method to analyze what they have found in an attempt to derive truth. Their findings are presented to elected representatives who make higher policy decisions. These decisions are then implemented at the micro level by public administrators who may utilize analytic techniques such as operations research or decision analysis to achieve the objectives intended in the policy.

However, at both of these levels, the scientific model falls short because it fails to take into account elements that cannot be measured scientifically. This is where administrators need to rely upon their senses and imagination. As a field of study and as an area of practice, public administration needs both the rigor of scientific inquiry and the quality of aesthetic expression. A carefully organized report that contains a balanced accounting of the issues it presents is pleasing to our sense of order. We also appreciate findings that result from a rigorous study based upon the application of sound methodological principles.

Practical demands, with their emphasis on usefulness, play an important role in the determination of beauty. Santayana comments on how our imagination refines the various forms it sees: "The horse's legs are said to be beautiful because they are fit to run, the eye because it is made to see, the house because it is convenient to live in."[3] The sense of order and design that the union of beauty and utility confers provides harmony in our lives. Public administrators sometimes have to choose between competing and worthy demands. The unsettling feeling accompanying these decisions may be alleviated if managers learn to see beauty in the way they handle demands. Appreciation of simple activities that have potential to transform disorder into harmony can enrich the work environment and restore a sense of balance. Santayana reminds us that every experience can "be observed with curiosity and treated with art."[4] If art imitates and enriches all aspects of life, a great gift awaits us.

HARMONY AND BALANCE IN THE GREEK TRADITION

Western culture is heavily influenced by the beliefs of ancient Greece. Fritjof Capra writes that the disciplines of geometry, philosophy, and art were founded on the assumption that uniformity brings harmony and balance. From the Greeks we learn that the world is arranged according to symmetrical patterns. Our perception of beauty and truth is based upon the concept of perfection through symmetry. The teachings of Pythagoras, who lived in Greece in the sixth century, B.C., live in today's prevailing belief that everything in the universe is related in a numerical sequence.[5]

The Pythagorean values of proportion and regularity have influenced the structures of our administrative systems. Cost-benefit analysis is widely acclaimed as providing a balanced approach to important macro-level policy questions of equity and efficiency. Double-entry bookkeeping and balanced budgets are examples of how we apply the concept of symmetry to decision making at the micro level. Attempts to balance performance against output in service delivery is another example. Public agencies promote behavior among employees that is consistent with the values of an administrative ethic. They institute procedures and take steps to ensure balance between intended policy outcomes and actual results. In short, the concepts of numerical symmetry have provided us with a solid foundation for administrative practice. If, however, the model were completely satisfactory, this book would not have been written.

THOUGHTS ON THE JAPANESE AESTHETIC

The simplicity and grace that are characteristic of the Japanese aesthetic tradition emanate from religious and spiritual values of Confucianism, Buddhism, Shintoism, and Taoism. According to Kitabatake Chikafusa, Japan is the only country in Asia that has always been ruled by an unbroken lineage tracing its origins to the "seed of the heavenly gods." Whereas China lost its divine rule when legendary emperors renounced their heirs and appointed "wise" men to the throne, Japan's unbroken line of ascendancy resulted in an "ever renewed Divine Oath."[6]

Divine Origins

Will Durant traces the inception of Japan's divine tradition to the mating of the last two surviving gods, Izanagi and her brother Izanami. Their union produced a daughter named Amaterasu, who was born from Izanagi's left eye. She was accorded the title Great Goddess of the Sun and, with the passage of time, produced a grandson named Ninigi. Amaterasu sent Ninigi to rule, bestowing upon him the virtues of the imperial regalia that have been handed down in direct succession ever since.[7]

According to Chikafusa, the descendants of Ninigi govern through inherited qualities received from such sources as reflections from the mirror of the sun, which provides honesty. Gentleness comes from the essence of the moon contained in a jewel, which offers compassion; and strength and resolution emanate from the substance of the stars contained in a sword, which furnishes wisdom. The light from the sun and the moon are reflected in the mirror and illuminate that which is incomprehensible, thereby providing the virtues of compassion and decision to those who gaze within. Illumination is inherited by "all sovereigns and ministers who receive the . . . highest object of all teachings."[8]

Edwin O. Reischauer and John K. Fairbank propose that honesty, compassion, and wisdom, combined with the ritual purity of primitive religions, are foundations of Japanese aestheticism. They go on to say that historically, the palace where government was administered and the shrine where worship was carried out shared the same word—*miya*. Likewise, "the early Japanese word for government, 'matsurigoto,' literally means 'worship.' "[9] The interweaving of aesthetic and religious values provides a richness to the fabric of Japanese life.

Harmony and Balance

Japanese culture is also known for its deep appreciation of the beauty inherent in nature and in the stillness of clean, simple lines as reflected in its architecture. The love of simplicity and gentle beauty is evidenced in the tea ceremony, which Kakuzo Okakura tells us has been called "a religion of aestheticism" since it was introduced in the fifteenth century. Daily life is exalted by the elaborate ritual of this ceremony. Beauty and balance grace the movements of the tea master as the dipper is lowered into the kettle to revive the "youth of the water." The "philosophy of tea" symbolizes the Japanese view of man and nature. The ceremony fosters hygiene, thereby promoting cleanliness; economy, because it is not costly; appreciation of the small and mundane in proportion to the universe, because it is simple; and democracy, because all segments of society participate.[10]

The tea ceremony invites an attitude that time can be suspended so that individuals may take pleasure in the beauty of a simple act and appreciate ordinary accomplishments. This relates to public administration. Many of its daily tasks are commonplace and imperfect. If we can be less critical of their prosaic nature, we may begin to appreciate the beauty that exists in simplicity. Just as the slow movements of the pouring create the atmosphere of the tea ceremony, so the tone of voice in which an administrator answers the telephone, for example, influences the quality of the ensuing interaction.

The aesthetic ideals contained in the ritual of the tea ceremony are expressed in the word *yugen*. Ryusaku Tsunoda and associates explain that simplicity and stillness lie at the core of everything in life. Whatever we do has meaning beyond the moment and in this sense is eternal. This profound awareness represents mystery and has a spiritual dimension transcending time and space. "There is yugen in the sight of a tea-master dipping water into a kettle with simple movements that have about them the lines of eternity."[11] Slowness of movement and grace of line distinguish Japanese aestheticism. We may begin to unravel the mystery of how to make better decisions when we add a dimension of grace to administrative practice. If a simple gesture carried out by one human being serving another touches upon the universal, how profound our profession!

THOUGHTS ON THE CHINESE AESTHETIC

The influence of Confucius on Chinese administration is examined by Reischauer and Fairbank. They note his integrity and practicality. Confucius taught his pupils how to rule and how to live a moral life. Government officials in early China were expected to uphold values appropriate to a gentleman, such as integrity, righteousness, loyalty, altruism, and love. The norms of the ruling elite required orchestrating a balance between these inner moral virtues and the outer virtues of culture and polish. Rulers were therefore expected to adhere to the dictates of moderation and balance. Authority brought with it responsibility to set an example of ethical and moral behavior.[12]

Confucian values are similar to the virtues borrowed by Western culture from the Greeks. American public administration has historically advanced a comparable value system. Although loyalty, integrity, and righteousness are often honored more in the breach than in the practice, we continue to espouse them. The virtues of moderation and balance are promoted to help us mediate between political realities and administrative necessities. But, of course, we do not always attain these ideals. The general breakdown of manners in American society contributes to an appearance of impoliteness and disinterestedness among government employees. In the eyes of Confucius, diamonds in the rough were not enough. As he said, "Uprightness uncontrolled by etiquette becomes rudeness."[13]

Confucius designed a social system intended to infuse political power with high principles and learning. Like Aristotle, he believed that if rulers engaged in finer pastimes, such as listening to music, they would aspire to higher virtues associated with moderation and consideration of others. Ritual and etiquette served as external forms through which inner attitudes were developed. The profession of public administration in the United States is also committed to high principles and learning. We have master's degree programs in the discipline and in related fields at many universities. Considerable energy is expended in improving our knowledge base. Yet little effort is spent in understanding how we can aspire to a more cultivated way of practicing our profession. We produce technically trained, professionally oriented individuals, but have virtually no standards of personal conduct to transmit to students. If we are to avoid becoming a profession that ignores development of its members' higher qualities, then we will continue to be subjected to the negative image of the public servant as an inconsiderate "diamond in the rough."

THOUGHTS ON THE TAO

Confucius called his teachings the Tao, the Way to ethical conduct in government. When his followers took over, they limited the freedom of the ordinary people through social conformity and centralization of power. Society became rigid and overly moralistic. Despotism overtook reason, and the people found themselves increasingly at the mercy of dictatorial rule. Tired of the pressures to conform and of being treated as inferior, they adopted their own version of the Tao that stressed the importance of the individual. Their metaphysical Taoism differed substantially from Confucian philosophy. Aesthetic expression, previously repressed by the rigidity of Confucian society, was encouraged and began to flourish. The Way of the common man, predicated on the pattern of nature, was the force uniting everything in the universe. Impersonal laws, not social laws made by human beings, defined the perfect society. The mixture of Confucian positivism and Taoist mysticism defined the ruler in classic China so that the poet and the bureaucrat were not necessarily distinct individuals.

Grasping the Tao

The mystical concept of the Tao may appear to our rational and definitive perception of the world as nothing more or less than what we see. Objectivity and analytical reasoning are the foundations of our discipline. We abhor the indecisiveness of ambiguous and vague explanations. Logic rather than intuition, and control rather than uncertainty, provide security in our well-legislated society. The unpredictable forces of nature threaten us because we perceive them as beyond our control.

Western society is predicated upon the assumption that what we can see, hear, and touch is within our grasp, and if we try hard, we may be able to determine the direction of events. This requires constant attention to the physical world in order to reduce the uncertainty that it imposes. Our bureaucracies depend upon rules to control behavior and processes to direct activities. Empirical studies help us analyze unpredictable events. Complex methodologies are devised to measure successes and document reasons for failures. We think, we hypothesize, we test, we measure, and we analyze results. Our conclusions rest upon carefully circumscribed sets of events that we have assembled. We convince ourselves that we have captured microcosmic samples of the real world upon which we base our decisions. Our system is rational and logically constructed, but also must accommodate the vagaries that are characteristic of political demands.

Our administrative culture is rooted in the precepts of the scientific method, which have served us well in many respects. It is when we are faced with the continuing dilemma of weighing rational truths against political uncertainties that science seems to fail us. When this happens, the vague and mystical lessons of the Tao are potentially helpful because they capture things that are beyond the scope of reason and rationality. The Tao can put us in touch with a deeper reality and the wisdom of trusting our inner stirrings. The policymaker who knows when to cease logical argumentation and simply allow the natural unfolding of events is wise.

The concept of the Tao is impossible to define. Most of the literature on it nevertheless attempts to provide a description. To the Western mind, these explanations are very difficult to relate to the processes of daily living. This is because we believe that the individual who takes control and is committed to action will contribute the most to the world. Knowledge based upon intelligence and learning is our key to success.

Ironically, in its simplicity the Tao is complex. Raymond Smullyan writes, "The Tao never commands, and for this reason, is voluntarily obeyed." Reischauer and Fairbank comment that when life is lived in conformity with "the totality of the natural processes," we achieve the essence of the Tao. When we awaken to what is natural, our behavior becomes spontaneous and voluntary, and we instinctively succumb to the meaning of the Tao. Smullyan argues further that there is a certain natural spontaneity that brings with it understanding "which comes direct from one's true 'unborn nature'—which is the important one." Bureaucracies are not known for promoting innovation and creativity, which are the results of spontaneity at its best.[14]

Harmony and Balance

When we consciously aspire to achieve harmony, we make changes in the natural order of things. For example, in standard public administration, protocols are designed to improve productivity, restructure reporting relationships, and influence decision making. The Tao teaches that accomplishment results from the harmony that follows from spontaneity, not from the chaos resulting from control. Philip Rawson and Laszlo Legeza describe the Taoist perception of harmony as the natural outcome of a continuous pattern of movement and change that can neither be ordered by individuals nor prescribed by convention. The world is a united entity from which nothing is excluded and in which separation does not exist. The endless stream of activity does not distinguish between organic and inorganic material. Harmony results from the complexity of this continually evolving process, not from what appears to be static reality.[15]

Modern administrative systems attempt to impose integration and balance through uniformity, repetition, and completion. We perceive administration as the profession dedicated to restoring order to a chaotic, untidy world. When we succeed in attempts to impose structure and meaning on disorder, we see perfection and beauty. When our efforts do not succeed, we see inadequacy and error, and tighten administrative mechanisms. The undesirable conditions are often alleviated, but the ambiguity remains. We continue to believe that the world can be controlled once we perfect an expedient strategy that will balance the opposing forces responsible for all the trouble. At the macro or policy-making level of public administration, we have the example of the failure of Great Society programs designed to eliminate some domestic problems. Attempts to restore order internationally are not noted for their resounding successes either.

In Taoism, beauty and perfection do not rest upon symmetrical patterns. Since everything is united, uniformity and repetition are unnecessary. Nothing is ever complete, and repetition stifles imagination and new ideas. The goal of Taoism is conformity to nature rather than adherence to personal or governmental convention. Harmony in nature is expressed through cycles that fluctuate between calm and storm, as reflected in the changing seasons. Appreciation of the natural order requires acceptance and expectation of change. The fierce storm is as natural to life as the gentle breeze.[16]

In order to discover beauty in our daily activities, we need to cultivate our powers of perception and truly experience the tasks we perform. We are unable to appreciate the aesthetic quality of our actions when we devote all our attention to analysis and reason. Pleasure in the ordinariness of life opens us to fresh insights and broadens our view of the world. The professor who brings a loved dog to class and the manager who prunes an African violet carefully placed in the office have much in common. Having retained their childhood joy, work and play are one for them.

The Aesthetic of Silence

The Taoist master Hua-ching Ni tells us that the Tao is "beyond conceptual understanding and existence . . . silence is how one may understand its nature." Consider the quiet beauty of Japanese pottery, painting, and architecture. Thomas Hoover writes that the art of Japan relies upon the insight of the viewer for definition and completion. In other words, art is internalized so that the viewer becomes identified with the object of attention. The "aesthetic quality" of the Japanese tradition allows us to develop our powers of perception and appreciate the form of our creations, attributing meaning and purpose to the most common objects.[17]

In short, the Tao is everywhere and in everything. This sense of unity creates a respect for every object and activity, leading to a glorification or beautification of all things from high to low. When we supplement our impressions with insights that lie beyond reason and logic, we elevate our thinking and add another dimension to administrative competence.

In the words of Rawson and Legeza, Taoism aims for "harmony between the components of the dialectic situation, leading to harmony between each man and his turbulent universe, and an ultimate tranquillity."[18] Contemporary public administration is often referred to as crisis management. Most government offices are so noisy that it is impossible to attain the silence and stillness necessary to perceive the essential beauty in every task. Also, the "aesthetic of silence" that permeates Japanese philosophy is as foreign to human relationships in America as it is to American art. Our frame of reference for interaction is predicated upon direct verbal communication that is often confrontational. This behavior is in marked contrast to the more suggestive style of communicating found in the Oriental countries and contributes to the discord we experience in all facets of our society.

"THE ART OF BEING IN THE WORLD"

How do we apply the lessons of the Tao (assuming we want to), if we are unable to contain its meaning within a framework that satisfies the logical requirements of our Western tradition? Actually, there is little difference between our organizational values, which emphasize control, division of labor, and expertise, and the Confucian Way. However, there is not much sense in looking toward the Eastern aesthetic for enlightenment if we confine our search to elements that are already part of our own value system. We must risk new things. Taking a risk is similar to planting a seed. But half a seed will not produce half a crop. Likewise, overlooking the metaphysical interpretation of the Tao means leaving half of its wisdom behind.

Okakura says that Taoism is the "art of being in the world." This inspires us to adapt to change and to find beauty and meaning in ordinary activities.[19] Beauty may well be in the eye of the beholder. And if we believe that our perceptions create beauty in the world, we will have learned an invaluable lesson from the East to enrich our lives.

Raymond Blakney interprets an ancient Chinese poem attributed to Lao-tzu as describing the qualities found in the ideal man as he went about his business:

Like men crossing streams in the winter,
        How cautious!
As if all around there were danger,
        How watchful!
As if they were guests on every occasion,
        How dignified!
Like ice just beginning to melt,
        Self-effacing!
Like a wood-block untouched by a tool,
        How sincere!
Like a valley awaiting a guest,
        How receptive!
Like a torrent that rushes along,
        And so turbid![20]

Ideal persons have developed their innate capacity to be receptive and open to life. They see beauty and truth as the essence of everything that is around them. In the rush of living and working, they embody harmony and balance. This capacity is in all of us. It requires only encouragement and support to manifest itself in our daily lives. We owe public administrators, and ourselves, at least that much.

NOTES

1. George Santayana, *The Sense of Beauty* (New York: Charles Scribner and Sons, 1896), 14.

2. Ibid., 22.

3. Ibid., 157.

4. Ibid., 221.

5. Fritjof Capra, *The Tao of Physics*, 3rd ed. (Boston: Shambala, 1991), 257.

6. Ryusaku Tsunoda, William Theodore de Bary, and Donald Keene, eds., *Sources of Japanese Tradition* (New York: Columbia University Press, 1958), 279.

7. Will Durant, *Our Oriental Heritage* (New York: Simon and Schuster, 1954), 829–30.

8. *Sources of Japanese Tradition*, 280–81.

9. Edwin O. Reischauer and John K. Fairbank, *East Asia: The Great Tradition* (Boston: Houghton Mifflin, 1962), 471, 473.

10. Kakuzo Okakura, *The Book of Tea* (Rutland, Vt: Charles E. Tuttle, 1956), 3, 4, 26.

11. *Sources of Japanese Tradition*, 285.

12. *East Asia: The Great Tradition*, 488–89.

13. Ibid., 71–72.

14. Raymond M. Smullyan, *The Tao Is Silent* (New York: Harper & Row, 1977), 187–88; *East Asia: The Great Tradition*, 74.

15. Philip S. Rawson and Laszlo Legeza, *Tao: The Eastern Philosophy of Time and Change* (New York: Avon Books, 1973), 7–12.

16. Edward S. Schafer, *Ancient China* (New York: Time-Life Books, 1967), 62; *The Book of Tea*, 69, 71.

17. Hua-ching Ni, *Attaining Unlimited Life* (Los Angeles: College of Tao and Traditional Chinese Healing, 1989), 81; Thomas Hoover, *Zen Culture: How Zen Has Influenced Art, Architecture, Literature, Sports, Ceramics, Theatre* (New York: Random House, 1977), 226.

18. *Tao: The Eastern Philosophy of Time and Change*, 12.

19. *The Book of Tea*, 44.

20. Lao-tzu, *The Way of Life*, trans. Raymond B. Blakney (New York: Mentor Books, 1955), 67. Translation copyright © 1955 by Raymond B. Blakney, renewed © 1983 by Charles Philip Blakney. Used by permission of Dutton Signet, a division of Penguin Books USA Inc.

Part III

Commentaries on Bureaucratic Values in the Arts

4

Regimentation and Rebellion in *One Flew Over the Cuckoo's Nest*

Elsie B. Adams and Frank Marini

THE CRITICAL POSTURE OF THE BUREAUCRATIC NOVEL

It is commonly said that art and artists are repelled by organization and bureaucracy. The usual picture is of artists who find bureaucracy dehumanizing and choose to portray the essence of human life as freedom from the restraints and structure one finds in highly organized behaviors and institutions. It is common to find novels such as Joseph Heller's *Catch-22* or Ken Kesey's *One Flew Over the Cuckoo's Nest* (hereafter *Cuckoo's Nest*) described as portraying bureaucracy as inflexible and inhuman and as offering idiosyncratic and highly personalized life-styles as examples of free, human interaction.

For example, Howard McCurdy, who believes that the critical posture of the modern bureaucratic novel often rests on "the doctrines of existentialism," sees the fictional alternative to bureaucracy in terms of autonomy and freedom. He describes the hero of *Cuckoo's Nest* as "an outlaw of sorts," challenging the order and authority of the organization. The chief authority figure of the novel is understood as motivated by challenge to her authority, "determined to maintain her rigid procedures," engaged in entrapment of the hero, and finally emerging victorious through his lobotomization.

McCurdy's interpretation of the novel is referred to here partly because it is the interpretation of someone in the field of public administration who has attempted to make the connection between fiction and public administration. In this and other interpretations, McCurdy has attempted to show the field how the values, sentiments, sensitivities, and philosophical underpinnings of works of fiction can illuminate and inspire public administration. A related—and more important—reason for reference to McCurdy's interpretation of *Cuckoo's Nest* is that it presents the usual interpretation of bureaucracy as essentially a negative in human life rather than a positive. McCurdy interprets a chief message of the novel as dealing with the personalistic abuse of bureaucratic power, which he rightly characterizes as the reverse of the essential theoretical value and purpose of bureaucracy:

> In theory, bureaucracies are designed to reduce the opportunity for misused authority. They are supposed to eliminate particularism, favoritism, nepotism, and any other types of behavior that are irrelevant to the official objectives of the organization. Novelists such as . . . Kesey clearly do not buy this argument. As they see it, bureaucratic government increases the opportunity for organizational pathology.
>
> Bureaucracies vest enormous power in the hands of individuals under the pretense that the vesting is done rationally. . . . In the eyes of the novelist, large institutions hand over to individuals a form of technology that vastly expands their tendencies to practice mischief, while the impersonality of the bureaucracy shields them from personal responsibility for their acts.[1]

It is certainly true that *Cuckoo's Nest* has come to be regarded as a classic negative statement about bureaucratic organization and institutional life. Indeed, Kesey's portrait of the rule-bound, inflexible nurse who heads the mental hospital that is the setting for the novel seems to be a textbook example of bureaucratic rules replacing institutional purpose. But it is not our purpose here merely to restate what is readily apparent in *Cuckoo's Nest*—the extremely negative view of bureaucracy that emerges from numerous confrontations between the rule-breaking hero and the Big Nurse (as she is called)—though that is our starting point. We want to focus on what this particular work of art can contribute to our theoretical understanding of public administration. Especially, we want to focus on what it can contribute to the theory of bureaucracy and to the question of values.

THE STORY OF *ONE FLEW OVER THE CUCKOO'S NEST*

A chief difficulty in analyzing the novel is encountered in an element that is also a brilliant creative stroke: the novel is narrated by one of the

inmates in the mental hospital. We see all events, understand all characters, and receive all commentary from the point of view of Chief "Broom"
Bromden, an American Indian who has been mentally crippled by racist
encounters in his childhood and by despair over a manipulative, controlling, conforming society. Part of the genius of *Cuckoo's Nest* lies in making
the narrator one of the victims of the organizational machinery attempting
to grind everyone into a smooth pattern. But this narrative ploy creates a
severe problem when we attempt to locate the "reality" of the novel. Chief
Bromden, moving in and out of blinding and numbing fogs, seeing a world
controlled by gears and cogs and wires and occupied by humans who
transform into machines and back again, announcing from the outset of
his story that "it's the truth even if it didn't happen," is (to put it mildly) a
less than reliable narrator.[2]

But Chief is the only narrator we have. All we can do is to note from
the outset that what we know of the hospital (indeed, of anything in
Cuckoo's Nest) is filtered through the consciousness of a madman.[3] Thus,
while one may find insight in Chief's descriptions of the mental hospital
and the wider society as part of a great mechanical "Combine," one should
not forget that Chief sees this as literally and not metaphorically true, and
that he often sees humans as literally machines. This point of view greatly
complicates reliable understanding of the story for critical and analytical
purposes, and should make us cautious about condemning the Big Nurse
out of hand and about accepting unquestioningly the heroic stance of her
antagonist.

The story of *Cuckoo's Nest* focuses on one patient's brief period in a ward
of a mental institution. The hospital ward is described as a frighteningly
efficient but dehumanizing machine under the command of the Big Nurse,
whose primary objective, according to the narrator, is to produce individuals who are "adjusted to surroundings." Her control is seen as extending
both within and beyond the hospital on a "web of wires," which she attends
"with mechanical insect skill" to create "a world of precision efficiency and
tidiness like a pocket watch with a glass back" (30). Her watchwords are
"follow the rules" and "enforce discipline and order" (28, 171, and passim).
The sterile, precise, rigid world she inhabits is represented by the stark,
white walls and bright tube lights of the hospital, the starched uniforms of
the Big Nurse and her attendants, and the hospital policies that discourage
any deviation.

Into this rule-bound, structured milieu steps the hero, Randolph P.
McMurphy. He is a refugee from a prison farm who has been sent to the
mental hospital for treatment as a psychotic. Whether he has feigned

insanity in order to lighten his workload and ameliorate his boredom, or whether he is actually mentally ill, we do not know. McMurphy confronts the hospital administration and challenges its rules with the loud mouth of a circus pitchman and the audacious courage of a western gunslinger. It is this confrontation that produces the major conflict in the novel—between the Big Nurse, representing organizational rigidity and impersonality, and McMurphy, seen by the narrator as the champion and savior of the hospital inmates.

Time and again McMurphy challenges hospital policy. *Why* must all patients brush their teeth at the same time each morning? (85). Why can't the attendants eat with the patients? (93). Why can't the music piped into the ward be turned down? (95). Why can't the inmates watch television in the afternoon (instead of the customary evening viewing) during the World Series? (105). To all these questions, the Big Nurse and her attendants seem obdurate. The Big Nurse, in her insistence on adherence to rules—not to mention her use of electroshock therapy or of lobotomy—to control ("adjust") her patients, seems to have lost sight of the healing purpose of the organization she heads.

Patient McMurphy is a bigger-than-life character who enters the ward with bravado and leaves through a sacrificial and Christ-like death. He is the clear hero of the novel, and though flashbacks and other devices extend the story a little beyond his brief stay, it is McMurphy's encounter with the institution and with the Big Nurse that temporally frames the story. McMurphy's braggadocio and his insistence that personal freedom and play are values worth wresting from rules and structure contrast sharply with the Big Nurse's insistence that order, regularity, and rules are necessary for the welfare and the eventual healthy adjustment of the patients entrusted to her and the institution. The picture presented is clear, and in black and white: the Big Nurse represents repressive order while McMurphy represents the freedom of unrestrained self-expression. It is not surprising that some commentators have seen the central conflict as repressive bureaucracy versus self-realization.

But if we would apply the story to our own interests in public administration, we should consider nuances other than the black-and-white, unidimensional interpretation. Several questions may elicit nuances of interpretation. Is the ward a bureaucracy or an antibureaucracy (i.e., are the values depicted in the ward and in the Big Nurse the values of bureaucracy or the distortions of bureaupathology)? Are the countervalues represented by McMurphy and his actions the values of freedom and self-actualization, or are they values of a darker kind? If one examines the values offered in opposition to the Big Nurse and her administration—the values articulated by the narrator and exemplified by the hero of the novel—one can scarcely avoid asking what negative results may accrue to these values. Specifically, does the novel suggest that the expression of free and autonomous individualism may be as dysfunctional as organizational rigidity? If so, in what ways and to what effect? It is our thesis that the novel forces us to reexamine not only our concept of bureaucracy but also our attitude toward authority as decentralized to the individual alone.

BUREAUCRATIC THEORY AND *ONE FLEW OVER THE CUCKOO'S NEST*

Bureaucratic theory as it has informed public administration has an important genesis and various aspects. First, there is the more or less objective social science theory of bureaucracy (traditionally exemplified in public administration literature by the work of Max Weber). Second, there is a body of emendations and addenda to such theory contained in commentary upon that theory, much of which criticizes the rigidity and the impersonality of bureaucracy and calls attention to phenomena such as the displacement of values. Examples are Philip Selznick, Alvin Gouldner, Robert K. Merton, Anthony Downs, Vincent Ostrom, and Frederick Thayer;[4] the literature of "new public administration";[5] and the literature of "Minnowbrook II."[6] Third, there are polemics for and against bureaucracy (e.g., Charles Goodsell, Ralph Hummel).[7] Fourth, there is the popular view of bureaucracy that is informed by, and perhaps in turn informs, the scholarly and professional literature; this view can readily be found in contemporary mass media, everyday vocabulary, political rhetoric, and academic and nonacademic civic discourse. *Cuckoo's Nest* is a good example of this fourth view.

In *Cuckoo's Nest* the formal organization of the hospital is powerfully portrayed as a device for control and resocialization. The role of the rules, the procedures and policies, the power structure—indeed, the mental institution and to an extent the whole society—is to "adjust" those who are ill-adjusted to their social life so that after adjustment they will better "fit" their social lives. In contemplating bureaucratic theory, though, we should be mindful of the fact that all social institutions are arguably institutions of socialization, resocialization, and "adjustment," and that the vision of a human being freed from the bonds of social institutions may not be the angelic figure often attributed to Rousseau and other allegedly naive idealists. Rather, it may be the dangerous and capricious figure to whom

Thomas Hobbes called attention. *Cuckoo's Nest* provides us with ample illumination for reflecting upon this question.

While reflecting upon *Cuckoo's Nest*, we should also consider whether the story is one about the problems of bureaucracy or one about the problems of the absence of bureaucracy. There has been a general tendency to assume that the failings of the Big Nurse and of the mental ward are bureaucratic failings. But one could argue just as readily that such failings have to do with personalistic and arbitrary action for which bureaucratic organization could be an ameliorative if not a preventive. For example, the Big Nurse's power, when it seems excessive, appears to be rooted in the failure of her superiors to perform their organizational functions, inappropriate manipulation of friendship (notably, but not solely, her supposed power and invulnerability because of a long-standing close friendship with the hospital's superintendent), and the seemingly personalistic rather than professional approach to discipline and treatment. In short, rather than a picture of bureaucracy, the hospital appears to be more nearly a picture of the problems connected with a nominally bureaucratic organization in which bureaucracy is regularly circumvented for personal purposes and private power.

One of the technical elements of bureaucratic theory has to do with the hypothesized tendency of bureaucracy to lead to a displacement of goals so that maintaining the trappings of bureaucracy comes to replace the official purpose for which the organization exists. Commentators (including those for whom the language of bureaucratic theory and displacement of goals is not the natural language) regularly see in the hospital and in the Big Nurse of *Cuckoo's Nest* a picture of obsessive concern with personal power and control, and with rigid discipline replacing the goal of patient treatment. The parallel with the theoretical perspectives of Robert K. Merton and others who discuss dysfunctional aspects of bureaucracy is striking. As Merton points out:

Discipline, readily interpreted as conformance with regulations, whatever the situation, is seen not as a measure designed for specific purposes but becomes an immediate value in the life-organization of the bureaucrat. This emphasis, resulting from the displacement of the original goals, develops into rigidities and an inability to adjust readily. Formalism, even ritualism, ensues with an unchallenged insistence upon punctilious adherence to formalized procedures. This may be exaggerated to the point where primary concern with conformity to the rules interferes with the achievement of the purposes of the organization, in which case we have the familiar phenomenon of the technicism or red tape of the official.[8]

It is easy to view the hospital and specifically the Big Nurse as setting aside human values and the good of patients for the good of the organization or for personal power aggrandizement. Yet it is not clear that the rationale the Big Nurse steadily offers in terms of maladjustment, mental illness, and resocialization is implausible and insincere in terms of the good of the patients or, indeed, of the hospital's function of striving for the good of the patients. The Big Nurse can and does give reasons and explanations for every rule about which she is questioned—and these reasons and explanations are plausible and plausibly related to the hospital's official purpose and a concern for the health of the patients.

In fact, if we step back a bit (and outside the novel) and attempt to understand the Big Nurse's ward from a point of view other than Chief's— say, that of a conscientious hospital administrator or attendant—we can perhaps see a rationale for some of the rules and procedures of the hospital. Admittedly, the use of electroshock or of radical surgery is out of favor in contemporary treatment of mental illness, but it was not so long ago that these were accepted (though one hopes never routine) therapeutic procedures.[9] Concerning the rules in force in the hospital, we could defend the necessity for proceeding in an orderly way—for establishing a daily schedule and sticking to it. The encounter between an attendant and McMurphy over brushing his teeth provides an extreme (and highly amusing) example of the rule-bound organization versus the autonomous individual. McMurphy is told that he cannot brush his teeth when he wants to, that the toothpaste is locked up. He seeks a reason for this policy, observing (in mock horror) that if the toothpaste were not kept under lock and key, "people'd be brushin' their teeth whenever the spirit moved them. . . . And, lordy, can you imagine? Teeth bein' brushed at six-thirty, six-twenty—who can tell? maybe even six o'clock" (85).

Put that way, the toothbrushing policy seems absurd. But, as we know, an organization such as a hospital, attending to the needs of many patients, has to operate according to a schedule of some sort. Perhaps it can make adjustments for human differences from time to time, but as a rule it must adhere to a preestablished routine—else some patients may be neglected, supplies may be misplaced, supervision may be inadequate. Though from the outside we can perhaps agree that McMurphy should be permitted to brush his teeth whenever the spirit moves him, we can also see that, from the point of view of the hospital staff, some sort of orderly schedule needs to be maintained. It is, after all, a mental hospital requiring constant monitoring of at least some of the patients.[10]

In short, one can profitably walk back and forth between the concerns of bureaucratic theory and the novel. And such crosswalking suggests interesting questions and insights about bureaucratic reality and bureaucratic theory.

THE VALUES EMBODIED IN THE NOVEL

A key element of much of the discourse of bureaucratic theory—social scientific, academic, and professional, as well as political, rhetorical, and civic—is the question of values. It is widely asserted that bureaucratic values are dehumanizing, controlling, conformist, rigid, and dysfunctionally impersonal. Frequently, the values held to be counter to these are asserted to be values of freedom, individual autonomy, passion, self-actualization, self-expression, and flexibility.

At every point *Cuckoo's Nest* rejects as dehumanizing attempts to "adjust"; the hospital ward is seen as a factory designed to turn out a product suitable to a mechanized, conformist society. As Chief explains, after release of a patient: "Something that came in all twisted different is now a functioning, adjusted component. . . . Watch him [the cured patient] sliding across the land with a welded grin, fitting into some nice little neighborhood" (40). *Cuckoo's Nest* recounts the story of Mr. Taber, who comes to the hospital asking questions and causing trouble and who leaves, after a lobotomy, "a *new man*," well adjusted to society: he makes love to "the doped figure of his wife," has two children, goes bowling on Mondays. "When he finally runs down after a pre-set number of years, the town loves him dearly and the paper prints his picture helping the Boy Scouts last year on Graveyard Cleaning Day, and his wife gets a letter from the principal of the high school how Maxwell Wilson Taber was an inspirational figure to the youth of our fine community" (40). Mr. Taber becomes "normal," living a totally unremarkable life without questioning any aspect of it, even statistically predictable (his death is "pre-set").

The same tendency to reduce human beings to ciphers and their lives to a predictable pattern is attacked in another memorable passage in the novel, when Chief sees "a *train* stopping at a station and laying a string of full-grown men in mirrored suits and machined hats, laying them like a hatch of identical insects, half-life things coming pht-pht-pht out of the last car" (203). These insectlike look-alikes go from the train to "five thousand houses punched out identical by a machine and strung across the hills outside of town, so fresh from the factory they're still linked like sausages" (203); nearby is a school with "five thousand kids in green corduroy pants and white shirts under green pullover sweaters" (204). The account concludes, "All that five thousand kids lived in those five thousand houses, owned by those guys that got off the train. The houses looked so much alike that, time and time again, the kids went home by mistake to different houses and different families. Nobody ever noticed" (204). It is with a shudder of horror that Chief shares this glimpse into suburban commuter life.

Again, if we move outside the novel and to a different point of view, a number of questions assert themselves: Is it necessarily wrong to be "normal" (as Chief implies in his examples of Mr. Taber and of the look-alike community)? Is "twisted" a desirable alternative way to spend one's life? Can we assume that adjustment to norms—even though it means conforming to social expectations—is always a mechanical and manipulative process? However we answer these questions, at the heart of the values of *Cuckoo's Nest* is the view that "normal" is uniform and inhuman and that idiosyncratic behavior is a preferable alternative.

If a too-well-regulated society is the target of the attack, how, then, is the alternative depicted? In order to answer this question, we turn to the climactic event in the novel, an all-day fishing trip organized by McMurphy and attended by sundry hospital inmates (including Chief), a doctor, and a prostitute friend of McMurphy. In the course of this trip, the men solve various problems confronting them and return at the end of the day transformed—not "the same bunch of weak-knees from a nuthouse" of the morning (215).

McMurphy organizes the trip over the objections of the Big Nurse, signing up the men and arranging for two prostitute friends to chaperone and provide cars. The first obstacle—the failure of one of the women to show—is overcome when the hospital doctor agrees to drive a staff car for the trip. A second obstacle—the hostile reception that the green-uniformed men meet at a local gas station—is overcome through McMurphy's bravado threats. Claiming that the men are "hot off the criminal-insane ward" and fabricating their violent crimes, McMurphy bullies the gas station attendants into respect for and fear of the men, and provides "food for thought" for one of the inmates: "Perhaps the more insane a man is, the more powerful he could become" (202). A third obstacle—the fact that the captain of the rental boat demands a waiver clearing him of responsibility for the passengers before releasing the boat to them—is overcome by direct action: McMurphy steals the boat. A day at sea of beer-drinking and deep-sea fishing culminates in a grand "scramble of action" that contrasts at every point with smoothly functioning routine:

the men yammering and struggling and cussing and trying to tend their poles while watching the girl; the bleeding, crashing battle between Scanlon and my fish at everybody's feet; the lines all tangled and shooting every which way with the doctor's glasses-on-a-string tangled and dangling from one line ten feet off the back of the boat, fish striking at the flash of the lens, and the girl cussing for all she's worth and looking now at her bare breasts, one white and one smarting red [from the punishment of trying to reel in a hooked fish]—and George takes his eye off where he's going and runs the boat into that log and kills the engine. (211)

The men, following McMurphy's lead, start to laugh, "swinging a laughter that rang out on the water in ever-widening circles, farther and farther, until it crashed up on beaches all over the coast, on beaches all over all coasts, in wave after wave after wave" (212). This fishing trip offers the antidote to the regimentation of the Big Nurse's ward and world: confusion, tangled lines, swearing, struggle, bare rather than confined breasts—topped by a kind of cosmic laughter. McMurphy's values seem to be freedom and play (understood as chaos or escape from order).

From another point of view, the fishing trip is dangerous, illegal, irresponsible in almost every way, as is another break for freedom that occurs on the hospital ward when McMurphy manipulates a black watchman, sneaks two prostitutes into the hospital, and breaks into the medical supplies to provide the alcohol for a wild party. The novel would have us believe that the fishing trip and the ward party are liberating and empowering experiences.

Whether or not the rough-and-tumble style of McMurphy is desirable is a matter for debate. However, McMurphy's methods—questioning the rules, metaphorically tangling the controlling wires, smashing through barriers, playing and laughing at life—in the world of the novel are effective means of combating a programmed, sterile, brutal society. McMurphy undeniably creates, through leadership, example, and self-sacrifice, an atmosphere in which Chief can break free of the hospital and other inmates are restored to a degree of self-esteem and, in some cases, to life on the outside.

The individual pitted against the overpowering machine, resisting its attempts to formulate and limit him, is an attractive (if exceedingly romantic) notion, even to those of us who are uncomfortable with chaos as an alternative to order. But much less attractive is the overall view of humanity offered by both the hero and the narrator of the novel. Insisting on the importance of human idiosyncrasy and autonomy, *Cuckoo's Nest* denies that importance to both women and blacks, shockingly stereotyping both.

If *Cuckoo's Nest* can be seen, as some critics have asserted, as an archetypal battle of the superhero against gigantic forces of evil, there is no escaping the fact that that evil is represented by women, and especially by a woman who takes on almost mythic significance in the figure of the Great Mother. Even her label—the Big Nurse—is suggestive, as are the frequent references to her oversized breasts (which she is portrayed as attempting to conceal in her starched white uniform). She is not, however, the archetypal nurturing Mother but the terrifying femme fatale—a castrator and destroyer of men. It is disturbing to find that, in a novel which condemns a society that controls and dehumanizes, that society is symbolized by a woman. Admittedly, at one point in the novel Chief quotes McMurphy, stating "that there's something bigger [than the Big Nurse] making all this mess"; and Chief himself says that it is "the nation-wide Combine that's the really big force, and the nurse is just a high-ranking official for them" (165). These disclaimers are significant, but they cannot obscure the fact that McMurphy's (and Chief's) principal antagonist is the Big Nurse. (She has a name, incidentally: Nurse Ratched; but she is depersonalized into "the Big Nurse" in most references to her.)

In an interesting conversation between inmate Harding and McMurphy, Nurse Ratched is identified as "a ball-cutter," after which McMurphy explains, "I've seen a thousand of 'em, old and young, men and women. . . . people who try to make you weak so they can get you to toe the line, to follow the rules, to live like they want you to" (57). Significantly, here (as in the comment on "the nation-wide Combine" above), both "men and women" are identified as the castrators. But again we have to note that there are no such men in the novel; the male attendants work at the Big Nurse's command, and the doctor stands in awe of her. When we look for the villain of the piece, we find the Big Nurse.

The only "good" women in the novel are the prostitutes (women to be used sexually by McMurphy and his friends) and a kindhearted nurse in the Disturbed ward, who offers the opinion that "all single nurses should be fired after they reach thirty-five" (234). The other women in the novel, like the Big Nurse, are like figures out of Philip Wylie's *Generation of Vipers*.

Manhood in the novel is defined as phallic power, manifested in sexual encounters with women and in stereotypical macho behavior (fighting, gambling, hard drinking, tough talking, big-game fishing, etc.). In the course of the novel, some of the inmates (after the fishing trip and after the wild party in the ward) reach such manhood.

Yet manhood is a state denied to the black characters in *Cuckoo's Nest*, who are consistently called "boys" by the narrator and who are—next to

Nurse Ratched—the most hateful (and hated) characters in the novel. Why does *Cuckoo's Nest* make all three of the Big Nurse's assistants black? Chief's account suggests that the three were selected by the Big Nurse because of their ability to hate and because "The blacker they are . . . the more time they are likely to devote to cleaning and scrubbing and keeping the ward in order" (31–32). These comments pinpoint a deplorably racist attitude, which is also reflected in the Chief's and McMurphy's use of racist epithets to refer to the ward attendants.

The celebration of McMurphy as the embodiment of freedom, self-actualization, and humane concern for fellow patients, which seems to be part of the reaction of some commentators and probably the first reaction of many readers, must be seriously called into question. His racism and sexism (even giving due consideration to the fact that the novel was written in the 1960s) are raw, blatant, brutal, and truly ugly. In *Cuckoo's Nest* we are presented with a disarmingly appealing iconoclastic hero who looks on women as "twitches" and on black men as "coons." We find an argument for coming to manhood in a conformist society but are offered as a model for manhood a stereotype out of a Marlboro ad. As Marcia L. Falk astutely observes, *Cuckoo's Nest* "never once challenges the completely inhuman sexist structure of society, nor does it make any attempt to overthrow sexist or racist stereotypes."[11] To a contemporary reader it warns that the man cut loose from rules may present a threat to society as serious as that of the big controlling bureaucracy in his manifestation of some of the ugliest aspects of human intolerance, including unthinking denigration of women and blacks.[12]

BUREAUCRACY, BUREAUPATHOLOGY, AND OTHER PATHOLOGIES

The popular understanding of bureaucracy portrays the essence of bureaucracy in terms that a serious student might characterize as bureaupathology. That is, the word "bureaucracy" commonly conveys none of the theory of bureaucracy and its functionality; rather, it conveys the perversions and dysfunctions of bureaucracy as though these were its essence. The role of popular art (literature, film, television, journalism, cartoons, and pop culture expressions like bumper stickers and T-shirts) in creating and sustaining this image of bureaucracy has undoubtedly been significant. The situation has evolved beyond the point where one could say—as Dwight Waldo did in 1962—that a popular pejorative notion conflicts with a scholarly theoretical concept and that popular understanding is a misunderstanding of the specialized terms of a professional vocabulary.[13] The present situation is that the popular understanding of the word has substantially eroded and replaced the theoretical understanding even among scholars who are avowedly specialists in the theory of bureaucracy. Thus one can find simplistic ideological treatments of bureaucracy in the professional literature of public administration.

Cuckoo's Nest illuminates how popular art can contribute to such a state of affairs. The novel stereotypes not only the principal characters and bureaucracy but also the whole of organizational and societal life. Of course, we cannot ignore the fact that Chief is the narrative source of McMurphy's story. We are constantly reminded that it is Chief who fears "adjustment" and "normality" and who admires McMurphy precisely *because* "he's out of control" (84). As we observed at the beginning of the chapter, this point of view calls into question all the information in the novel and makes locating the values of the novel a very slippery job indeed. To complicate matters, *Cuckoo's Nest* is a novel that undercuts itself. An obvious attack on regimentation and soulless conformity, it offers in contrast a pathological hero who manifests some of the most antisocial attitudes in modern fiction.

Perhaps the most powerful image to emerge is that of a dysfunctional organization dominated by a professional who lets her nurturing role as nurse be overshadowed by a need for power and control. The hospital ward and the wider society outside are seen as similarly unfeeling, uncaring, and manipulative, forcing everyone into preset patterns. In opposition to this is the autonomous individual, ultimately crushed by the big society but nevertheless questioning the rules and disrupting the machine precision of the hospital/society as a way of asserting freedom. Unfortunately, this individual—as represented by McMurphy and reported by Chief—holds such a racist and sexist view of humankind that we are forced to wonder if the "twisted" individual is really better than the "adjusted" conformist. Whether intentionally or not, the novel offers a sobering view of certain antisocial attitudes of the individual flying free from organizational constraints.

The narrator of the novel makes clear which choice he prefers between the organizational machine and this individual. Our choice is more difficult. McMurphy is hardly a heroic model. Similarly, we cannot with confidence offer the Big Nurse as a public administrator worthy of emulation. Perhaps we should refuse to choose between compulsive order and chaos, between the flawed individual operating without restraint and the crippling forces of a repressive society, and should insist upon other alternatives and models for both individual behavior and social organization.

It may be that bureaucracy itself should not be neglected as one of the alternatives to the picture *Cuckoo's Nest* projects. For in spite of the conflation in rhetoric of bureaucracy and bureaupathology, and in spite of the postulated tendencies of the former to evolve into the latter, bureaucracy itself may be, ironically, a principal preventive of the very abuses and behaviors so frequently attributed to it. Bureaucracy as Weber treated it, for example, is part and parcel of the general tendency of certain societies away from personalistic, nonrational, magical, arbitrary, and in some cases anarchic traits and toward regularized and relatively predictable traits resting in reasoned explanation.[14] This evolution was closely related to that of predictable legal systems and rules whose goal was to diminish the prevalence of whim and wildness in human beings' treatment of one another. It is also closely related to evolution in notions of science and professionalism; only a profound misunderstanding equates the capricious end of this evolutionary path with art, creativity, and freedom. Bureaucracy and its related phenomena may still be one of the best hopes we have against prejudicial, chaotic, and irresponsible expressions of mad action masquerading as freedom. *Cuckoo's Nest* is a useful work from which to contemplate such questions.

NOTES

1. Howard E. McCurdy, "How Novelists View Public Administration," in *A Centennial History of the American Administrative State*, ed. Ralph C. Chandler (New York: Free Press, 1987), 543–74, quote at 562.

2. Ken Kesey, *One Flew Over the Cuckoo's Nest* (New York: New American Library [Signet], 1962), 13. All page references in the text are to this edition. Many readers will be familiar with the film based on the novel. Our essay deals exclusively with the novel and not with the film, which differs from the novel in so many ways that it makes an entirely different statement and produces an entirely different effect.

3. The generic problem represented by author intention, point of view, "meaning," and statements that may be reliably communicable intersubjectively is, of course, not unique to this particular novel. Indeed, exploring such issues is a significant industry.

4. Philip Selznick, *TVA and the Grass Roots: A Study in the Sociology of Formal Organization* (Berkeley: University of California Press, 1949) and *Leadership in Administration: A Sociological Interpretation* (Evanston, Ill.: Harper & Row, 1957); Alvin Gouldner, *Patterns of Industrial Bureaucracy* (Glencoe, Ill.: Free Press,

1954); Robert K. Merton, *Social Theory and Social Structure*, enl. ed. (New York: Free Press, 1968); Anthony Downs, *Inside Bureaucracy* (Boston: Little, Brown, 1967); Vincent Ostrom, *The Intellectual Crisis of American Public Administration* (University: University of Alabama Press, 1973); Frederick C. Thayer, *An End to Hierarchy! An End to Competition!: Organizing the Politics and Economics of Survival* (New York: New Viewpoints, 1973).

5. The literature that can be subsumed under the "new public administration" label directly or by extension is extensive and debatable. It would include Frank Marini, ed., *Toward A New Public Administration* (Scranton, Pa.: Chandler, 1971); Dwight Waldo, *Public Administration in a Time of Turbulence* (Scranton, Pa.: Chandler, 1971); and H. George Frederickson, *New Public Administration* (University: University of Alabama Press, 1980).

6. The literature of Minnowbrook II has been described, briefed, and promised; but for the moment it is confined to H. George Frederickson and Richard T. Mayer, eds., "Minnowbrook II: Changing Epochs of Public Administration," *Public Administration Review* 49 (March-April 1989): 95–227. Mary Timmins Bailey and Richard T. Mayer, eds., *Public Management in an Interconnected World: Essays in the Minnowbrook Tradition* (New York: Greenwood, 1992), is also pertinent.

7. Charles T. Goodsell, *The Case for Bureaucracy: A Public Administration Polemic*, 3rd ed. (Chatham, N.J.: Chatham House, 1994); Ralph P. Hummel, *The Bureaucratic Experience*, 4th ed. (New York: St. Martin's Press, 1994).

8. Robert K. Merton, "Bureaucratic Structure and Personality," in his *Social Theory and Social Structure*, p. 253.

9. Note in this regard Mary Frances Robinson and Walter Freeman, "Glimpses of Postlobotomy Personalities," and Arthur P. Noyes and Lawrence C. Kolb, "Shock and Other Physical Therapies," in *One Flew Over the Cuckoo's Nest: Text and Criticism*, ed. John C. Pratt (New York: Penguin [Viking Critical Library], 1973), 477–97 and 498–505, respectively.

10. To these observations defending schedules and routine, Chief would argue that they are merely reflections from someone "Outside" who has been "adjusted" into conformity by the Combine.

11. "Letter to the Editor of *The New York Times*," in . . . *Cuckoo's Nest: Text and Criticism*, p. 451.

12. Some might argue that the racism in the novel is mitigated by the fact that the narrator is an American Indian whom McMurphy befriends. Moreover, a black attendant, Mr. Turkle, is included in the ward party, though he does not escape racist labeling in McMurphy's references to him. Yet the strong racist undercurrent of the novel is clearly seen in the portraits of the Big Nurse's black attendants. Compare the various accounts of the attitudes of Kesey and his Merry Pranksters in Tom Wolfe's *The Electric Kool-Aid Acid Test* (New York: Farrar, Straus & Giroux, 1968).

13. Dwight Waldo, "Bureaucracy," in *Collier's Encyclopedia* (1962 ed.), vol. 4, 732–39.

14. Max Weber, *Economy and Society: An Outline of Interpretive Sociology*, ed. Guenther Roth and Claus Wittich (Berkeley: University of California Press, 1978).

5

Insights into Bureaucracy from Film: Visualizing Stereotypes

Marc Holzer and Linda G. Slater

THE OYSTER BED WAR

The sun is setting away from the oyster beds in the pungent marshes leeward of the barrier islands. A low darkness creeps along the coastline, imposing an eerie stillness.

A sharp rat-tat-tat shatters the truce as night envelops the last vestiges of day. Five hundred yards inland, on higher ground prime for development, a construction crew finishes work on a deck overlooking the low-country marsh. The burly foreman reviews the blueprints under the glare of his headlights—blueprints that detail an eight-foot-wide dock penetrating the marshes right over the critical bedding areas for the sensitive oysters.

The battle lines are drawn as sharply as the blue lines on the construction diagram.

Oyster beds have been destroyed by development all along the southern coastline. Environmentalists and oyster lovers are enraged. Yet the landowner who paid big bucks for shore property wants, and feels he's entitled to, deep-water access. Docks are going in all along the bay sides of similar islands.

Who can save the endangered oyster before its bed is shattered and its environment polluted by oil, gasoline, and Twinkie wrappers?

Enter the Coastal Council, whose chairman handles his gavel as surely as the foreman his hammer. Rat-tat-tat. Permit denied! The public oyster beds are protected by state and federal mandates. Docks will not be built along this island. Thick files document the decision and the testimony and research supporting it. Appeals will be filed, but the oysters will not be disturbed tonight.

This is a real-life drama, straight off the public record. Will the competent, quiet heroics of the Coastal Council be immortalized in film? Maybe. But in the fictionalized version, the bureaucrat would be incompetent, the foreman would be bribing the government inspectors, the landowner would wear black clothes and smoke a cigar, and a local environmentalist would save the day and the innocent oysters, with a wild boat chase thrown in. This is *The Milagro Beanfield War* (a movie in which local activists save farmland) transplanted to the marshes of South Carolina.

UNFORGIVING IMAGES

The media are crucifying the public sector. Virtually all depictions rework stereotypes to excess: a torrent of unflattering images teaches the public that government employees are incompetent, callous, and corrupt. The composite image is vivid and powerful: in print, over the air, on the stage or the screen. From the restrained *New York Times* to the tabloids, from the local newscast to the world news, from the small screen to the silver screen, the image is unmistakable and the language consistent. News stories focus on the negative and dysfunctional, and champion the victims of bureaucratic red tape. Headlines blare scandals. Editorials castigate bureaucrats for their inability to control the "system." Government bureaucrats are "incompetent officials," "tangled in red tape," "uncaring." They incessantly "shuffle papers" and render "arbitrary decisions." The attack is ceaseless and merciless; the only exceptions seem to be the obituaries, in which the deceased officials may finally (but futilely) be praised for "public service." Positive accomplishments by live public servants are usually considered neither newsworthy nor entertaining.

Beginning with the youngest readers (or even nonreaders), the cartoonist's assault on bureaucracy is incessant and devastating. Nationally syndicated comic strips reinforce a negative image of public service daily in black and white, and in color in the Sunday papers: "Broomhilda," for example, rails against dehumanization by society; citizens fight back against onerous paperwork in "Goosemeyer"; "Doonesbury" portrays the Pentagon as a blissful pawn of lobbyists. Cartoons that accompany newspaper editorial and opinion pieces offer those commentaries to older readers, typically illustrating a "Bureau of Bureaucracy," "Red Tape," "The Runaround," or unintelligible "Government Speak." A popular bumper sticker states, "Crime Wouldn't Pay If the Government Ran It."[1]

Cinema wields the heaviest hammer. Motion pictures—first as theater films and then as videos in rental outlets—promote and feed on the negative stereotypes of the bumbling bureaucrat. The movie M*A*S*H (and the very popular television series of the same title, which continues as reruns) highlights bureaucratic nonsense in the military, with a substantial dose of sarcasm. Unthinking military bureaucrats—unnecessarily officious, obstinate, and formal—are easily outmaneuvered, outwitted, and outflanked. This unflattering image of bureaucratic bumbling is so ubiquitous and so pervasive that the public adopts the premises of inefficiency and corruption, excesses and waste, without objectively balancing the dysfunctions with successes, accomplishments, or even routine operations. Moviemakers and television scriptwriters would improve their craft by crossing the Values Bridge and seeing beyond the narrow confines of stereotypical casting. Public administrators are not the only ones who could benefit from the bridges of Illumination and Inspiration.

THE CAMERA'S IMPACT

There are many reasons films can have a damaging effect on public perceptions. Foremost is the vast size of the audience. The more outlandish (e.g., *E.T.*), the more antiestablishment (e.g., *Do the Right Thing*), or the more violent (e.g., *Serpico*) the movie, the more people of all ages it attracts to the theater or video rental outlet. In each of these three films, for example, the audience is exposed to inept, self-serving, brutal, or corrupt public officials and agencies. Even the most polarized points of view are legitimized by films whose only purpose is to attract viewers.

A related factor is the "half-life" of a successful film. No longer do theatrical releases play at first-run and then second-run movie houses, then sit on a shelf to await a TV premiere and occasional rerun before fading into obscurity. As videos they live on indefinitely, entertaining the public. A prime example is *Raiders of the Lost Ark*, an ever-popular video rental. In addition to taking us on vicarious adventures, it tells of the incompetence of government officials, Nazi and American. Indiana Jones outwits the Nazis, then loses the invaluable Ark of the Covenant to his own government's bureaucrats—who unthinkingly relegate it to a huge warehouse with assurances of safekeeping. Will it remain there for several more millennia?

Movies go beyond other forms of fiction to combine visual and auditory dimensions. The visual image is encompassing, immersing. It allows for the total suspension of disbelief so the viewer can become a vicarious participant in the situation or conflict. The sound track manipulates emotions through choice of music (patriotic march or romantic ballad), through volume, and through intensity of beat, rhythm, or sound bite. The speed and complexity of the production can lead to a charged reality. Films can also manipulate time and "enhance" history, facts, or even logic.

All of this is important because in films and videos, unlike written fiction, the perspective is prechosen and imposed on the viewer. The imaginative interpretation has largely been decided by the director, who can take off from the text or script upon which his film is based to create a vehicle for reform, criticism, or satire through creative manipulation of visual images and sound track or the pacing of the production. A good example is Spike Lee, who writes, directs, and sometimes appears in loud, fast-paced, and visually abrupt films that often project anger and impatience at a bureaucratic system that has failed blacks. Throughout *Do the Right Thing*, Radio Raheem's boom box blasts "Fight the Power"—right up to his senseless murder by cops responding to a street fight.

LET'S GO TO THE MOVIES

Which movies utilize enduring images, directorial bias, and technical creativity in order to institutionalize bureaucratic stereotypes and assault the public servant? Some examples illustrate the argument for films' negative role in bureaucracy in terms of such organizationally important factors as values, leadership, decision-making models, and organizational structure.

In *Ghostbusters*, which underscores the popular image of "bureaucrat as buffoon," an official of the Environmental Protection Agency obnoxiously demands to inspect a storage facility for ghostly spirits. Rejected because he did not use the magic word "please," he returns with a court order. Told that his actions will surely endanger the populace, he opts for rules and regulations, ordering the facility to be shut down. Even though his actions almost lead to disaster, the agitated bureaucrat still clings to the letter of the law. He is finally removed by the mayor, who opts for live, grateful voters over mindless procedures. The enduring message is that bureaucrats are dangerously incompetent.

In *Catch-22*, a World War II bureaucratic farce that was first a novel and then a movie, corruption is prevalent, accountability nonexistent, and the treatment of individuals callous. The war's goals are replaced by those of profit and individual comfort. The interests of the illicit M&M Syndicate become more important than military success or soldiers' lives. Similarly,

Colonel Cathcart continually increases the number of dangerous missions required of his men, solely to enhance his own reputation. Perhaps the most important theme in the movie, as in the novel, is the ludicrous nature of bureaucratic rules; the image of circular reasoning is so powerful that "Catch-22" has become a common phrase in our language.

In *The Band Played On*, an HBO made-for-TV movie, progress on a cure for AIDS is hampered by bureaucratic infighting and timidity. Although the federal Centers for Disease Control (CDC) make great progress on identifying the causes of AIDS in the early 1980s, and can recommend prevention strategies, their work is hindered. Committees question their methodology. A key scientist at the National Institutes of Health is more interested in his reputation and power. Superiors within CDC are conditioned by traditional, incremental strategies; they lack the imagination and initiative to push for adequate funding for research. The chief seeker of a cure finally resigns, in disgust, to pursue his work with private funding.

Star Wars, as discussed in Chapter 1, provides an excellent illustration for crossing the Values and Leadership bridges. The evil Empire initially uses a mindless bureaucracy to its advantage. Under a Weberian model, its legions can be described as coldly efficient; its information networks, as pervasive; its technological achievements, as superior. But the Rebellion ultimately triumphs by being much less bureaucratic—more motivated and innovative. In both *Star Wars* and *The Return of the Jedi*, individual initiative and on-the-spot innovation defeat seemingly impervious forces. The Empire's bureaucrats are stereotypical ciphers, unable to think, to react, to adapt.

In *Stand and Deliver*, a dedicated math teacher overcomes the skepticism of burned-out colleagues and the harassment of the disbelieving, bureaucratic Educational Testing Service (ETS), which, relying on flawed and biased computer "analysis," accuses his minority students of cheating. ETS bureaucrats force the teacher's entire class to repeat an advanced placement calculus test. Fortunately, the students succeed under even greater pressure, but only due to their teacher's David-like efforts in opposition to the bureaucratic Goliath.

In *Mister Roberts*, the obstinate imposition of discipline conveys the inflexible image of the military mind. Although Doug Roberts, the cargo officer of a World War II transport ship, is anxious to see combat, his requests for transfer are routinely denied by a stupid, petty captain. The compulsively authoritarian officer not only trashes Roberts's requests but is pathologically inflexible—ruling solely on the basis of Weber's legal-rational model. The crew is forced to respect the authority of his office but refuses to accord him any respect as a leader or motivator. Its members finally forge the captains's signature on Roberts's request to transfer, with unintentionally tragic consequences; he is killed in action.

In *One Flew Over the Cuckoo's Nest*, discussed in its' original novel form in the previous chapter, patient McMurphy disturbs the routine procedures of a mental hospital. The film version presents the staff as particularly callous and control-oriented. Nurse Ratched, in particular, is the epitome of a narrow-minded functionary. The crux of the movie is that her authority is challenged by McMurphy's informal power. Her custodial assumptions are in direct conflict with a humanistic orientation toward patient/staff relations. Ultimately, Nurse Ratched and the organization triumph in the harshest terms, and McMurphy's power is negated by subjecting him to an irreversible and unnecessary lobotomy.

VISUALIZING STEREOTYPES

As noted in Chapter 1, published analyses have examined the role of fiction—including films—in molding the image of government and the public servant. In one contribution to this literature Dwight Waldo identified three types of fiction directly related to public administration: bureaucratic fiction, in which the plot is centered on bureaucratic relationships; administrative fiction, involving decision making within an organization; and the self-explanatory political fiction. Many of the novels used as his examples, such as *A Bell for Adano*, are also the basis of feature films.[2]

Marc Holzer, one of the authors of this chapter, constructed a "Matrix of Concern in Fiction," in which he categorizes pessimistic views of bureaucracy's impact on individual values. This framework can be used to analyze the values imputed to bureaucracy in film. In an intraorganizational sense, bureaucracy not only stifles (e.g., Gilbert's and Sullivan's *H.M.S. Pinafore*, as an operetta and movie) but also demoralizes or corrupts (e.g., Melville's "Bartleby the Scrivener," also a PBS movie). In terms of extraorganizational relationships, clients are generally treated as impersonal objects (e.g., Butler's "Pigs Is Pigs," also a cartoon), but may also be the objects of unjust decisions (Dickens's "Containing the Whole Science of Government"). The films also suggest that an individual bureaucrat's reactions to such dysfunctional environments may range over disinterest, impotence, cynicism, and resignation.[3]

Lawrence L. Downey has noted that fiction can explore conflicts in three predominant areas, and this is true in films as well: legitimization of authority (e.g., *The Caine Mutiny*); relationship of organizations to their external environment (e.g., *Agnes of God*); and relationship of organizations to their internal environment (e.g., *An Officer and a Gentleman*). David A. Gugin expands on the conflict issue, focusing on fictional treatments of morality and ethics. He places these subjects in two general categories: external and internal. The external category deals with accountability and responsiveness to intent or traditional norms, while the internal subgroup is concerned with individual ethics or morals in conflict with organizationally demanded behavior.[4]

Thus, moral and ethical conflicts are at the heart of many of the negative public sector stereotypes embodied in films. The clear-cut right vs. wrong choice is muddied when individual preferences or practical solutions conflict with abstract rights—or when group ethics differ from organizational policy and mission. These themes are illustrated, to the detriment of the public sector, in Joseph Ruben's gritty 1989 film *True Believer*. The pot-smoking antihero Eddie Dodd, a fighting liberal lawyer, takes on the system to prove a Korean youth was wrongfully convicted of a gang murder. As the plot unwinds, the cops are revealed to have framed the youth to protect a valuable informant who actually committed the hit; and the district attorney went along to assure indictments of a Colombian drug ring, sacrificing the little guy to serve the "greater good." In this film, the public is as much the victim as the youth. The oppressor is the "system."

What makes the vital role of the bureaucrat so hard to capture in films in a positive sense? Part of the answer lies in a lack of public understanding of the essential nature of public service. An interesting paradox is evident in an analysis of society's negative preconceptions of government in contrast to its demands and expectations for ever greater levels of service. The Volcker Report (of the National Commission on the Public Service) noted that the public expects government "to keep the peace with other nations, resolve differences among our own people, pay the bills for needed services, and honor people's trust by providing the highest levels of integrity and performance." Public servants build bridges, keep vital statistics, treat AIDS patients, issue food stamps, fight crime, bury garbage, inspect meat, explore the moon . . . the list goes on and on. Yet, as Eileen Siedman wrote in 1984, "The American public's love-hate relationship with its government produces demands for services, assistance, and protection while denigrating the people, processes, and costs necessary to meet those demands."[5]

What the public knows and understands about government and the public servant, beyond personal experience, is what it reads in the newspaper or sees on the screen. An important factor in the film portrayal of public bureaucracy is a movie studio's goal to make money. Films are looking for the heroic gesture or the incredible dysfunction to rivet audiences to their seats. Public sector heroes certainly do appear in films: firefighters, crusading cops, Elliot Ness and his federal crime fighters, tactical teams dealing with terrorists, and rescue missions into crumbling subway systems. While positive statements on loyalty, bravery, and integrity emerge from films such as *Rain Man*, *Patton*, *Gorillas in the Mist*, and a slew of "war" movies, these same pictures also portray institutional rigidity, military obsession, and bureaucratic red tape in ways that demean the public sector.

The problem is that bureaucrats who are busy designing environmentally sound landfills or financing a transportation system with municipal bonds are rarely making the heroic gesture, and their jobs are too complex for the public to understand fully. Headlines may deplore higher property taxes attributed to the recommendations of bureaucrats, but the bureaucrats' contributions to the community will probably not be captured on film. Real bureaucrats are most often just practicing what Charles E. Lindblom calls "muddling through," making decisions incrementally without a "grand plan" or epiphanic breakthrough.

Nancy Murray refers to the Confucian sense of moderation in Chapter 3, suggesting the modern bureaucrat's need to find a balance between political realities and administrative necessities. But these are not the public servants portrayed in films. Until they make mistakes and are perceived as dysfunctional managers, they are ignored by the public. Failure to detect asbestos, approval of a dangerous drug, misdiagnosis of a critically ill patient—these are examples of situations in which bureaucratic decision making is held hostage to angry public reaction. When put before the public in an entertainment medium, the image of incompetence becomes institutionalized and is rarely balanced by any kind of portrayal of the vast positive role of the public sector. A more balanced depiction of public sector decision making in films would strengthen the Values Bridge and contribute significantly to the practice of public administration.

PERSPECTIVES ON REALITY

The relationship of films to reality is dichotomous and paradoxical. Clearly, films reflect and enlarge reality for multiple purposes. Reality, less obviously, is influenced and molded by films. Exploring these perspectives draws into focus the ominous nature of the effect of movies on public service.

It is in the nature of fiction depicted on film that it plants its seed in a ground of truth with which the viewer can identify, then grows to expand his or her mind to new horizons. The major public dysfunctions, thus, become fair game for the camera shot, as in *One Flew Over the Cuckoo's Nest* or *Catch-22*. But the audience also has personally encountered the officious tax collector, the self-righteous cop, the clueless motor vehicle office clerk, and finds even exaggerated portrayals of such bureaucrats realistic.

Thus, part of the problem may be in the present nature of public bureaucracy. David Osborne and Ted Gaebler think we need to "reinvent government" so as to encourage hierarchically organized administration (operating with inflexible rules and fiscal checks) to become more entrepreneurial, in order to lead by persuasion and incentives rather than power and control. The present obsession with control is decried in the June 1993 report of the National Commission on the State and Local Public Service, issued after two years of research by current and former government officials. The Commission offers proposals to "move us away from an encrusted and outmoded system of command and control and its rule-bound management that emphasizes constraints and process at the expense of mission and results." This report shares a frustration with government as "a system undergoing death by a thousand paper cuts." Cinematic satire or harsh screen depictions, such as those cited earlier, may play a role in hastening these reforms.[6]

In another sense, films are a reflection of, and reflect upon, the times in which they are produced. Their social and political climates constitute a palette from which a writer or director creates comment, criticism, observation, satire—even the framework for reform or change. This phenomenon is evident in the plethora of movies related to the Vietnam war and its aftermath. Unlike the world wars, this involvement was unpopular, political, and considered a failure. Films about it reflect alienation (*The Deer Hunter*), horror and disorientation (*Apocalypse Now*), and social stigma (*Coming Home*). It was not until almost two decades after the U.S. troops pulled out that acceptance and understanding were socially evident and thematically present in films related to Vietnam. The 1989 release *In Country*, with Bruce Willis, reflects sympathy and comprehension of the psychological trauma experienced by the Vietnam veteran. That same year Brian DePalma held Americans to a full moral accounting for the Vietnam involvement in his film *Casualties of War*. In *Good Morning, Vietnam* we have two major messages: the Vietnamese are individuals with morally worthwhile goals, and the Army is an organization of bureaucrats who are insensitive to the psychological needs of the populace as well as those of their own troops.

Michael Sragow, writing for *Mother Jones*, sees a more sinister effect of society and politics on films. His premise is that political climate shapes their content and even their social commentary. In a creative indictment of the Reagan–Bush era, Sragow contends that the political emphasis on attitude and image over thought and substance produced "movie making that can be codified and quantified—and sold to the same sort of people who buy paintings to match a color scheme." He finds that, politically and cinematically, the common themes reflected the bland, the simple, the unreal, the sentimental, and the benign. Emotional complexities were ignored in favor of "inspirational" denouements, as in *Dead Poets Society*, when the prep school kids "atone for betraying their free-spirited teacher by standing on their desks and calling him Captain (after Whitman's Lincoln, not Captain Kangaroo)."[7]

The late 1980s and early 1990s saw the rise of the counterculture films. The work of Spike Lee draws on street experience and a reverse racism to offer stark commentary on prejudice, urban blight, and human dignity. Lee attacks establishment views and power structures, such as the welfare system and the police, while forcing the viewer to consider alternative perspectives. *Boyz N the Hood* (1991) portrayed the same social reality, softened by positive family values and the teasing possibility of breaking the cycle.

Films mirror, often with creative distortion, public perception and popular attitudes. Perceptions are a personalized reality, dynamic concepts that grow tangentially with an abstract "truth." Films manipulate facts and concepts to the extent that reality becomes what viewers perceive it to be. If the public is consistently presented with the media image of mediocre bureaucrats who are unprofessional and inflexible, that in essence is what those bureaucrats become—not just in the eyes of the public but in the bureaucratic professional identity. The negative perception becomes self-perpetuating; the films create the reality.

This same perception allows films to rewrite history. *Mississippi Burning* examines racism in the South. Based on an actual incident involving the disappearance of civil rights activists, it simplifies and whitewashes the involvement of the FBI, in this case creating federal heroes in conflict with corrupt, bigoted local officials. But initiative and unorthodox (i.e., illegal) behavior are glorified in an "ends justify the means" portrayal that the film fails to question.

Motion pictures can thus go beyond entertainment to affect public policy. *The Grapes of Wrath* helped build a constituency for social welfare programs by condemning corrupt local bureaucracies—such as police in league with Oklahoma banks to evict luckless farmers, and with California growers to exploit the new migrants. Oliver Stone's *JFK* suggested there was something terribly wrong with our government, charges that have generated a vigorous debate and helped build pressure to open files on the assassination. *Star Wars*, as discussed in Chapter 1, inadvertently helped create a public demand for and support of a very expensive space-based strategic defense initiative. More recently, *Free Willy* rode the waves of political correctness to galvanize animal rights activists against big business, in this case businesses that capture killer whales, or other marine mammals, ostensibly for educational purposes but also to lure tourists and their money to marine entertainment centers. John Wayne and Clint Eastwood have done their share to win public support for military might. Charles Bronson probably played a role in increasing law enforcement budgets in cities across the nation.

SO WHAT?

Are we making too much of the movies? Maybe that's the point. The manipulative role of films in society and the insidious constancy of the motion picture industry's assault on government and the public servant have transformed what may be, on the surface, innocent entertainment into a force threatening the very quality of public service. Affected are productivity and efficiency, as well as recruitment and retention.

Movies, in short, have reinforced the public's long-standing, poor image of government. The American culture's long fascination with the embarrassing and the inept has fostered a dark perception of our public life in general. This has led to a crisis in the public service, deterring the "best and the brightest" from government careers and breeding the self-fulfilling prophecy of mediocrity. Citizens have been conditioned to believe that public servants exhibit both low competence and low productivity. Politicians have been encouraged to demean their own employees and dismantle their own agencies. As a consequence, many public servants have become discouraged or demoralized. Leonard D. White's 1926 conclusion still holds: "Two ideas are widely held by the American taxpayer. He believes that there is an extraordinary number of useless or overpaid public officials and he is convinced that most government employees are lazy and incompetent. . . . The city, state, or federal employee . . . thinks of the years of faithful service which he has performed, well hidden from the windows where 'the public' peers in . . . and is not unlikely to shrug his shoulders, thinking, 'What's the use.' "[8]

Contemporary attacks on the bureaucracy in films range from the naive to the malicious, and are more than annoying. Unceasingly demeaning the value of public service, reinforcing an image of "government as incompetent," they not only help to undermine support for the public sector but also create important consequences for compensation, recruitment, and retention. The message to potential and present managers is that the public service—under attack by the private sector and the "fall guy" for the failures of elected officials— is not an attractive place in which to work.

Aaron Wildavsky concurs that the message society gives to public servants is an ambivalent one. On the one hand, public service is the highest aspiration a citizen can have. On the other hand, bureaucracy is the problem, not the solution.[9] This contrasts with the situation in many other countries. The public service is held in high esteem in the industrial democracies of Western Europe, the British Commonwealth (particularly Canada and Australia), and Japan. A Twentieth Century Fund study, *The Government's Managers*, contrasts the century-old American habit of disparaging the civil service with the high respect in which the public service is held elsewhere:

In those nations [industrial democracies], the most promising students are attracted to the civil service. And members of the mandarinate are often tapped to head major organizations in the private sector. . . . But despite the growth of government and the increasing complexity of its responsibilities, the careerists in the civil service, the men and women who run the federal government's agencies and departments, have rarely won much in the way of the rewards—in either public esteem or in monetary compensation—that their counterparts abroad regularly receive. . . . Comparatively few of the government's senior managers, even with their superior qualifications, go on to top positions in the private sector.[10]

We agree with the Twentieth Century Fund that "demeaning civil servants not only is harmful to morale, it also makes it increasingly difficult to attract and keep the kind of independent and imaginative career professionals who are critical for the future well being of the nation." The Volcker Commission reported that college honor society students preferred employers (perceived as providing challenging work and the opportunity for personal growth) that were nongovernmental: academic institutions, small business/professional firms, and large corporations. The federal service was ranked only a distant fourth, followed by state/local government and the military. Among those who have entered government, a 1988 survey of management attitudes in the federal government concludes that the constant criticism public servants receive does in fact bother the respondents, who feel the perceptions are ill-founded.[11]

By undermining the general confidence in public servants' competence and productivity, the movie industry has helped to create a climate in which the best of the capable, young, educated, ambitious administrators or technicians are shunning government and looking to the private sector for employment. The most qualified of our young people should be performing the challenging and meaningful jobs in the field of public administration. Yet all too often the negative marketing provided by the media, especially films, turns potential applicants off to any thought of seeking a government job.

The messages in movies should not, however, be dismissed just because they are predominantly negative. Nancy Murray's discussion of the Tao in Chapter 3 suggests that the acceptance and expectation of change are part of the natural order. Movies can play as great a role in effecting a needed change in the expectation of performance in public sector jobs as any other single social force. The Coastal Council's members may never get to be the heroes in the oyster bed war, but the public administrator needs to be portrayed as knowing from which side to mount the white horse.

Bureaucracy's critics—reporters, artists, writers, and film directors—are a societal asset insofar as they have assumed the responsibility for persistently addressing the full and subtle range of ethical issues within public organizations. They are warning us that public bureaucracies are often dysfunctional; enervating and inefficient; the antithesis of creativity; cancers in our social fabric. Moviemakers and other creative artists portray the clean, well-lit buildings that house our bureaucracies as some of the most dangerous places in our society. And because entertainment is a palatable conveyor of criticism, the messages in movies (as well as in cartoons, novels, and other forms of artistic expression) may be especially effective in generating a dialogue within a bureaucracy, or between bureaucrats and clients. The foil might be a movie such as Marie, which portrays government as corruptly suppressing the truth. The film would enable us to cross the Values Bridge and discuss the writers' or directors' messages. Bureaucrats, knowledgeable critics, and citizens might even be invited to comment. The ensuing dialogue could illuminate the implicit solutions suggested by filmmakers: problem-solving approaches that puzzle the public sector and may account for its failure to respond to critics. Government too often fails to untangle red tape, to eliminate waste, and to treat its clients and employees humanely. From the perspectives of members of the public and their moviemaking surrogates, avoidable human tragedies are all too routine. Messages that bureaucracy stifles productivity cannot be dismissed as simplistic, for many social science theories are grounded in the same assumptions. Osborne and Gaebler, and many others, argue that the old bureaucratic model must give way to an entrepreneurial approach to public administration.[12]

Those same tensions—bureaucratic control versus individual initiative— have been resurfacing for decades. They have staying power because the problems of bureaucracy are still unsolved, because the organizational sciences have not been able to change most organizations, because bureaucracy is still perceived as violating the public trust. Perhaps that inadequacy is due in large part to a choice of one medium, print, and one slice of that medium, textbooks and journals, as the locus of debate. But the cinema offers another as yet unexploited means for drawing attention to our most basic organizational concerns, and sometimes it underscores the same models that students of government also recommend. Many of the movies cited above suggest remedies to the traditional bureaucratic management that often produces unanticipated and tragic consequences. The classic *Grapes of Wrath*, for example, presents an effective federal bureaucracy—a humanely administered work camp—as an alternative to society's failures toward migrant workers. In *Brubaker* a newly appointed prison warden and reformer experiences the Wakefield State Prison bureaucracy disguised as an inmate. Uncovering a corrupt deal between the outgoing warden and the prisoner-trustees, he gains the respect of abused inmates and harnesses the informal system for the purpose of effective reform. In *An Officer and a Gentleman* the drill instructor, Sergeant Foley, is in full control in pursuit of a narrow goal: to produce the most physically fit, most disciplined officers possible. That approach, in accord with the Navy's emphasis on control and subordination, often succeeds. But below the authoritarian veneer is an examination of the group, of informal cohesion and interpersonal motivation. In these three cases the movies are exploring alternative views of organizational efficacy. Perhaps consideration of those alternatives can be accelerated if students of organization also become students of film.

NOTES

1. Marc Holzer, "Visual Perspectives on Bureaucracy: Art, Cinema, and Photography," paper presented at annual conference of the American Political Science Association, Washington, D.C., 1991.

2. Dwight Waldo, *The Novelist on Organization and Administration: An Inquiry into the Relationship Between Two Worlds* (Berkeley: University of California Press, 1968), 5–23.

3. Marc Holzer, "Unorthodox Administrative Commentary," *The Bureaucrat* 3 (July 1974): 116–29; *Literature in Bureaucracy: Readings in Administrative Fiction*, ed. Marc Holzer, Kenneth Morris, and William Ludwin (Wayne, N.J.: Avery Publishing Group, 1979), ix.

4. Lawrence L. Downey, "The Use of Selected Fiction in Teaching Public Administration," paper presented at the first national conference on Public Administration, the Arts, and the Humanities, the New School for Social Research, New York City, 1987; David A. Gugin, "Bureaucratic Decision Making and Bureaucratic Ethics: An Argument for the Novel," paper presented at the annual meeting of the American Society for Public Administration, Boston, 1987.

5. National Commission on the Public Service, *Leadership for America: Rebuilding the Public Service* (Washington, D.C.: The Commission, 1989), 1; Eileen Siedman, "Of Games and Gains. . . ," *The Bureaucrat* 13 (Summer 1984): 5.

6. David Osborne and Ted Gaebler, *Reinventing Government: How the Entrepreneurial Spirit Is Transforming the Public Sector* (Reading, Mass.: Addison-Wesley, 1992); National Commission on the State and Local Public Service, *Hard Truths, Tough Choices: An Agenda for State and Local Reform* (Albany: Nelson A. Rockefeller Institute of Government, State University of New York, 1993), 23–24; "Hard Truths, Tough Choices," *Governing* 6 (August 1993): 48–49.

7. Michael Sragow, "Gross Projections," *Mother Jones* (January 1990): 23–29.

8. Leonard D. White, "The Personnel Problem," in *Classics of Public Personnel Policy*, ed. Frank J. Thompson (Oak Park, Ill.: Moore, 1979), 23–24.

9. Aaron Wildavsky, see quote in *The Bureaucrat* 19 (Fall 1990): 17.

10. *The Government's Managers: Report of the Twentieth Century Fund Task Force on the Senior Executive Service* (New York: Priority Press, 1987), v, 3.

11. *The Government's Managers*, 4; Leadership for America, 197; Jack Jabes, "Qualitative Results: 1988 Survey of Management Attitudes in the Federal Government," *Optimum* 20–22 (1989–90): 32.

12. *Reinventing Government.*

6

The Administrator–Viewer Reviewed, Through Film

Morton Kroll

THE ADMINISTRATOR–VIEWER

The viewer in this instance is the public administrator, the woman or man who works within the public sector and makes or contributes to decisions and actions that affect public policy, writ large or small. In this chapter I shall examine the ways in which motion pictures might stimulate responses relative and relevant to the work of public managers.

It is both the blessing and the bane of American public administration that public administrators cannot readily be stereotyped. Despite frequent and continuing attempts, we have not really evolved an administrative class. Political leaders, from presidents on down the elected ladder, have all too often punitively blasted "the bureaucracy" as made up of managers and their minions who get in the way of successful policy implementation, insensitive to the needs of their communities as well as of their political masters. The brushes used to paint this picture have been broad yet anecdotal, defying empirical evidence or analysis. "Bureaucracy" and "bureaucrat" have long had a pejorative popular meaning.[1]

Films, especially American films, have tended to adopt a negative concept of bureaucracy. In the previous chapter, Holzer and Slater analyze these cinematic portrayals and their consequences, especially upon their audiences. Recognition of the bleak portrait painted by films of the public service raises the question of the utility of this vibrant, popular art form (or, perhaps, its disutility) for public managers. Can inspiration, stimulation, even solace be drawn from them? The answer we assert with great

clarity and assuredness is "It depends." It depends upon who the administrator is, his or her circumstances, and, most of all, his or her degree of
receptivity to films or even to a single motion picture. Of course, any
dramatic incident may strike a chord of response and reaction. On the other
hand, it is possible to develop an analytical mind-set, a desire and capacity
to integrate a film, or some aspect of it, into one's professional experience.

As many levels of meaning may be read into a good motion picture as
there are levels of comprehension within the audience. We're all familiar
with the observation that it depends on "the mood I'm in." This certainly
has relevance for the understanding and empathy the administrator derives
from a film, especially if he or she selects it for entertainment or enlightenment. It may be coincidental, even accidental, if a "message" is derived
by the administrator, unless that person is oriented to view motion pictures
as rich sources of insight and information.

One of the suggestions of this chapter is that the public administrator
who sees society as a whole, who grasps the interrelation among its parts,
its complex connections and dependencies, who sees his or her persona in
this context, has much to gain.

With apologies for adding to anyone's jargon, let me suggest the term
"administrator–viewer" to describe the person attuned to viewing films in
this way. Active, analytical viewing is the key to this process. It involves
consciously sensitizing one's mind to the meaning a given film holds for
the professional insight—indeed, inspiration—one gains from it. A film,
as much as a novel, drama, painting, or poem, can provide enlightenment
and deep pleasure if actively studied.

As the twentieth century draws to a close, we recognize the growing
importance of motion pictures, especially with the advent of VCRs and the
burgeoning availability of sound and imagery through digital channels. It
is commonplace to note that we are all living through a communications
and information revolution. Public administrators, like others in society,
must understand that not only are methods of gathering, processing, and
communicating information rapidly changing, but new interactive processes utilizing these systems are emerging. Greatly increased access to
untold numbers of newly created works brings virtually instant exposure of
phenomena, such as films, to wider audiences.

Among those now in supervisory and administrative roles, many managers have been acculturated to include motion pictures as an integral
aspect of their cultural, informational, educational, and professional environment. The film is implicitly recognized as an art form whether or not it

is appreciated as such by the viewer. My use of the term "art" includes bad art as well as good art.

A further purpose of this chapter is to stimulate greater reciprocity between the moviemaker as artist and the public administrator. From the perspective of the viewer, one can think of the benefits to be derived from active viewing as involving, first, an empathic understanding of the complexities of situations presented in films and the consequent dilemmas facing the characters in them; and second, the film characters as individuals. We see events, we see the environment of the story through the eyes and psyches of its personalities. We gain an appreciation of how critical events in one's life effect change. Vicariously, the viewer experiences the dilemmas of others from a close-up portrayal of their lives. The analytic step to be taken is to note similar situations one knows about in one's experience or reading and how these might be resolved.

Films thus can help public administrators across the Values Bridge so that they become more aware of the subtleties inherent in the interplay between complex situations and individual personalities. The essence of public management involves this interplay, and the arts, including motion pictures, induce the administrator to understand and see himself or herself as part of this dynamic relationship.

In this chapter I shall examine, first, the manner in which films relate to the diverse people engaged in public administration. I then proceed to a review of the cultural and subcultural contexts of films and their meaning for public administrators. I move on to a consideration of the time dimension in films. I then proceed to an examination of the individual in cinematic treatments in the context of public service. Consideration of ethical dilemmas and the interaction between the individual and community as depicted in movies logically follows. By way of a synthesis I have related the analysis to the bridges in this book's theoretical framework and consider, in conclusion, the role of the public administrator as artist.

THE RECOGNITION OF MEANING IN FILMS

Let us assume an array of public administrators from all sorts of jurisdictions, bombarded by public policy and management situations. The spectrum of personalities and the nature of the problems that present themselves defy easy classification. These range from foreign policy and national security questions to urban violence, epidemics, infrastructural deterioration, and the chronological cycles of public budgets, the legislative process, and electoral politics. These are but a glimpse of part of the array of policy areas and their administrative components that constitute the everyday demands and challenges that permeate the public management function. The federal, state, or local administrator, as the cliché has it, is "involved." This person may be a frontline supervisor or a senior administrative assistant secretary in a large agency. Given the diversity of persons and personalities who perform these functions, we do not have any predictive data as to how any of them will react to a given film. The nature and degree of influence, stimulation, even inspiration, are as varied as the persons, their positions, and their official and personal circumstances.

What is out there, in the cinematic medium, that can offer edification, insight, and inspiration to anyone who devotes a professional life to public employment and its attendant headaches and responsibilities? At the outset, we must differentiate between the filmmaker's intent and the uses to be made of the finished work. The two are not necessarily in sync. The primary creative force behind a film, be it director, writer, and/or producer, may have a specific artistic purpose. The goal may or may not be directly tied to a social or political thesis. For the administrator-viewer, the insight or stimulus may be triggered by a single scene, personality, or bit of information. A viewer might ruminate on a film as follows: "I was sitting there, watching this movie about an air force general who didn't take into account what the losses of so many of his men and aircraft would mean, despite the success of the mission, to his own organization. It dawned on me that's exactly what's happening at the office, and the more I thought about it, the more I saw parallels between the film and my experience. I could hardly sleep that night. By morning I had my next step worked out. Of course, it wasn't anything like the movie, but I wouldn't have thought about the resolution that soon if I hadn't seen the picture."

The mind-set of the viewer, the capacity and willingness to accept art as part of one's experience, leads to relevant appreciation. Art enriches only to the extent that the beholder is willing to receive and interact with its meanings. In this way, art inspires the viewer to come to terms with his or her values as they reflect personal and professional experiences. In other words, art inspires the beholder to cross the Values Bridge.

MOTION PICTURES AND CULTURES

Of course, an understanding of a culture and/or subcultures (such as those of organizations and institutions in differing environments) can enrich the viewer's perspective. Cultural diversity has become a self-conscious preoccupation, particularly as portrayed in contemporary films. They obviously reflect the values and behavior of the culture that produces them. This is so whether the culture is internal to our society or that of another country.

Spike Lee's *Do the Right Thing* (1989) depicts African-American life from an inside perspective. Through its vivid imagery the film presents racism as an urban phenomenon in contemporary terms. This film, and others, such as *Boyz N the Hood* (1991), transport the viewer into the intimacy of the environment. One cannot help but grasp the dilemmas and the problems that produce enraged reactions in some, negative behavior in others, embattled challenges in still others. The meaning of family, or its absence, the influence of adults on children, the impact of external forces such as economic exploitation and the drug "culture" are conveyed in dramatic cinematic form.

The Native American plight is carried through comedically in *Powwow Highway* (1988) and dramatically in *Thunderheart* (1992). In both films the portrayal of public officialdom is negative. In *Thunderheart*, however, the hero, part Native American and an FBI agent, takes on a corrupt colleague and roots out the evil, to the advantage of his people and the FBI. Cleaning bureaucratic house is a prevalent theme in current movies. But the perspectives that the artistic lens focuses upon, in both of these films, are the values and attitudes of a people deprived and dispossessed.

Stand and Deliver (1988), one of the few films produced thus far concerning the Hispanic-American, or Latino, population, focuses on secondary education. A Hispanic-American high school math teacher teaches, and then tutors, his mainly Latino students to score high marks on their college entrance exams, over the strenuous objections of his immediate supervisor. The teacher relates to his students bilingually and biculturally, and is able to stimulate their interest, motivation, and desire to work toward their goal. The film addresses, furthermore, the impact of such achievements on the family and social lives of the students. What is fundamentally important to the administrator–viewer is that the successful implementation of this educational policy could never have occurred without a thorough understanding of the values of the people affected.

From its cultural purview, this film criticizes the rigid behavior within institutional structures, in this case a high school in Los Angeles. The hero is the person who overcomes bureaucratic obstacles to benefit the group he serves. It is worth noting the reaction and behavior of the minority communities to a well-meaning and, in this instance, successful program. Mainstream achievement can clash with traditional values of the minority group effected, a dilemma the administrator must understand and address.

The public administrator inevitably deals with people of varying cultural orientations. The values contained in these must be woven into the administrator's, must be added to the mix of his or her constitutional commitments to public life in a democratic society.

Motion pictures are produced in most parts of the world: industrial, developing, urban, rural, and all categories in between. There are established film industries on nearly all continents. Much can be gained if, upon seeing a "foreign" film, the viewer asks, "What does this movie tell me about these people? How do they think about the relation of their situation, their condition, to the community or public parts of their lives, including their bureaucracy?" Pursuing these questions can enhance our enjoyment of a good movie by our reflections upon it.

At times an American-made film, shot on location in another country, can offer a rich array of insights. *City of Joy* (1992) deals with the travails of an American physician working in an impoverished section of Calcutta: the frustrations, problems faced, the ingenuity with which he "makes do" with the meager resources at hand. His developing relationships with individuals in the community provide a decidedly upbeat impression when one considers the film as a whole. While not a motion picture for the fainthearted, it portrays the gamut of the doctor's feelings and responses under horrid conditions: from revulsion and frustration to adjustment and as much achievement as one could hope for. As his relationships and involvements grow, his work becomes more effective. It is this combination of professional objectives with one's personal awareness, including one's own history, that makes for effective action in any community.

No matter how it is defined, the community to which the public administrator inevitably relates constitutes a distinct subculture with its unique, identifiable qualities and dynamics. A public official continually experiences a virtually organic relationship to her or his community. In a small jurisdiction (including the classroom where the Teaching Bridge is crossed), this can be a very direct interaction. The classic film *High Noon* (1952) allegorically typifies the case wherein the official is unappreciated, even unrecognized, until he performs the heroic act that saves the community. In some respects this theme provides a classic plot outline for many movies. *In the Line of Fire* (1993) affords another example of the hero, unsung until the very end, who suffers rejection that nearly overcomes his single-minded pursuit. In other films the hero must unearth the corruption in his work environment, as in *Thunderheart*, wherein the Native American FBI agent must cope with the hostility of his fellow Native Americans while unearthing the corrupt behavior of the agent in charge.

Occasionally a film provides a portrait of community. One depiction is in the classic British comedy *Tight Little Island* (1949), in which the community contests the government in salvaging a shipwrecked vessel loaded with whiskey. Its actors appear to the viewer more as an ensemble than as one or several characters. In such films no single personality stands out, or stars.

UNDERSTANDING TIME AND CHANGE

Cultural diversity is never static; it changes with time. And if we take a historical glimpse, we find this change reflected in films. The making of motion pictures is more than 100 years old. Film has evolved from a brief amusement to a full-fledged medium. The viewer can observe the evolution of attitudes toward public life, its problems, and its personalities that spans a considerable period of time. Viewing made in the 1930s and 1940s, offers a perspective on the values, actions, and politics of the times. We see where we were in relation to where we are.

The simplistic theme of *Mr. Smith Goes to Washington*, made in 1939, compared with a film such as *Bob Roberts*, released in 1992, reveals how sophisticated and cynical moviemakers have become, and no doubt their audiences as well. At the same time, it is clear that underlying values, the acceptance of the ideals of a democratic republic, have not changed. The evidence today is presented in a more pejorative manner. The "good guys" are still identifiable, and what is good remains unchanged from the standard of the 1930s. By the 1990s, however, it has become much harder to find these virtues through the thicket of violence so often offered. The contemporary attitude toward American politics is caricatured in *The Distinguished Gentleman* (1992), which satirically pulls together the often conflicting stresses on a congressman. If the view of elected officials is so rendered and the portrayals are believed, what does this tell us about perceptions of the civil service, labeled "the bureaucracy"? In an era of "trickle down" theory, the cynical perception of the political process certainly "trickles down" to the public service.

In a 1965 essay on administrative fiction, I noted the function of time in novels such as Lawrence Durrell's *The Alexandria Quartet*.[2] This series depicts the perspectives of the principal characters with respect to events affecting them over an extended period of time. Each person sees these happenings differently; an occurrence that looms large to one person is not even recalled by others. Kurosawa's classic film *Rashomon* (1951) uses differential perception in treating rape and murder. To the administrator–

viewer such a film suggests the need to appreciate that different participants, in recalling a given event or transaction, might each view a critical
action entirely differently. The recognition of this phenomenon calls for
analyzing the reasons for these varying perceptions, including those of the
administrator–viewer himself or herself.

THE INDIVIDUAL IN FILMS

Motion pictures thrive on personalities. The classic movie hero is the
individual who overcomes obstacles, frequently within his or her own
camp, to achieve whatever objectives are delineated. The antihero as hero
has emerged in recent decades as a popular prototype. The acclaimed John
Le Carré television series, based on his novels *Tinker, Tailor, Soldier, Spy*
and *Smiley's People*, is about George Smiley, a British administrative official
who heads his nation's major intelligence network.[3] Smiley is low-key,
vulnerable, perceptive, at times brutal and conniving, generally admired
by his colleagues and subordinates, and respected by his political superiors.
The Le Carré novels, and their adaptations for film, deal with the period
dominated by the Cold War. The Soviet enemy was the primary and
seemingly ineradicable target. Smiley's major antagonist was Karla, his
Soviet counterpart. A major theme of this series is the corruption endemic
to a world system that requires deception, violence, and a host of immoral
actions as its modus operandi. The impact of the Circus, as Smiley's agency
is labeled, on its personnel, from operatives to clerical staff, is disastrous.
Smiley is an unhappy man despite his successes. He is an effective bureaucratic leader within the British establishment. He is a tough and resourceful
commander in the field, camouflaged by mild manners, a diffident exterior.
But make no bones about it, he is a twentieth-century hero.

In viewing these television dramatizations one sees the Policy, Leadership and Teaching bridges looming, with possibilities for greater understanding available if they are crossed. Smiley's persona enables him to
maintain his organization through a profound understanding of his subordinates and an ability to match personality to task. In *Tinker, Tailor, Soldier,
Spy* he suffers a terrible failure by finding a spy, or mole, in his midst who
has intruded upon his personal life—his marriage, in fact. It is a lesson that
perhaps plunges him more deeply into his work. In *Smiley's People*, George
Smiley achieves his goal of the surrender of his archenemy. But it is a sad
accomplishment.

The study of these films leads us to the Values and Leadership bridges.
Internal and external values are relevant. External values involve a grasp

of the culture of the Cold War and the Soviet system for waging it. Internal values deal with the manner in which Smiley is able to understand and work with his motley crew and his skill in functioning within the complexities of British bureaucracy. Leadership concerns the requisites for decision making and the motivation for exercising power. It is doubtful that many viewers would empathize with Smiley, yet he strikes a sympathetic chord. Why? To what extent are we, as managers, as public officials, aware of this personal connection between our private and public lives? How much of our private lives provides stimulus and inspiration for the work we do? Some of us watch Smiley and see a piece of ourselves in his character. Others may find him repulsive, a bit too quaint. Yet Le Carré forces us to see this difficult tension between one's intimate self and the administrative life.

Hollywood continues to grind out its share of superhero heroes. Superman and Batman still reign. Indiana Jones provides the slightly more credible prototype. The myth of the godlike, invincible savior remains as a conditioning agent. And there is always Luke Skywalker, "the hero supreme" of Chapter 1. The enormous popularity of *Star Wars* points to the prevailing need for mythological supermen, no matter how rational our society. It may be because of that very rationality and the impossibility of its achievement that the fantasy of superheroes is required.

The human being, singular or plural, is the critical element in all administrative behavior. He or she is both means and end. All of the rational systems of analysis and techniques for data gathering, maintenance, and action are mechanisms created and used by human beings in making and implementing countless decisions and functions. Often we do not know the complex factors that play upon the human decision to act, even in the most routine ways. In a motion picture, the personal lives of the characters are laid out as in "real life." The fact that the FBI agent in *Thunderheart* is Native American affects his behavior as a federal officer. The fact that the Secret Service agent is growing old in *In the Line of Fire* (1993), and that he clings to his guilt about a perceived failure years before, when he could not prevent the assassination of President Kennedy, are critical factors affecting his behavior as an agent.

The public administrator, for the most part, sees the people with whom he or she works primarily in the context of the job, the office, the substantive work situation. Over time one gets to know one's colleagues personally and, perhaps, gains an understanding of the vital relationship between their private and public lives. Our vocabulary is not without its revelatory formulas: "Got up on the wrong side of the bed?" "What's eating her?" Whether it is a hangover, a love affair, a passion for power, prejudice, or fatal illness, the story unfolds before the viewer's eyes. What must be recognized, and is illustrated in films and other stories, is that private behavior certainly affects the substance and quality of public behavior.

ETHICAL DILEMMAS

Motion pictures as reflections of the lives of human beings are loaded with ethical questions. Clear-cut depictions of right and wrong are commonplace. Corruption is a common evil in contemporary movies, perhaps because of its dramatic and visible element. The haunting ethical dilemmas that arise in the seas of gray are rarer. The agony of sending men into battle is dramatically posed in the Australian film *Gallipoli* (1981) and in *Memphis Belle* (1990). The status of war overrides the value of the lives of one's comrades, thus posing one of the ethical dilemmas of all civilization. Related to this is the classic question of the limits of the nation-state, or lesser jurisdictions, over individuals, something rarely addressed in films.

In *Hidden Agenda* (1990) the protagonist, at the climax of the film, unearths a major, politically engendered crime. He must decide between walking away from the truth—but securing the remaining few years of his career as a police officer—and exposing the conspiracy, thereby incurring dismissal from the service, notoriety, and the loss of financial security. It is an agonizing decision with intense pressure from both sides, one of the strongest depictions of ethical conflict portrayed in any film.

The classic motion picture *The Caine Mutiny* (1954) tells of the overthrow of a skipper in the U.S. Navy during World War II. The anatomy of the mutiny is seen through the personalities and relations of the men involved. The officers are subjected to a court-martial and are cleared of wrongdoing. At a celebration afterward, the officer who successfully defended the mutineers privately dresses down his colleagues for ruining the life of a career officer. The viewer is jolted to understanding the incident from the perspective of the loser.

Box office popularity can inform the administrator–viewer about public values, tastes, and attitudes, ballyhoo and public relations strategies aside. Thus, the success of such films as *In the Line of Fire* and *The Fugitive* in the summer of 1993 reveals public empathy for the character we have designated as the nonhero hero. American filmgoing audiences, by and large, empathize with a figure who challenges unfairness, injustice, and prejudice, and who acts upon strongly held beliefs. The valiant, if vulnerable, underdog is the character with whom many viewers, themselves often pursuing unattainable dreams, identify.

MOTION PICTURES AND THE BRIDGES

This book began by proposing five bridges to connect public administration and the arts. For the administrator–viewer, the five bridges are virtually inseparable; each is an essential component. In the course of the examination I have touched upon elements that provide the substance of these bridges from the public administration perspective. A motion picture is an art form, and the administrator–viewer can draw knowledge and insight from a variety of films as he or she relates these to the art of public management.

The Theory Bridge

Aesthetically, a fine film reveals a unity, the amalgam of many components. The story, its people, its circumstances, and a particular setting come together in a comprehensible work. Moviemaking is an architectonic art, in that it demands the shaping of numerous skills into a whole that makes artistic sense. Despite the banalities of the commercial purposes of most movies, like most art forms, the making of motion pictures from concept to screening has its own rules that, generally speaking, must be learned. Motion picture innovators have deviated from and developed this art in dynamic ways. But the reality of the medium is that the work has its form and function and utilizes a mix of component skills. Orson Welles once observed, according to Steven Bach, that "a poet needs a pen, a painter a brush, and a filmmaker an army."[4]

It may seem odd to some, but public administration bears a certain resemblance to moviemaking. Virtually all bureaucratic efforts require an amalgam of people and resources. Like the filmmaker, the administrator must design his or her team and resources in the most effective manner to achieve the organization's objectives. No matter how rigid or literal the constraints, the administrator, like the moviemaker, has a wide range of choices with regard to people and method in the design and selection of tasks. The "art of public administration" entails, as Charles Goodsell notes in Chapter 2, developing and utilizing the materials at hand.

The Values Bridge

Most American films reflect American values. In a sociopolitical context, the virtues of community, ethnicity, and living in harmony with the environment have emerged in recent films. On the other side of this values coin are films that describe the evils of racism, environmental destruction, and war.

The overriding quality of films centers on the worth and plight of the individual. Almost always it is through his or her eyes and psyche that the story is told. We see characters as persons, individuals, much as we view people to whom we relate in group or individual transactions. To be sure, films use, often abuse, stereotypes, but the central character in a film is personalized, individualized. Good and evil are thus personified as good guys and bad guys, competent and incompetent, honest and false, effective managers and incompetent blunderers.

An idealized political value system is frequently portrayed by its antithesis. Films from *All the King's Men*, made in 1949, to *Bob Roberts*, made in 1992, deal in their differing ways with corruption in the political process. They deal with the loss of virtue, with corruption rather than the more direct affirmation of constitutional values. *Mr. Smith Goes to Washington* (1939), made by the director Frank Capra in a more innocent age, deals with political corruption in a moralistic way. The virtues of democratic institutions and practices, the values of the Constitution, are inherent in most American films that treat political problems.

Imagination and creative spirit are strongly upheld as values to be sought by everyone. These are often presented as a codicil to democratic virtues. The entrepreneurial spirit pitted against enormous odds, as in *Tucker: The Man and His Dream* (1988), is not always victorious but is often admired. Films are frequently critical of institutions that oppress individual freedoms. The repressive components of industrial and corporate life that have been portrayed in films are as far apart in time as Charlie Chaplin's *Modern Times* (1936) and *Working Girl* (1988).

Given the interaction of public administration and public policy, the public administrator, like many of the public servants in the films we have touched upon, brings to his or her work a set of acculturated values. These include an internalized set of constitutional beliefs that guides him or her through the policy maze of current legislation and implementation as well as the pressures that emanate from them. Films enlighten the public official through their portrayal of a given action situation. For example, in *City of Joy*, the viewer can sense the tensions that are set up between the professional values of the physician, and his personal life and reactions in an alien and hostile situation. Part of the art of administration certainly entails coping with difficulties that challenge constitutional and professional values.

The Leadership Bridge

Crossing this connector is a more complex issue in studying films. Historical figures are frequently idealized, if not idolized, from D. W. Griffith's biography *Abraham Lincoln* (1930) to the more sophisticated film *Abe Lincoln in Illinois* (1934), and then on to *Young Mr. Lincoln* (1939). Lincoln, in all of these films, is imbued with the attributes of an American folk hero: tough, diligent, intelligent, one who leads by example and humility.

A classic cinematic study of leadership is the monumental *Lawrence of Arabia* (1962, reissued in 1992). In it, T. E. Lawrence is portrayed as brilliantly successful in achieving his objectives. Like other leaders, he defies "regulations," seizes opportunities, takes enormous, seemingly irresponsible risks, and succeeds in a sensational manner. Yet the viewer is left seriously wondering whether this larger-than-life character is not at least half mad!

Bear in mind that motion pictures are a dramatic art. The medium does not reflect for the viewer; it presents to the viewer. The consequent meaning is in the eye of the beholder. We see more the manifestations of leadership, its visual impacts, perhaps its motivating relationships—not a deep, thoughtful analysis. The exception is rare—for example, Kenneth Branagh's version of Shakespeare's *Henry V* (1989).

The Policy Bridge

As for the policy bridge, films themselves tend to be simplistic and superficial. Yet, as Howard McCurdy points out in Chapter 12, films have been known to inspire policy actions, or at least to spur them on. Often, what is inferred from the visual version leads to policy reflection. Motion pictures can be realistically brutal, as are the rash of films that appeared in the 1980s and early 1990s that focused on urban blight, plight, and violence. They offered their tragic story with the conclusion, in public policy terms, to be drawn by the administrator–viewer, among others. In effect, the filmmaker says, "This is the situation. What are you going to do about it?"

The Teaching Bridge

My use of the term administrator–viewer presumes a certain condition-ing toward looking at films analytically. Motion pictures offer a rich storehouse of situations, problems, and personalities. They can pose policy questions that, viewed in light of one's experience, can be helpful and stimulating. The integration of films into the public administration cur-riculum as part of the literature of courses as diverse as organization theory, policy analysis, decision making, policy and program planning, personnel and human resources, cannot help but enrich instructors and students alike. A serious film merits serious consideration.

Unquestionably, administrator–viewers will recognize the utility of mo-tion pictures as case studies. The viewer has the opportunity to observe the story within the disciplined continuum of plot. A recent remake of *Memphis Belle* (1990), based on a true story about a bomber crew during World War II that engaged in heavy and dangerous bombing runs over Europe, delves into the personalities of its officers and men. Casualties in the Eighth Air Force were as close to catastrophic as one could imagine. Yet this crew of one bomber, this mixture of officers and men, combining great skill and compatible combat personalities, survived more than their share of mis-sions. Unquestionably, luck played a major role, as it always does in war. At the same time, these men faced incredible odds on many of their raids. In the film, we see them differentiated as individuals as well as members of an organization.[5]

A very different film that lends itself to case analysis is *Working Girl* (1988). While the story deals with the private, corporate sector, its essence is readily applicable to life in public agencies. It concerns the drive to move up the ladder, or pyramid, in the organization, the willingness of one woman to incur enormous personal risks to get out of her menial role. She violates trust and lies about her position all the while displaying consider-able skill and talent. Ironically, for a time the young woman gets away with her falsehoods, but then incurs the wrath of her former boss when she is found out. While the morality of the film is questionable, the realization of the woman's fantasy is certainly attuned to the times. Furthermore, it is clear that the central figure is emulating the behavior of her boss as well as adhering to the mores of the financial world. Who does not see himself or herself as achieving his or her dream in the organization, public or private?

Could viewing a film such as *Working Girl* suggest to an administrator an appreciation of a situation within his or her office? Might not the thought run thus: "This movie reminds me of Shirley's vigorous assertiveness, her energetic initiative, her tendency to take over whether or not she's asked or directed. Does she know how transparent her ambition is? On the other hand, to what extent is she following my lead? Where have I fallen short as her supervisor? Don't I encourage her assertiveness, even aggressiveness? I should talk to her about it. I ought to think about this. Maybe I have fallen short of setting a good example and working more closely with people like Shirley. Anything I can do about that?"

THE ADMINISTRATOR AS ARTIST

We must be careful not to overemphasize the question of what art can do for the public manager. Perhaps, as can be inferred from Charles Goodsell's argument in Chapter 2, it would be equally appropriate to ask what the public administrator can do for (or with) art. That is, how can the manager make his or her work more artful? How can the creative balance be gained, the integration of forces and action in a way that has a unity of resolution and purpose?

The professional life of the public administrator is made up of a complex, varying array of concerns and involvements. Helping to implement functions assigned the agency or jurisdiction, sustaining the integrity and accuracy of actions, entail not only rational-technical functions but also myriad relationships and interactions. These relationships between and among people involved in a policy sphere are at the core of successful motivation and action. The managerial experience demands an understanding of human dimensions up and down the lines of function and authority.

The administrator–viewer carries the knowledge and burdens of office. Some of the films I have mentioned make it seem that the burden of one's innermost self can be equal to one's public demands. No matter how the equation of private to public works out, it varies greatly with individuals. It is vital for the administrator to understand himself or herself in the context of role.

What can be learned from films, among other art forms, are the components that constitute the public administrator's palette, the ever-changing combination of the social equivalent of colors. These entail interactions with subordinates, peers, and superiors within the office, or unit, as well as with persons immediately involved in the policy determination, support, and oversight (i.e., legislators, their committees and staffs). Depending upon the nature of administrative tasks, the interactions may involve groups as diverse as clientele and community representatives, media jour-nalists and even litigants.

All of these, and other human factors, constitute the professional life and activities of the administrator–viewer. As such attributes are integrated into his or her person, they blend with other aspects of life to make up the total personality.

If art and creativity are melded into the persona, society and the administrator are the richer for it. The administrator–viewer, through analytical observation of motion pictures, gains a broader perspective on an exceedingly complex world. Furthermore, art provides a storehouse of ways of looking at and dealing with people and phenomena that further enriches understanding and action.

NOTES

1. Charles T. Goodsell, *The Case for Bureaucracy: A Public Administration Polemic*, 3d ed. (Chatham, N.J.: Chatham House, 1994); Gregory B. Lewis, "In Search of Machiavellian Milquetoasts: Comparing Attitudes of Bureaucrats and Ordinary People," *Public Administration Review* 50 (March–April, 1990): 221–26; Francis E. Rourke, *Bureaucracy, Politics and Public Policy*, 3d ed. (Boston: Little, Brown, 1984); William G. Scott and David K. Hart, *Organizational America* (Boston: Houghton Mifflin, 1979).

2. Morton Kroll, "Administrative Fiction and Credibility," *Public Adminis-tration Review* 25 (March 1965): 80–84.

3. John Le Carré, *The Quest for Karla* (New York: Knopf, 1989). This omnibus volume contains three novels, including *Tinker, Tailor, Soldier, Spy* and *Smiley's People*. These are available on video but are sometimes difficult to obtain.

4. Steven Bach, *Final Cut: Dreams and Disaster in the Making of Heaven's Gate* (New York: William Morrow, 1985), 7.

5. It is interesting to compare this version with the original documentary, put together by the famous director Billy Wilder, which lacks the depth of characterization of the later, fictional movie. In the context of this chapter, we might ask whether dramatizations do a better job of conveying the "feel" of reality than do some documentaries.

Part IV

Insights for Administrative Leadership from the Arts

7

Lessons in Leadership from Shakespeare

Catherine R. Gira

A MIRROR FOR MODERN MAGISTRATES

Today's public administrator, seeking advice about management or leadership, has many options from which to choose—from a countless array of books, articles, and videotapes to costly professional development seminars and workshops. Some of these resources portray the effective administrator as manager of time (e.g., the "one-minute" manager); others depict the executive as overseer of quality (as in total quality management); as horticulturist (adept at "cultivating" and, when necessary, "pruning" managerial "decision trees"); as technician (periodically called upon to "reengineer" the organization); or as change agent, transformer, or visionary.

Useful as some of the advice provided by these resources may be, we know that there is no simple "how to" manual for something as complicated as leadership. Yet, from the time of Plato's *Republic* to our own time, leaders and would-be leaders have sought—and writers have sought to provide—words of wisdom on the elusive art of leadership.

In Shakespeare's time, monarchs in England and on the Continent could look to Thomas Elyot's *Book of the Governour*, Niccolò Machiavelli's *The Prince*, Baldassare Castiglione's *The Book of the Courtier*, the anonymous *A Mirrour for Magistrates*, and similar treatises for practical advice. (Both Machiavelli and Castiglione, in English translation, were widely read by Elizabethans.) Small wonder that such books flourished, given the widely recognized travails of monarchy. Sojourning at Woodstock, in a rustic and bucolic setting, Queen Elizabeth I reputedly remarked, "The milkmaid's lot is better than mine, and her lot merrier."[1] Years later, in her final speech to Parliament, she said: "To . . . wear a crown is a thing more glorious to them that see it than it is pleasing to them that wear it."[2] Shakespeare said it more succinctly and more directly: "Uneasy lies the head that wears a crown." (*Henry IV, Part 2*, III.i.31).[3] Rather than compose a manual for monarchs, however, Shakespeare chose through his plays to hold a mirror up to life, wherein we may observe why some leaders succeed, despite the burdens of office, and why others fail.

With the exception of Henry V (and even he is the subject of some disagreement among Shakespearean scholars), Shakespeare tended to define the qualities of a good leader principally by negation—that is, by identifying common deficiencies of failed leaders. If we reflect on those deficiencies, we can arrive at certain positive maxims for those who aspire to be effective leaders. This chapter will define a kind of "mirror for modern magistrates," derived from exempla in selected works of William Shakespeare, principally *Richard II, Henry IV, Henry V*, and *King Lear*.

AVOID SELF-DELUSION

Avoiding self-delusion is closely allied to the classical admonition "Know thyself." Again and again in Shakespeare's plays, we meet tragic characters whose sense of self is predicated initially on illusion and whose journey toward self-understanding is excruciatingly torturous.

Richard II, for example, refuses in the early scenes of Shakespeare's play to accept either his mortality or his vulnerability. A wastrel king who squanders money on lavish parties, fashions from Italy, and foolish wars, Richard levies heavy taxes on the common people, fines the nobility for petty grievances, and confiscates property illegally, thus leading the realm to both moral and economic bankruptcy. (In many ways, he reminds us of the corrupt savings and loan administrators in our own time who used positions of power and trust to exploit and confiscate what was not rightfully theirs.) Some historians note that Richard's irresponsible behavior may be attributed in part to his early upbringing, which did little to prepare him for kingship. But in Shakespeare's play Richard invokes the so-called divine right of kings, declaring, even as Henry Bullingbrook's forces advance and Richard's deposition nears:

> Not all the water in the rough rude sea
> Can wash the balm off from an anointed king;

> The breath of worldly men cannot depose
> The deputy elected by the Lord. (III.ii.54–57)

Richard's self-identity, to this point, is defined solely by his position as king. Take away that position, take away the mantle of "divine right," and what remains is a hollow man, inheritor of a hollow crown. "For you have but mistook me all this while," he laments prior to his deposition, yet

> I live with bread like you, feel want,
> Taste grief, need friends: subjected thus,
> How can you say to me, I am a king? (III.iii.174–77)

It is only when he no longer wears the mask of kingship that Richard can begin to realize himself as a man, but by then it is too late to reclaim his royal legacy.

Like Richard II, King Lear moves progressively from self-delusion to self-awareness, from a fixed belief in his own infallibility to the realization that, stripped of the trappings of kingship, he is "no more but . . . a poor, bare, fork'd animal" (III.iv.107–8) and that the very hand his old friend Gloucester would kiss in deference "smells of mortality" (IV.vi.133). Irascible, unpredictable, and unyielding throughout the early scenes of the play, Lear believes, as Richard does, that he is favored by the gods, whom he frequently invokes, and that he can command Nature, including the elements, to do his bidding. Puzzled by Lear's outburst of anger against Cordelia, his favorite daughter, and his decision to exile her, Regan, one of his evil daughters, remarks perceptively, "he hath ever but slenderly known himself" (I.i.293–94).

Having abdicated both the throne and his proper role as father to Cordelia, Lear is left with no clear identity. The Fool, in his wisdom, addresses him thus: "I am better than thou art now. / I am a Fool, thou art nothing" (I.iv.193–94). Moments later, Lear queries, "Does any here know me? This is not Lear. . . . Who is it that can tell me who I am?" "Lear's shadow," the Fool aptly replies (I.iv.226–31).

Lear's journey toward self-knowledge takes him through literal and metaphorical tempests, through physical agony and madness. When the storm within him finally abates and he is reunited with Cordelia, Lear recognizes himself as "a very foolish fond old man" (IV.vii.59) and begs Cordelia to forget and to forgive him for the wrongs that he has done her. Then and only then can he lay rightful claim to those titles he had formerly worn but only superficially deserved: a loving father and "every inch a king." Unfortunately, Lear's restoration is short-lived, and with the death of Cordelia he once again reels back to the beast, literally howling as he carries her lifeless body onto the stage in the final scene.

Richard II and King Lear demonstrate that titles alone do not define the person and that true empowerment comes from within, not from the office one inherits or acquires. To believe otherwise is to engage in dangerous self-delusion. Unlike the royal positions held by Richard II and King Lear, positions in public sector bureaucracies do not belong to incumbents. The public administrator who is wise enough to learn from crossing the Leadership Bridge will accept the challenge of self-reflection and attain genuine power.

PREFER TRUTH TELLERS TO FLATTERERS

A close companion of delusions of grandeur and overweening pride is vanity. Both Richard II and Lear prefer the company of sycophants who tell them only what they want to hear. Richard's uncle, John of Gaunt, berates him: "A thousand flatterers sit within thy crown" (II.i.100). Northumberland observes, "The King is not himself, but basely led / By flatterers" (II.i.241–42). One of the gardeners who tends Richard's royal gardens states metaphorically, with an intuitive wisdom that Shakespeare frequently affords to commoners:

> The weeds, which his [the King's] broad-spreading
>   leaves did shelter,
> That seem'd in eating him to hold him up,
>   Are plucked up root and all by Bullingbrook. (III.iv.50–53)

Earlier, in a similar but rather mixed metaphor, Bullingbrook had described the flattering hangers-on in Richard's court as "The caterpillars of the commonwealth, / Which I have sworn to weed and pluck away" (II.iii.166–67).

The consequences of Richard's vanity and fondness for flattery are profound. None of his closest companions attempts to dissuade him from seizing Henry Bullingbrook's lands illegally or from waging a costly and meaningless war against Ireland. Given Richard's temperament in the early scenes of the play, however, it would have been inconsistent for him to heed such advice, had it been given. He certainly pays no attention to his uncle, John of Gaunt, who on his deathbed admonishes Richard for his foolishness and his profligacy. Like many failed leaders, Richard prefers to surround himself only with "yes men" who feed his ego and feed on his largesse.

Unlike Richard, Lear is surrounded by several loyal truth-tellers: his daughter Cordelia, his good friend Kent, and his court Fool. These he chooses to banish or ignore, preferring to reward dissembling flatterers. At the outset of the play, Lear unexpectedly announces a contest in which, ostensibly, he will award shares of the kingdom to his daughters, in proportion to the degree of filial love they are willing to express publicly. Goneril, his eldest, and Regan, the middle daughter, play the game, although it is apparent early on that it is rigged. Rather than wait to hear all three daughters' responses before dividing the kingdom, he awards prizes after each speech, dispelling any lingering illusion among the players that the contest is real and the outcome yet to be determined. Cordelia refuses to be a part of the charade, protesting that she cannot "heave" her heart into her mouth (I.i.91–92) and that, were she married, she would love her husband and, therefore, could not love her father "all" (I.i.104).

The penalty for Cordelia's honesty is repudiation and exile. Kent, close friend and counselor to Lear, suffers a similar fate when he dares, as Lear characterizes it, to come "between the dragon and his wrath" (I.i.122). Kent accuses Lear of folly and madness, but Lear will not heed the truth. As the Fool later remarks, when Lear threatens to whip him for his cryptic criticisms, in Lear's mind "Truth's a dog must to kennel; he must be whipt out . . . " (I.iv.111–12).

Even Machiavelli, whom Elizabethan authors (including Shakespeare) considered the quintessence of evil, warned princes against flattery, observing that "Courts are always full of flatterers . . . this plague of flattery is hard to escape . . . there is no way to protect from flattery except by letting men know that you will not be offended at being told the truth."[4] Although Shakespeare overtly ascribed Machiavellian traits only to his villainous or duplicitive characters, principally Richard III, he and Machiavelli shared the view that leaders who prefer flattery to truth are ill-prepared to deal effectively with reality or adversity. Ambition untempered by personal honesty and self-knowledge causes administrators to believe the steady stream of flattery that inevitably follows high office. Public administrators who know that the cornerstone of truth is the foundation of the Leadership Bridge are spared the unctuous fawning of favor seekers.

THERE CAN BE NO HEAD WITHOUT A BODY

Common analogies for the ruler in Shakespeare's time included that of the king as head of the body politic and as father of the kingdom. Thomas Pickering wrote in 1609: "Upon the condition of the Familie, being the Seminarie of all other Societies, it followeth that the holie and righteous government thereof, is a direct meane for the good ordering, both of Church and Commonwealth."[5] When the head of state—or of any organization—forgets his or her responsibilities to the body general, then isolation, suffering, and defeat almost inevitably follow.

Richard II so offends and loses touch with his people that, following his deposition, he is subjected to ridicule and disdain as commoners throw dust and rubbish on his head (V.ii). Alone in prison just before his death, Richard engages in some introspection and comes to the realization that he has "wasted time." Even then, however, he seems not to understand that he has failed to fulfill his obligations to that body of which he had been the head.

By contrast, Lear—the madness raging within him and a tempest raging about—comes to realize that he has been negligent in ministering to the needs of the less fortunate of his people:

> Poor naked wretches, wheresoe'er you are,
> That bide the pelting of this pitiless storm,
> How shall your houseless heads and unfed sides,
> Your loop'd and window'd raggedness, defend you
> From seasons such as these? O, I have ta'en
> Too little care of this! (III.iv.28–33)

Lear learns painfully that he has been unjust and unloving as a father, both to Cordelia and to his subjects. Like Gloucester, his blinded mirror image, he comes to see "feelingly." As one Shakespearean scholar has observed, "The need for kindness, or the natural love which binds all human beings in distinction from the rest of creation, was the conviction which unified all his [Shakespeare's] moral beliefs." The fulfillment of leadership, thus defined, is "the grace and well-being which individual action can bring to the lives of others."[6] Lear eventually comes to understand his deficiencies in that regard; Richard II does not.

Of all Shakespeare's kings, only Henry V is portrayed as a monarch closely in touch with his subjects. As Hal, the madcap Prince of Wales, Henry in his youth chooses as his close companions the fun-loving and somewhat degenerate patrons of the Boar's Head Tavern, led by that old iconoclast, Sir John Falstaff.

Although we learn in Hal's first soliloquy in *1 Henry IV* that he is prepared to abandon his frivolous life-style when the time is right, in the meantime he enjoys observing the high jinks of his low-born friends, for whom he has genuine affection. They, in turn, dub him "King of Courtesy" and vow that, when he becomes king, he "shall command all the good lads in Eastcheap," home of the Boar's Head (II.iv.10–15).

Eventually, Hal must set aside the pleasure of Falstaff's company and the carefree life of the tavern to assume the awesome responsibility of leading his country. Even as he does so, he remains the "king of courtesy," in the sense that Castiglione used the term in his *Book of the Courtier*, written in 1528. Castiglione's portrait of the "perfect courtier" included the traits of modesty, humaneness, and "grace." The courtier, Castiglione wrote, should be "pleasing and lovable to all who see him"; at the same time, he must be "bold, energetic and faithful to whomever he serves."[7]

Whereas Henry IV confesses to his son that he manipulated the commoners to win their support, Hal's devotion to his people runs deep. "I stole all courtesy from heaven," Henry IV admits, "And dress'd myself in such humility / That I did pluck allegiance from men's hearts" (*1 Henry IV*, III.ii.50–52). His son wins allegiances not by feigning courtesy to advance his own ambitions but by living it.

On the eve of the battle of Agincourt, Henry V walks among his troops, not as their king but as a man: a fellow soldier who goes by the transparently disguised name of Harry le Roy. One might say, somewhat irreverently, that Shakespeare's Henry V knew the value of "managing by walking around" long before Tom Peters and Robert Waterman popularized the phrase in *In Search of Excellence*. The Chorus describes the scene in these words:

> For forth he goes, and visits all his hosts,
> Bids them good morrow with a modest smile,
> And calls them brothers, friends, and countrymen.
> . . . freshly looks and, and overbears attaint
> With cheerful semblance and sweet majesty;
> That every wretch, pining and pale before,
> Beholding him, plucks comfort from his looks:
> A largess universal, like the sun,
> His liberal eye doth give to every one,
> Thawing cold fear, that mean and gentle all
> Behold . . .
> A little touch of Harry in the night. (IV. prologue 32–47)

Some modern critics have read this glowing description of Henry V as ironic, but sources such as Edwards Hall's *Chronicle*, from which Shakespeare derived his portrait of Henry V, are even more eulogistic, portraying him as "immaculate" and "liuying without spot." To most Elizabethan audiences, Henry V was an unqualified national hero, deserving of the titles that Shakespeare's Chorus bestows upon him: "star of England" and "mirror of all Christian kings."

Queen Elizabeth, like Shakespeare's hero, understood well that the leader is powerless without the support of the people, that the head cannot function independently of the body. In her last address to Parliament, she said: "Though God hath raised me high, yet this I count the glory of my crown: That I have reigned with your loves."[8]

PREPARE TO SPEND SLEEPLESS NIGHTS

Queen Elizabeth was doubtless right in speculating that the milkmaid's life is "merrier" than that of a queen. Whether Shakespeare's monarchs inherit the role legitimately through right of primogeniture, or whether they seize it through criminal acts, virtually all suffer sleepless nights. Murderers like Macbeth and Richard III lack repose because of guilty consciences, as does Henry IV, who has the blood of Richard II on his hands. But even Henry V, who was off sowing his wild oats in taverns when his father made his march on Richard II, observes, like Elizabeth I, that no king "can sleep so soundly as the wretched slave" and that the "heart's ease" other men enjoy is denied the ruler, who must "bear all" (*Henry V*, IV.i.233–68).

In our own time, we have come to express this concept of ultimate responsibility in the less elegant adage "The buck stops here." Queen Elizabeth, Shakespeare's Henry V, and Harry Truman well understood the fact that, especially in times of crisis, the leader needs to inspire and empower others to engage in a common enterprise. At the same time, as one critic has observed, "Power, at best, is a glorious burden."[9] Ultimately, it is the leader who bears responsibility for the success or failure of the organization, be it the state, a public agency, a corporation, or a university. Small wonder that with that responsibility come occasional, or frequent, restless nights. After all, acceptance of ultimate responsibility for everything under his or her supervision is the mark of a true public servant.

MAINTAIN A SENSE OF HUMOR

Few of Shakespeare's failed leaders—with the exception of Richard III, who takes demonic delight in his ability to deceive and manipulate his trusting victims—have a sense of humor. Although Henry Bullingbrook moved among the populace "with familiar and humble courtesy," "topping his bonnet" to an oyster wench to gain support for deposing Richard II, and although as Henry IV, newly crowned, he was amused by the sight of his ancient Uncle York and his wife feuding loudly and comically for his attention over whether to punish or pardon their wayward son, Henry IV becomes generally humorless as the burdens of kingship mount, describing himself as "wan with care."

Henry V, on the other hand, loves a good laugh. As the youthful Prince Hal, he plays harmless practical jokes on Falstaff and his companions and on Francis, the tavern serving boy. Before he is called to undertake the serious business of war (which he does with valor), he mimics the hothead rebel, Hotspur, and, later, his stern father and Falstaff in a famous mock-king scene at the Boar's Head. After his coronation, when he moves among his troops as "Harry le Roy," he meets and quarrels with a common soldier whom he later tricks and then rewards with a glove full of golden crowns. His wooing of Princess Katherine of France following his victory at Agincourt is laced with wit and humor. Although Katherine is inevitably his for the asking by virtue of his victory, Henry chooses to woo her and win her through his charms.

The lesson to be learned from Henry V's leadership is to maintain a sense of perspective; an ability to laugh at oneself, as well as others; and a genuine joie de vivre. The importance of these qualities has not gone unnoticed by modern organizations in search of new leaders. Included in the attributes frequently sought in postings for leadership positions in corporations and other institutions is a sense of humor. Among Shakespeare's kings, only Henry V would have really qualified.

PREPARE TO LET GO

A story familiar to senior administrators in higher education is about a retiring dean who left to his young successor three envelopes to be opened as needed at successively difficult moments on the job. Eventually, the young dean had recourse to all three envelopes. The message in the first one read, "Blame the old dean." The message in the second one read, "Promise a reorganization." The message in the third one read, "Prepare three envelopes." Like many jokes, as Freud was wont to remind us, there is an element of truth at the core of this story. It is the maxim that the leader should prepare ultimately to give up a particular position of leadership, a maxim that relates closely to the admonition to avoid the self-delusion of infallibility.

In Shakespeare's *King Lear* we see the dangers inherent in a leader's wanting to step down yet not wanting to let go. Lear is old and tired. He wishes at the outset of the play "To shake all cares and business" of his office and confer them "on younger strengths" (I.i.39–40). At the same time, he really does not want to transfer leadership to his daughters. After exiling his favorite daughter, Cordelia, he resolves to spend alternate months with his other two daughters and their husbands, to whom he has given directions to divide the kingdom between them. But he will not come alone. With him will be one hundred knights as fellow house guests. (One can understand why Goneril and Regan do not welcome this arrangement!) Lear also demands the same respect from his former subjects that he had when he was king. He beats his daughter's servant for chiding his Fool, calls irritably for his dinner, and, as Goneril says, "still would manage those authorities / That he has given away" (I.iii.17–18).

Lear's situation is not necessarily typical; many leaders leave an organization when they leave a position, but not infrequently some are promoted from within. We are all familiar with the CEO who becomes chairman of the board, the dean who becomes provost in the same institution, or the vice president who is promoted to president. Nothing could be more damaging to an organization than leaders who, like Lear, would have it all, assuming responsibility for a new role while refusing to let go of the old. That way, as Shakespeare would have said, "madness lies," not only for the individual but for all those within the organization whose loyalties are inevitably tested and divided.

CODA

Although Shakespeare did not explicitly set out to compose in dramatic form a manual for monarchs, it is true, nonetheless, that some of the observations in his "mirror for magistrates" did not go unnoticed. Queen Elizabeth, smarting over her own political embarrassment at the Earl of Essex's rebellion in 1601, following a vainglorious and ill-fated invasion of Ireland which she sanctioned, later declared "Know ye not that I am Richard?" Presumably not by coincidence, the scene depicting Richard's deposition did not appear in subsequent printed versions of the play during

Elizabeth's lifetime. Richard's deposition was clearly one reality the queen did not wish to see mirrored in her own time.

As all administrators know, time is a precious commodity: time to get things done and, more important, time to reflect on what has been done and what needs to be done. Amid the plethora of "how-to" publications vying for the attention of contemporary administrative leaders, it is worth noting that Shakespeare's plays provide no easy formulas, no simplistic prescriptions for success. What they can do is make static ideas dynamic and convert generalized labels to vivid examples. In short, they provide, if we are willing to reflect on them, profound and timeless insights about leaders, the art of leadership, and life itself.

NOTES

1. M. M. Reese, *The Cease of Majesty: A Study of Shakespeare's History Plays* (London: Edward Arnold, 1961), 137.

2. Roy Strong and Julia Trevelyan Oman, *Elizabeth R.* (New York: Stein and Day, 1971), 62.

3. All act, scene, and line references to Shakespeare's plays are from *The Riverside Edition*, ed. G. Blakemore Evans (Boston: Houghton Mifflin, 1974).

4. Niccolò Machiavelli, *The Prince*, trans. and ed. Robert M. Adams (New York: W. W. Norton, 1972), 67.

5. Robert Pierce, *Shakespeare's History Plays: The Family and the State* (Columbus: Ohio State University Press, 1971), 6.

6. *The Cease of Majesty*, 113–14.

7. Baldassare Castiglione, *The Book of the Courtier*, trans. Charles S. Singleton (Garden City, N.Y.: Doubleday, 1959), 29–34.

8. *Elizabeth R.*, 62.

9. *The Cease of Majesty*, 137.

"I See It Feelingly": How Imagination Transforms Leaders

Stephen R. Kuder

THE POWER OF IMAGINATION

Crossing the Leadership Bridge connecting public administration and the arts permits one to witness a poignant scene from Shakespeare's *King Lear*. Two utterly defeated leaders, King Lear and the Earl of Gloucester, meet for the last time on the storm-racked heath. Neither is dressed for success: the maddened Lear is almost naked and crowned with flowers; the blinded Gloucester is all disheveled. Lear, realizing that Gloucester is now blind, says, "yet you see how this world goes." Gloucester replies: "I see it feelingly."[1]

What accomplishes this fusion of seeing and feeling, of knowledge and emotion? In a word: imagination. It is imagination that allows the two old men, educated by suffering, to see the world feelingly and thus discover the essence of true leadership.

The poet Robert Frost is said to have defined education as hanging around until you catch on. "Hanging around" has a nice, informal ring to it; we can imagine ourselves as students again, browsing leisurely as though scholarship had returned to its Greek root—*skholē*, meaning "leisure." "Catching on" adds an emotional connotation to understanding; we can imagine Archimedes, having just discovered the principle of specific gravity, dashing out of the baths shouting "Eureka!" The teacher's part in this educational transaction was approached by Mark Van Doren when he said, "The art of teaching is the art of assisting discovery." This, no doubt, entails some hanging around, too.

Education has also been defined as a slow process of disillusionment. "Slow process" certainly echoes Frost's hanging around. And "disillusionment" offers a corrective to the optimistic ring of Frost's catching on. As we shall see, disillusionment is the educational environment of tragedy, for the great tragedies of literature assist the transformation that only suffering can bring. As the blinded Gloucester says: "I have no way, and therefore want no eyes; / I stumbled when I saw. Full oft 'tis seen, / Our means secure us, and our mere defects / Prove our commodities" (IV.i.18–21). As every leader's experience shows, prosperity can give the illusion of certainty, and suffering proves beneficial.

The pedagogical question before us as students of public administration is how we can best discover, or catch on to, the meaning and development of leadership. Or, perhaps better, since illusions about leadership abound, where we can best hang around, best experience the suffering of flawed leaders, and thus "see feelingly" how the world of leadership goes.

We must admit, first, that the usual pedagogical methods in leadership studies are based almost entirely upon theory. For our purposes here, we can echo a critique quoted by Warren Bennis:

As we survey the path leadership theory has taken, we spot the wreckage of "trait theory," the "great man" theory, and the "situationist" critique, leadership styles, functional leadership, and, finally, leaderless leadership, to say nothing of bureaucratic leadership, charismatic leadership, group-centered leadership, reality-centered leadership, leadership by objective, and so on. The dialectic and reversals of emphases in this area very nearly rival the tortuous twists and turns of child-rearing practices, and one can paraphrase Gertrude Stein by saying, "a leader is a follower is a leader."[2]

Leadership studies, we must admit, have had a bias toward theory and knowledge. They have neglected, or at best subordinated, the emotional or right-brain component of leadership. Albert Einstein, a knower par excellence, is said to have maintained that imagination is more important than knowledge. Anatole France took this thought a step further: "To know is nothing at all; to imagine is everything." Yet knowledge and imagination are not antagonistic: imagination is the fusion of knowledge with emotion, Gloucester's "I see it feelingly." Thought and emotion fused allow an imaginative person to empathize, or as the Sioux prayer puts it: "Great Spirit, help me never to judge another until I have walked for two miles in his moccasins."

DEVELOPING IMAGINATION

Where does the student of public administration discover and develop this imagination? As Mircea Eliade says, "All that essential and indescribable part of man that is called *imagination* dwells in realms of symbolism and still lives upon archaic myths and theologies"—and, we might add, upon the literature derived from these myths and theologies.[3]

If we allow ourselves the leisure to hang around two archaic myths in their literary forms—Sophocles' *Antigone* and Shakespeare's *King Lear*—we will see feelingly the deeper meaning of leadership each offers us.

Antigone

In *Antigone*, we experience King Creon effecting his own downfall through leadership errors that range from insecurity to miscommunication to obstinate pride. Conventional MPA and MBA case studies of leadership focus on these problems and offer solutions to them. Literature's contribution is to shock us with a recognition of the multiple levels of a human problem: emotional, psychological, religious, and political—and hence the problem's capacity for tragedy as well as solution. The reader (and in the case of a public administration student, a future leader) is confronted by the deep structure of leadership, and if the result is pity and fear, isn't that what tragedy is all about?

The plot of *Antigone* is simple enough. Creon is in his first day as king of Thebes after a violent civil war in which his two nephews, Eteocles and Polynices, have killed each other in the battle for the kingdom. Creon's first act as leader is to declare publicly that whoever buries the traitor Polynices will be executed. Antigone, the sister of Polynices, counters that there is a higher law than Creon's, and attempts to bury the body. Creon condemns her to death by starvation. Haemon, Creon's son and Antigone's fiancé, tries to reason with his father but is rebuffed; he leaves, uttering dire threats. Next, the blind seer Tiresias tries to sway Creon and is likewise stubbornly rebuffed. Only when Tiresias prophesies that the gods will punish him, does Creon realize that he must reverse his judgment. But it is too late. Antigone hangs herself, Haemon falls on his sword, and Creon's wife, Eurydice, hearing of her son's death, kills herself. In the final scene an utterly defeated Creon says: "My life is warped past cure."[4]

On the case-study level, this is merely another example of the pitfalls of autocratic leadership. We can easily list Creon's leadership errors, a few of which might be the following:

- He chooses as advisers yes-men who do not tell him the truth.
- He issues orders that leave no room for compromise.
- He imagines threats to his leadership everywhere.
- He refuses to take public opinion into account.
- He insists on policies that are no longer useful.

But on the deeper, imaginative level, Sophocles leads us into a tragic struggle in which no one can remain an innocent bystander. "Tragedy," Aristotle says in the *Poetics*, "is an imitation not only of a complete action, but of events inspiring fear and pity." For us as students of leadership, Creon's plight exerts a profound effect because it is that of every tragic protagonist, "a man who is not eminently good and just, yet whose misfortune is brought about not by vice or depravity, but by some error or frailty." Experiencing Creon's misfortune, we cannot avoid the pity and fear that Aristotle calls "catharsis": "pity is aroused by unmerited misfortune, fear by the misfortune of a man like ourselves."[5]

This realization that Creon is like us, is at the heart of our response to the leadership issues revealed in *Antigone*. Creon, in the final scene, is every leader who has suffered the "slings and arrows of outrageous fortune" because, as critic Northrop Frye reminds us, "The poet's job is not to tell you what happened, but what happens; not what did take place, but the kind of thing that always takes place. He gives you the typical, recurring, or what Aristotle calls universal event."[6] Thus Sophocles has the Chorus speak of the universal leader in the final words of the play:

> Our happiness depends
> on wisdom all the way.
> The gods must have their due.
> Great words by men of pride [*hubris* or *hybris*]
> bring greater blows upon them.
> So wisdom comes to the old.[7]

The universal leader's failure is summed up by Walter James Miller: "Creon, in short, was quite guilty of what the Greeks called *hubris*, arrogant pride, or the violent misuse of power."[8] Yet *hubris* is more complicated than this, as Edward G. Ballard points out:

Hybris, although often translated as "pride," is not felt as a sin. Yet it is a dangerous possession, for it dares much and is regarded by Aristotle as a flaw of the heroic character. Hybris is the quality of self-confident greatness which makes for heroic virtue. It is the mask of divinity which certain men tend to assume and which is destined to be torn from them to expose the suffering humanity beneath.⁹

We can behold in Creon the suffering which every leader risks when he or she dares too much, whether this is labeled *hubris* or simply failure of imagination.

King Lear

If the Chorus in *Antigone* utters Creon's epitaph in the words "So wisdom comes to the old," in *King Lear* we also experience on a deep imaginative level how aging leaders, Lear and Gloucester, struggle in parallel plots to attain that wisdom which comes only through seeing feelingly. Like Dante in the *Divine Comedy*, the two must plunge down from their leadership roles and slog through hell before they can finally soar (if briefly, before their deaths) to the recognition of what leadership really means. As with Creon, the pity and fear that we feel is that this recognition comes too late for them to become great leaders. Only we readers, as survivors, can profit through imagination.

Take Lear. An old man up against the ambition of youth. An autocrat thrown on the mercy of those he has lorded it over, his daughters Goneril and Regan, who flatter their way into leadership of his kingdom. A foolish person stripped of his power so that his folly shows clearly at last: "'Tis the infirmity of his age, yet he hath ever but slenderly known himself" (I.i.293–94). The leader driven mad as it dawns on him what his position-power really amounted to: "Thou hast seen a farmer's dog bark at a beggar? . . . And the creature run from the cur? There thou mightst behold the great image of authority: a dog's obeyed in office" (IV.vi.154–58).

Yes, Lear is the leader who gets what he deserves. He has sown his destiny and now reaps his own whirlwind. Doomed by his own free choices, he is surrounded by enemies because he has exiled his friends, the faithful and unflattering daughter Cordelia and the too-frank adviser Kent. Yet unlike Creon, who ends a broken man, Lear is able to hang on until he can catch on to the essence of true leadership. On the heath, with the wind's howling tuned to his own, we behold Lear's moment of discovery as he utters his most telling words:

> Poor naked wretches, wheresoe'er you are,
> That bide the pelting of this pitiless storm,
> How shall your houseless heads and unfed sides,
> Your loop'd and window'd raggedness, defend you

> From seasons such as these? O, I have ta'en
> Too little care of this! Take physic, pomp;
> Expose thyself to feel what wretches feel,
> That thou mayst shake the superflux to them,
> And show the heavens more just. (III.iv. 28–36)

This is the empathic moment of the imagination: feel what others feel so that you may respond to their needs. This is the transforming breakthrough into genuine leadership, the realization that autocratic selfishness must give way to distributive justice. And so Harold C. Goddard can say: "*King Lear* is the story of how a king in the worldly sense became a king in the fairy-tale sense, of how a bad king became a beautiful man."[10]

Lear's empathic breakthrough is echoed by Gloucester's remarkably similar moment of discovery as he prays:

> Let the superfluous and lust-dieted man,
> That slaves your ordinance, that will not see
> Because he does not feel, feel your pow'r quickly;
> So distribution should undo excess,
> And each man have enough. (IV.i.67–71)

Thus Gloucester, who has been physically blinded, is able to see Lear's truth: real understanding means to feel what others feel and to give each person what he or she needs. Public administrators who are sensitive to the needs of others understand an important component of the art of leadership.

Shortly after this, Lear and Gloucester meet for the final time. Lear realizes that Gloucester is blind and says what was noted earlier, "yet you see how this world goes." And Gloucester replies: "I see it feelingly" (IV.vi.147–49). And so we have it: seeing and feeling fused, knowledge and emotion united as imagination. True leadership discovered by old men who have suffered so much that they can see the world feelingly. As if to underscore this unity of seeing and feeling, Shakespeare ends the play with these words:

> The weight of this sad time we must obey,
> Speak what we feel, not what we ought to say:
> The oldest hath borne most; we that are young
> Shall never see so much, nor live so long. (V.iii.324–27)

So Shakespeare finally advocates the very thing that literature has to give: the empathic moment. Here we experience the deeper structure of human reality where knowledge and emotion are fused, where wisdom comes finally to those who suffer, where leaders walk in their followers' moccasins before judging.

IMAGINATION TRANSFORMS LEADERS

To see the world feelingly is how imagination transforms leaders. Eliade puts it this way: "To have imagination is to be able to see the world in its totality . . . hence the disfavour and failure of the man 'without imagination'; he is cut off from the deeper reality of life and from his own soul." A public administrator without imagination is fatally flawed and unable to approach the Leadership Bridge: "In some modern languages, the man who 'lacks imagination' is still pitied as a limited, second-rate and unhappy being."[11]

Stepping back from these two plays for a moment, what more can we say about imagination? To the point of transforming leaders: imagination can be developed. To the counterpoint: once developed, it can turn things upside down.

"The way to develop the imagination," according to Northrop Frye in *The Educated Imagination*, "is to read a good book or two." He adds, "The art of listening to stories is the basic training for the imagination." Thus, reading *Antigone* and *King Lear* rewards the student beyond the experience of leadership in action. It energizes: "The end of literary teaching is not simply the admiration of literature; it's something more like the transfer of imaginative energy from literature to the student."[12]

As a counterpoint to the positive things we have been saying about imagination, we must caution that it has a dangerous side: by its very nature it tends to be subversive. Like education itself, it is disillusioning. Even children's literature is sometimes subversive, according to Alison Lurie, "because its values are not always those of the conventional adult world":

Of course, in a sense much great literature is subversive, since its very existence implies that what matters is art, imagination, and truth. In what we call the real world, on the other hand, what usually counts is money, power, and fame. The great subversive works of children's literature suggest that there are other views of human life besides those of the shopping mall and the corporation. They mock current assumptions and express the imaginative, unconventional, noncommercial view of the world in its simplest and purest form. They appeal to the imaginative, questioning, rebellious child within all of us, renew our instinctive energy, and act as a force for change.[13]

Yes, much imaginative literature is subversive of conventional values. It suggests that the status quo, the "right way" of doing things, is downright not right. In the old primers Dick and Jane were always telling each other, "Look and see." Imagination says, Look and feel if you will experience a better way." Frye puts it this way: "The fundamental job of the imagination in ordinary life, then, is to produce, out of the society we have to live in, a vision of the society we want to live in." And this is at least mildly subversive because it implies that society is not all that it cracks itself up to be; its emperors—not to mention its other leaders of lesser note—rarely wear the golden clothing they think they do. Frye again: "The first thing our imaginations have to do for us . . . is to fight to protect us from falling into the illusions that society threatens us with."[14]

Read on, imaginative literature coaxes, and you will discover that the conventional is but a set of assumptions that have nothing to recommend them beyond their currency. To illustrate this truth we might recount, as Eliade does, "an episode in the legend of Parsifal and the Fisher King, concerning the mysterious malady that paralysed the old King who held the secret of the Graal":

It was not the King alone who suffered; everything around him was falling into ruins, crumbling away—the palace, the towers, and the gardens. Animals no longer bred, trees bore no more fruit, the springs were drying up. Many doctors had tried to cure the Fisher King, all without the least success. The knights were arriving there day and night, each of them asking first of all for news of the King's health. But one knight—poor, unknown, and even slightly ridiculous—took the liberty of disregarding ceremony and politeness: his name was Parsifal. Paying no heed to courtly custom, he made straight for the King and, addressing him without any preamble, asked: "Where is the Graal?" In that very instant, everything was transformed: the King rose from his bed of suffering, the rivers and fountains flowed once more, vegetation grew again, and the castle was miraculously restored.[15]

Eliade goes on to comment that "No one had thought, until then, of asking that central question—and the world was perishing because of that metaphysical and religious indifference, because of lack of imagination and absence of desire for reality."[16] Parsifal subverts the conventional protocol of the court and is able to change the cosmos. Everything is transformed. The same dynamic is repeated throughout great literature.

IMAGINATION SUBVERTS CONVENTIONAL THINKING

In the Hebrew Scriptures the prophets and prophetic literature fulfill the function of subverting what Walter Brueggemann calls the conventional "royal consciousness":

The same royal consciousness that makes it possible to implement anything and everything is the one that shrinks imagination because imagination is a danger. Thus every totalitarian regime is frightened of the artist. It is the vocation of the prophet to keep alive the ministry of imagination, to keep on conjuring and proposing alternative futures to the single one the king wants to urge as the only thinkable one.[17]

Prophetic literature both criticizes and energizes; it afflicts the comfortable and comforts the afflicted. All leadership, whether political or religious, is open to its critique.

In *Antigone*, as well, a prophet subverts convention. Here the convention is Creon's royal consciousness with its law-and-order assumptions. Tiresias, the blind seer, appears on stage as the prophet and at once proves Brueggemann's contention that "every totalitarian regime is frightened of the artist." He jolts the autocratic king into new action that, tragically, is too late for everyone but the audiences of two and a half millennia.

In *King Lear* we find another prophet of imagination who subverts conventional leadership: the Fool. He confronts Lear up to the very moment on the heath when the king enters through suffering and madness into a realization about what leadership really means. D. Verne Morland quotes L. C. Knight, who says that the Fool "speaks to (and out of) a quite different order of apprehension: His function is to disturb with glimpses of confounding truths that elude rational formulation."[18]

The Fool thus personifies the imagination's transforming function in the leadership arena: "to disturb with glimpses of confounding truths that elude rational formulation." *Antigone* disturbs us as leaders; so does *King Lear*. We begin to understand that truth lies beyond all the achievements of leadership theory, no matter how ingenious they may appear. The poet John Donne says:

> On a huge hill,
> Cragged and steep, Truth stands, and he that will
> Reach her, about must, and about must go;
> And what the hill's suddenness resists, win so;

> Yet strive so, that before age, death's twilight,
> Thy soul rest, for none can work in that night.[19]

When we do reach leadership–truth in moments of imagination, we are transformed and can say with Gloucester, "I see it feelingly."

IMAGINATION EDUCATES LEADERS

At the end of *Lear* all the leaders are deposed, either by death (Lear himself, Goneril, Regan, Cordelia, and Cornwall) or by abdication (Albany). In his abdication at the end of the play, Albany gives over leadership to Kent and Edgar. Is there a sense in which these two men are leaders because they have been educated in true leadership during the course of the play?

If so, the play describes how the education of a true leader must proceed. Kent immediately refuses the leadership role, but his education as leader parallels Edgar's; he is educated through the course of the Lear plot while Edgar is educated through Gloucester's plot. Their progress is identical, as we shall see, and thus Shakespeare emphasizes the steps to leadership through repetition as he had emphasized the process to seeing feelingly in both Lear and Gloucester.

The first step in their education to leadership is loyalty to their masters in face of all the wrongdoings suffered at their hands. While the others are exercising flattery and lies to seize power, they remain doggedly loyal to Lear and Gloucester, following them step by step through their sufferings on the storm-racked heath.

The second step in their education to leadership is connected with this devotion to loyalty; in fact, it makes this loyalty possible in the face of the blindness of their masters. It is the paradoxical strategy of disguise. Kent disguises himself as a serving man; Edgar, as the lunatic Poor Tom. In these disguises they are able to be loyal without any misunderstandings from their deposed masters. They can stand back, understand the whole situation, keep their own counsel, and suppress any aspirations for power or control. They disguise themselves in a profound humility (much as Dante must at the beginning of the Purgatorio if he is to climb the mountain to the Earthly Paradise) and function as servant-followers until the time is ripe to assume leadership. Shakespeare has used this disguise motif elsewhere to portray the wisdom of not committing oneself until others have proved their true intentions and the situation is fully understood. Rosalind in *As You Like It* disguises herself as a boy until she proves the love of Orlando to be true.

Disguising oneself allows a certain neutrality; it gives the character room to see feelingly until the time is ripe for action.

When Edgar says, "Ripeness is all," he is stating a principle that all potential leaders must ponder (V.2.11). Ripeness is an absolute necessity for every leader to exercise authority effectively. Only when Gloucester has suffered blindness and attempted suicide is he ripe to be the true father he never was before. And Lear must go through the intense suffering of the storm and imprisonment before he shows himself a true king.

This necessity of suffering is the third step in the education for leadership. Just as Dante needed to plunge into the punishing suffering of the Inferno and climb through the purifying suffering of the Purgatorio before becoming crowned and mitered as lord of himself, so Kent and Edgar must suffer exile in order to be ripe for leadership.

King Lear thus can be read as the story of how leaders are formed. The steps to true leadership can be taken while one is a servant–follower, as in the case of Kent and Edgar. But they can also come while one is a leader: Lear and Gloucester attain the stature of servant–leaders through the suffering in which they discover the value of loyalty and the need to see feelingly. Lear achieves this stature when he delivers his most touching speech, one that bears repeating:

> Poor naked wretches, wheresoe'er you are,
> That bide the pelting of this pitiless storm,
> How shall your houseless heads and unfed sides,
> Your loop'd and window'd raggedness, defend you
> From seasons such as these? O, I have ta'en
> Too little care of this! Take physic, pomp;
> Expose thyself to feel what wretches feel,
> That thou mayst shake the superflux to them,
> And show the heavens more just. (III.iv. 28–36)

Gloucester, as we have seen, parallels this insight when he says:

> Let the superfluous and lust-dieted man,
> That slaves your ordinance, that will not see
> Because he does not feel, feel your pow'r quickly;
> So distribution should undo excess,
> And each man have enough. (IV.i.67–71)

In the last speech of the play, Edgar (Albany is given these lines in some texts) says: "The weight of this sad time we must obey; / Speak what we feel, not what we ought to say" (V. iii. 324–25). Here speaking feelingly is added to seeing feelingly as the capstone of the true leader. And so in the play's conclusion, leadership reaches its full development. The time is ripe for Edgar to assume leadership. "Ripeness is all."

NOTES

1. William Shakespeare, *The Tragedy of King Lear*, in *The Riverside Shakespeare*, ed. G. Blakemore Evans (Boston: Houghton Mifflin, 1974), IV. vi. 147–49. Subsequent citations of the play in the text are from this source.

2. Warren Bennis, *On Becoming a Leader* (Reading, Mass.: Addison-Wesley, 1989), 39.

3. Mircea Eliade, *Images and Symbols: Studies in Religious Symbolism* (New York: Sheed and Ward, 1969), 19.

4. *Antigone*, in *Sophocles I*, ed. David Grene and Richmond Lattimore (Chicago: Phoenix, 1954), l. 1342.

5. *The Poetics*, in *Aristotle's Theory of Poetry and Fine Art*, ed. S. H. Butcher, 4th ed. (New York: Dover, 1951), ll. 1452a1.

6. Northrop Frye, *The Educated Imagination* (Bloomington: Indiana University Press, 1964), 63–64.

7. *Antigone*, ll. 1347–52.

8. Walter James Miller, *Antigone* (New York: Washington Square, 1970), 61.

9. Edward G. Ballard, "Sense of the Tragic," in *Dictionary of the History of Ideas*, vol. 4 (New York: Scribner's, 1973), 413.

10. Harold C. Goddard, *The Meaning of Shakespeare*, vol. 2 (Chicago: Phoenix, 1960), 141.

11. *Images and Symbols*, 20.

12. *The Educated Imagination*, 102, 116, 129.

13. Alison Lurie, "A Child's Garden of Subversion," *New York Times Book Review*, February 25, 1990, 34.

14. *The Educated Imagination*, 140–41.

15. *Images and Symbols*, 55–56.

16. *Images and Symbols*, 56.

17. Walter Brueggemann, *The Prophetic Imagination* (Philadelphia: Fortress, 1978), 45.

18. D. Verne Morland, "Lear's Fool: Coping with Change Beyond Future Shock," *New Management* 2, no.2 (1984): 23.

19. John Donne, "Satire III," in *John Donne's Poetry*, ed. A. L. Clements (New York: W. W. Norton, 1966), 60.

9

Art and Transformation in *Murder in the Cathedral*

Michael R. Carey

EXPLORING TRANSFORMATION THROUGH SYMBOLS

Poetry and drama, as do all art forms, draw upon symbols to express what is most true about people's lives. The symbols offered to the reader or the audience require a simultaneous standing in two worlds: the world of the symbol's literal meaning and the world of its conceptual meaning. Often readers and audiences must struggle to bring together the literal and conceptual meanings, but when they are bridged, the result is enlightenment and transformation. Such transformation is the object of art, as Shelley's comment that poetry "awakens and enlarges the mind" suggests. John Henry Newman speaks of the individual who, transformed by the experience of education, makes "a certain progress, and has a consciousness of mental enlargement; he does not stand where he did, he has a new centre, and a range of thoughts to which before he was a stranger."[1]

This "bridging" of the general and the particular, the abstract and the concrete, which produces such enlargement of the mind, is the underlying theme of this book. Moreover, T. S. Eliot's poetry, especially his verse drama *Murder in the Cathedral*, is a great manifestation of this theme. By illuminating the relationship between art and transformation, Eliot's play about Archbishop Thomas Becket affords the reader an opportunity to gain deeper insights into the processes of leadership.[2]

THE ART OF *MURDER IN THE CATHEDRAL*

Murder in the Cathedral begins with the return of Archbishop Thomas Becket to England after having been forced to live in exile for seven years by England's King Henry II. Part I of the play has the Chorus of Canterbury women waiting in dread for the arrival of Becket; they know that things will not go well for either Thomas or the Church, and that this also means things will not go well for them.

Also awaiting the arrival of Becket are the Priests of Canterbury Cathedral, who look to Thomas as their spiritual and temporal leader. They are concerned that Thomas will be destroyed by Henry if he is not careful, although they know that Becket is a strong-willed man.

Thomas arrives, and begins to prepare for the struggle with Henry and the probability of his death in the near future. Eliot has a series of Tempters interact with Becket, attempting to seduce him away from his mission of protecting the Church from Henry. These Tempters represent the operating logic of Thomas's life in the past: pleasure, power, and pride. The final Tempter is unexpected, however; he represents the present temptation of Thomas, who is willing to give up his life, not for the glory of God but for his own glory and for final victory over his adversaries. Eliot has Becket remark that this last temptation is the most significant betrayal: to do what one should do, but with the wrong motivation.

Thomas's reflection on the role of the martyr—his homily that makes up the Interlude between Part I and Part II—is the pivotal point for the whole drama. In the process of purifying his intentions, Becket underscores the fact that Christian martyrdom is never something that happens by accident, nor is it something that is due to the will of the martyr. Rather, the true martyr is the individual who has become the instrument of God and, paradoxically, has found authentic freedom in his or her willing submission to God.

Part II begins with the Chorus, more anxious now because Thomas's death draws closer. Four Knights loyal to Henry arrive at the Cathedral and, after some discussion, kill Thomas. They then explain their actions to the audience, using the ploy typical of tryants: no one regrets Becket's death more than they, but sometimes violence is necessary in order for justice to prevail.

The four Knights depart, and the Chorus descends into a deep, overwhelming depression that finally leads to a breakthrough and a new understanding of the meaning of Thomas's life and death for them. The play ends on a note of hope and renewal for the Chorus and for the audience.

TRANSFORMATIONAL LEADERSHIP

T. S. Eliot wrote *Murder in the Cathedral* for the Canterbury Festival of 1935, choosing to emphasize the inner spiritual struggle of the martyr rather than the outer political struggle between king and archbishop.[3] The themes present in Eliot's verse drama are most clearly connected to what is called "transformational leadership." The term has received its most insightful definition as part of the general concept of political leadership posited by James MacGregor Burns in a book titled *Leadership*.[4]

Burns attempts to explain leadership by viewing the process from a single perspective that integrates theories of leader behavior and follower behavior. Central to this perspective is the definition of the two types of leadership: transactional and transforming. Transactional leadership defines a process whereby "leaders approach followers with an eye to exchanging one thing for another." Transforming leadership, according to Burns, is quite different from the transactional variety in that the leader "looks for potential motives in the followers, seeks to satisfy higher needs, and engages the full person of the follower," which results in "a relationship of mutual stimulation and elevation" for both leader and follower. Both types of leadership are contrasted with naked, coercive power wielding that "objectifies its victims . . . literally turn[ing] them into objects."[5]

Use of the term "needs" by Burns is based upon the work of Abraham Maslow, who theorized a hierarchy of human needs. It is not until the lower-level "need" is satisfied, according to Maslow, that human beings move to the next higher-level need. For example, once physiological needs are satisfied, the need for security becomes important; and then, in ascending order, needs arise for belongingness, esteem, and finally self-actualization, or the fulfillment of one's potential.[6]

Besides Maslow's theories of human motivation, Burns uses Lawrence Kohlberg's theories of moral development to formulate his understanding of transforming leadership. Kohlberg identifies six stages of moral development. The first two are what Kohlberg calls the "preconventional level": here decisions regarding proper action are based upon an orientation to punishment and obedience, as well as the satisfaction of one's own needs. The next two stages are at the "conventional level," where appropriate behavior is influenced by the desire to conform and gain approval, by an orientation toward authority, fixed rules, and the maintenance of the social order. The final two stages are at a "postconventional level," where appropriate behavior is based upon principles that are logical, comprehensive, universal, and consistent.[7]

Burns integrates Maslow's and Kohlberg's theories to build upon his definition of transforming leadership and to examine moral leadership, which he views as going beyond simply satisfying the followers' wants or desires to actually being instrumental in producing the social change that will satisfy both followers' and leader's authentic needs. According to Burns, transforming leadership operates as a "relationship of mutual stimulation and elevation that converts followers into leaders and may convert leaders into moral agents."[8]

Burns's description of the relationship between transforming leader and follower is consistent with research done by Kohlberg and others which indicates that individuals who engage others at a higher stage of moral development in an ongoing dialectical relationship are stimulated to move to the next higher stage. One study showed that if people "were systematically exposed to moral reasoning one stage above their own, they would be positively attracted to that reasoning, and would, in attempting to appropriate the reasoning as their own, be stimulated to the next higher stage of moral judgment." Another study found that the shift to a higher stage was facilitated by "operative moral transacts [i.e.], exchanges in which the discussants do not simply assert their own opinions or paraphrase the opinions of the other, but rather engage each other's reasoning in an ongoing dialectic." This give-and-take dialogue is not unknown among professional administrators at federal, state, and local levels of bureaucracy.[9]

Another view of the developmental process is provided by Robert Kegan, who distinguishes between two personality structures: the self-as-subject (i.e., the structure by which people compose experience) and the self-as-object (i.e., that aspect of an individual's consciousness that itself may be examined consciously). Building his theory upon Jean Piaget's work in cognitive development, Kegan states that the subject self is so basic to human functioning that people typically are not aware of it. If the self-as-subject is thought of as the lens through which an individual views both the world and his or her inner experiences, then the *only* object not examinable by the lens is the lens itself.[10]

Being a developmentalist, Kegan views the relationship between the self-as-object and the self-as-subject as constantly changing. The frame of reference that is created by the subject at one stage of development later becomes, at a new stage of development, the object of a new frame of reference.

Subject–object relations emerge out of a life-long process of development; a succession of qualitative differentiations of the self from the world, with a qualitatively more extensive object with which to be in relation created each time; a natural history of qualitatively better guarantees to the world of its distinctness; successive triumphs of "relationship to" rather than "embeddedness in."[11]

Kegan outlines six stages of an evolutionary process of development: the Incorporative Stage, where the embeddedness is in reflexes, sensing, and moving; the Impulsive Stage, where the organizing process is limited to impulse and perception; the Imperial Stage, where the embeddedness is in needs and interests; the Interpersonal Stage, where there exists a sense of mutuality and interpersonal concordance; the Institutional Stage, where self-as-subject is embedded in personal values and autonomy; and the Interindividual Stage, where the organizing process is found in the interpenetration of systems. This evolutionary process is marked by a crisis produced when the old way of making sense of the world no longer works, a realization that the solution of this crisis will come only with a new way of "being" in the world. Moreover, anxiety and depression serve as a prelude to this new "being," finally followed by a shift in thinking, as what was the self-as-subject becomes object to a new subject.[12]

If Burns's and Kegan's ideas are combined, it might be said that leadership is a matter of consciousness; the authentic leader is "less embedded" in the self-as-subject than is the follower. This higher level of consciousness allows the leader to choose between being transactional and transformational. Both types of leadership require an understanding of what motivates followers in order either to manipulate them (transactional leadership) or to call them to higher levels of performance (transformational leadership). If the above-mentioned choice is for transformational leadership, and therefore for moral leadership, then followers are transformed by means of a dialectical relationship that results in a higher level of consciousness for them, eventually making them into leaders. On the other hand, if the choice is for transactional leadership, then followers and leader are limited to meager exchanges of valued items. Furthermore, both followers' and leader's present consciousness remains unchallenged.

For example, the city manager who must implement a low-cost housing program when residents have adopted the NIMBY stance (Not In My Back Yard) is faced with a moral challenge. As a transactional leader, the manager may negotiate political trade-offs, such as construction of a neighborhood park if residents accept a housing project. The transformational city manager, on the other hand, will engage residents in a dialogue designed to raise their sensibilities and moral consciousness regarding the plight of less fortunate citizens.

Coercive power wielding contrasts with leadership that flows out of higher levels of consciousness. Such controlling pseudo leadership lacks any connection to a greater consciousness of reality and, in fact, betrays an almost complete embeddedness in the self-as-subject, to the point that healthy human development is arrested. Burns states that "to watch one person absolutely dominate another is horrifying; to watch one person disappear, his motives and values submerged into those of another to the point of loss of individuality, is saddening."[13] Ironically, this ultimate coercion is often facilitated by the power wielder's creation of the illusion that he or she has greater consciousness of reality and/or sensitivity to followers' needs. There is no room in modern public administration for this type of irrational, oppressive behavior.[14]

ART AND TRANSFORMATION

With the foregoing concepts, it is possible to find in Eliot's characters examples of Burns's leadership types. For example, the Priests in the drama are the classic bureaucrats: as they wait for the arrival of the Archbishop, they view the imminent struggle in transactional terms, that is, as a matter of how much one has to bargain with politically.

The Priests' transactional approach to their leadership role vis-à-vis the Chorus makes them unwilling or unable to respond in any creative fashion to the Chorus, whose members are anxious and pessimistic about Thomas's entrance into Canterbury. The Chorus expresses its view of things in transactional terms related to more primal issues than those of the Priests. They talk of birth and death, marriages, taxes, and oppression; their sense is that they are left out of the action, and must simply witness events that ultimately will shape their lives. The only response the Priests have for the women is the equivalent of telling them to "put on a happy face" with which to greet the archbishop.

Thomas enters the play as a transformational leader. He tells the Priests not to criticize the Chorus: they have an understanding of reality that goes beyond their seeming confusion. He has a perspective on the world that allows him to understand the fears of the Chorus, yet he is able to place those fears in the context of the eternal. Eliot has Becket express this in a passage on the concept of suffering and action: the Chorus experiences action as suffering, yet its suffering is also action.

The Knights represent a power wielding that distorts the notion of relationship between leader and follower. Their entrance into the cathedral is drunken and loud. When questioned about their anger, which is directed toward Thomas, they respond in a very simple and linear fashion, calling him derogatory names. They complain to Thomas about his lack of gratitude for the honors and possessions the king has granted him. And finally, when Thomas is unmoved by their arguments and has responded to all of their accusations, they kill him.

After murdering the archbishop, the Knights appeal to the audience to justify their actions. They are completely different personalities now, arguing with a "pure" logic that they had nothing to gain from this murder—they did it because it was the right thing to do. One of them wonders out loud as to who really killed the archbishop, and concludes that Thomas was more responsible for his death than were the Knights. Like many coercive pseudo leaders, they attempt to justify their actions in the language of a higher consciousness to which they are still strangers. In a final attempt to overpower the minds of the audience, the Knights create a value of the separation of church and state, a value for which they argue they have been willing to kill and are willing to be imprisoned.

Leadership may be understood, then, in terms of the leader's and followers' levels of consciousness. Thomas represents a transforming leader who is less embedded in the self-as-subject than are any of the other characters; he understands the other characters, even though they do not understand him. The Priests are transactional leaders whose construction of meaning is more limited than that of Thomas but greater than that of the Chorus. They limit the leadership process to transactional approaches (e.g., through obedience to authority). The consciousness of the Knights is at the lowest of Kegan's stages: they equate their personal agendas with absolute truth and are unable to hold a conversation, much less a dialogue, with Becket about political issues.

Becket is aware that he is at a higher level of consciousness than are any of the other characters in the play. His initial speech to the Chorus about suffering and action has an air of condescension toward them and the Priests. His self-confidence may be viewed as proceeding from his having successfully integrated the self-subject and the self-as-object at various developmental levels. Each of these levels may be viewed as represented by one of the Tempters. The first Tempter speaks to Thomas of the life of worldly pleasure he engaged in as a young man, and this is roughly equivalent to Kegan's stage where needs and interests form the organizing process. The second Tempter argues that while selfish power is one thing, real power comes from allying oneself with those who have political power, as did Becket in his former alliance with the King. This may be viewed as the Tempter's urging Thomas's return to a stage, as Kegan describes it, where relationships and mutual obligations form the organizing process. The third Tempter attacks by proposing a return to embeddedness in values that go beyond relationship, characterizing the next stage in Kegan's hierarchy: overcome the King, the Tempter argues, for then you can side with the Normans who desire the rights of sovereignty against the King, who desires to expand his control.

Thomas, however, has already left all these limited perspectives behind; he is at Maslow's stage of self-actualization and Kohlberg's stage of universal principles. Thomas is not defined by values; to use Kegan's framework, he *has* values. However, a final Tempter comes unexpectedly, and offers a paradox that seemingly cannot be resolved by Thomas, even at the "highest" stage of making meaning. This final, unexpected temptation is simply for Becket to do what he plans to do: that is, resist the King, stand his and the Church's ground, and accept the fact that this action will lead to his death. But, the Tempter adds, Becket must also know that because of his actions, he will win an everlasting reward, and will see his persecutors receive an everlasting punishment. Becket's apparent selflessness, therefore, becomes subtle selfishness.

The fourth Tempter's insight into the limitations of his way of constructing meaning leaves Thomas deeply troubled. He wonders if there is any way for him to act without his ego getting in the way. The Tempter responds to Becket in the same way that Becket had earlier responded to the Chorus: he has an understanding of reality that goes beyond his seeming confusion.

His confusion is centered in the paradox of choosing both to act *and* to be an instrument of God's will, the tension between action and suffering, and is resolved by Thomas when he throws himself into the seeming absurdity of his situation and trusts in God. He tells the Priests that, if limited to results, every action could be shown to have good and bad consequences. What is left, therefore, is for action to transcend consequences and be grounded in the eternal, that is, in the will of God.

Using Kegan's theories, the paradox of suffering and action, of both willing an act and being instrumental to the will of God, is insolvable to Thomas from his present level of consciousness. Only through a shift in his way of constructing meaning can this paradox disappear, and that shift is from reliance on logic to faith. Thomas trusts in God's love and shifts to a higher level of consciousness, a level that can then integrate the paradox of suffering and action. Thomas becomes what Maslow calls a "transcending" self-actualizer, and starts thinking at what Kohlberg suggests is a "Stage 7" of moral thinking (i.e., having to do more with the "cosmic" than with the universal). Thomas makes a fully conscious choice to be a transforming, moral leader.[15]

In creating the Chorus for *Murder in the Cathedral*, Eliot draws upon the dramatic model of ancient Greek choruses. But rather than serving primarily as a device to reflect upon the struggles of the protagonist or as representatives of the community (as was the case in the majority of Greek dramas), Eliot's Chorus becomes transformed, experiencing a dramatic shift in consciousness.

The Chorus begins the drama at a level of consciousness that cannot make sense of what is happening. The Chorus has become used to being oppressed. But with the return of Thomas from exile, it cries out in fear of something more than oppression: it is afraid of transformation. The tremendous anxiety expressed throughout the play may be the same kind of anxiety that is present in an individual who is in the throes of a shift from one of Kegan's stages to another. Kegan writes:

My position amounts to a conception of depression as radical doubt, that which presents the possibility of "not knowing" with respect to the ultimate proposition: How do the world and I cohere? What is subject and what is object?[16]

In viewing the above position from a leadership perspective, the importance of the Chorus's depression is based not on the fact that its members view the world as no longer making sense to them; rather, the question becomes one of *how* they regain their equilibrium and shift to a new organizing process. This "how" is connected to the relationship that the Chorus has with its archbishop, Thomas.

In spite of the danger, the Chorus is attracted to Thomas and feels compelled to witness what will happen at the cathedral. The action of the Chorus may be interpreted as an attraction to a different way of constructing meaning, one that is not accessible to them at their current stage but for which they long. The Chorus engages Thomas in a dialectic, arguing that their old way is sufficient. Thomas responds both by acknowledging their truth and by calling them to a higher truth.

Thomas resolves his dilemma of action and suffering for himself; more important, as a transforming leader he expresses it to the Chorus in the Christmas Day homily during the interlude. He notes that it is fitting to celebrate the birth of the Savior with great rejoicing in a eucharistic liturgy that is a reenactment of the suffering and death of Christ. In a sense, those present at the Christmas liturgy will both mourn and rejoice, and for the same reason. Thomas relates these mixed feelings to the Chorus's mixed feelings about martyrdom, his martyrdom in actual death, and theirs in opening themselves up to God's will, telling them that martyrdom is always the design of a living God, in order to warn and lead people back to God.

One critic has pointed out that the problem with the homily in terms of the dramatic structure of the play is "its superfluity. The sermon is completely unnecessary to the play, and if it is removed we feel no loss."[17] Yet it is the presence of the homily that makes Becket a transformational leader. For after his own shift in consciousness, Thomas seeks to help the Chorus shift to another level of consciousness, and the homily represents the dialectic process mentioned earlier. Thomas becomes a leader who, as Burns says, is "so sensitive to the motives of potential followers that the roles of the leader and the follower become virtually interdependent."[18]

And the Chorus responds, praising God in the final passage of the play. Through its members' relationship with Thomas, both he and they have changed. What made them anxious at the beginning of the play is understandable to them at its conclusion. Thomas has helped them to become more fully conscious, so that his leaving them is not a disaster. Thomas *was* the leader whose entrance was longed for at the beginning, but the members of the Chorus *are* the leaders who exit at the end.

Inspired public administrators are like Thomas. They accept the challenge of transcending the self. They are able to engage in a dialectic that results in a shift of consciousness for all involved in the process. Such administrators must have the ability to see possibilities where none seem to exist, to be able to see connections where others see only differences. To work effectively, public administrators must see problems integratively, that is, "see them as wholes, related to larger wholes, and thus challenge established practices—rather than walling off a piece of experience and preventing it from being touched or affected by any new experiences."[19] By doing so, followers and leaders become indistinguishable from one another, and true participation in decision-making results. When moral responsibility is assumed by all actors on the public sector stage, the illumination and inspiration so desperately needed in the profession emerge.

NOTES

For assistance in preparing this chapter, I thank Franz K. Schneider, Timothy C. Soulis, Stephen R. Kuder, Yusif S. al-Hatlani, John Ney, and Mary Ann Grimes Carey.

1 ˙Percy Bysshe Shelley, *A Defense of Poetry* (Boston: Ginn, 1890), 13; John Henry Newman, *The Uses of Knowledge*, ed. Leo L. Ward (Arlington Heights, Ill.: AHM, 1948), 35.

2. The sources used for the work are *The Collected Plays of T. S. Eliot* (New York: Harcourt Brace, 1964); and T. S. Eliot and George Hoellering, *The Film of Murder in the Cathedral* (London: Faber and Faber, 1952).

3. For a description of the development of Eliot's play for the Canterbury Festival, see E. Martin Browne, *The Making of T. S. Eliot's Plays* (Cambridge: Cambridge University Press, 1969), esp. chap. 2, pp. 34–89. Another book useful in understanding Eliot's work is Grover Smith, Jr., *T. S. Eliot's Poetry and Plays* (Chicago: University of Chicago Press, 1950).

4. James MacGregor Burns, *Leadership* (New York: Harper, 1978). Burns's concepts have been developed by other writers, the most prominent being Bernard M. Bass, *Leadership and Performance Beyond Expectations* (New York: Free Press, 1985). See also Bass, "From Transactional to Transformational Leadership: Learning to Share the Vision," *Organizational Dynamics*, 18 (Winter 1990): 19–36.

5. *Leadership*, 4, 21.

6. Abraham H. Maslow, *Motivation and Personality* (New York: Harper and Row, 1954) and *The Farther Reaches of Human Nature* (New York: Penguin, 1971).

7. Lawrence Kohlberg, "The Cognitive–Developmental Approach to Moral Education," *Phi Delta Kappan*, 56, 10 (June 1975), 670–77.

8. *Leadership*, 4.

9. F. Clark Power, Ann Higgins, and Lawrence Kohlberg, *Lawrence Kohlberg's Approach to Moral Education* (New York: Columbia Univesity Press, 1989), 11, 13.

10. Robert Kegan, *The Evolving Self: Problem and Process in Human Development* (Cambridge, Mass.: Harvard University Press, 1982). In defining the self as object, Kegan points out that the root "ject" means "throw away from," so that the term "object" refers to that which "some motion has made separate or distinct from, or to the motion itself."

11. Ibid., 77.

12. Ibid., 119–20.

13. *Leadership*, 21.

14. For more discussion of this point, see Michael R. Carey, "The Transformative Nature of Christian Leadership," *Human Development* 12 (Spring 1991): 30–34; "Transformational Leadership and the Fundamental Option for Self-Transcendence," *Leadership Quarterly* 3, no. 3 (1991): 217–36.

15. See Maslow, *The Farther Reaches of Mankind*, esp. chap. 22. Kohlberg, in his "Stages and Aging in Moral Development—Some Speculations," *The Gerontologist* 13, no. 4 (1973): 498–502, says: "The concept of such a Stage 7 is familiar, of course, both in religious writing and in the classical metaphysical tradition from Plato to Spinoza. In most accounts the movement starts with despair. Such despair involves the beginning of a cosmic perspective. It is when we begin to see our lives as finite from some more infinite perspective that we feel despair. The meaninglessness of our lives in the face of death is the meaninglessness of the finite from the perspective of the infinite. The resolution of the despair which we call Stage 7 represents a continuation of the process of taking a more comsic perspective whose first phase is despair. It represents, in a sense, a shift from figure to ground. In despair we are the self seen from the distance of the cosmic or infinite. In the state of mind we metaphorically term State 7, we identify ourselves with the cosmic or infinite perspective; we value life from its standpoint" (p. 501).

16. *The Evolving Self*, 269.

17. Sean Lucy, *T. S. Eliot and the Idea of Tradition* (London: Cohen and West, 1960), 189.

18. *Leadership*, 21.

19. Rosabeth Moss Kanter, *The Change Masters* (New York: Touchstone, 1983), 27.

10

Poetry and Leadership: The Case of Lincoln

Dalmas H. Nelson

POETRY AND ADMINISTRATION

This chapter's preparation reflects a sharing of the book's premise that the vast, complex, somewhat mysterious subject called public administration can be illuminated by the vast, complex, somewhat mysterious realm of the arts—including fine poetry. Abraham Lincoln serves here as a case example of both a great poet and a great poetic subject. Belief about poetry's utility as an avenue of access to understanding rests on several grounds.

First, the poet may dramatize relationships, dimensions, and meanings starkly or graphically. Ralph Waldo Emerson's "Each and All," a forerunner of the environmentalist movement, illustrates the Policy Bridge.

> Nothing is fair or good alone.
> I thought the sparrow's note from heaven,
> Singing at dawn on the alder bough;
> I brought him home, in his nest, at even;
> He sings the song, but it cheers not now,
> For I did not bring home the river and sky;—
> He sang to my ear,—they sang to my eye.
> The delicate shells lay on the shore;
> The bubbles of the latest wave
> Fresh pearls to their enamel gave,
> And the bellowing of the savage sea
> Greeted their safe escape to me.
> I wiped away the weeds and foam,

I fetched my sea-born treasures home;
But the poor, unsightly, noisome things
Had left their beauty on the shore
With the sun and the sand and
       the wild uproar.[1]

Second, poetic language may provide concreteness and dynamism of extraordinary quality, as in the words of Herman Melville's Ishmael, in *Moby Dick*, who finds the skeleton of a whale that had been driven ashore by storm. Ishmael begins systematically to count and measure its ribs, then stops:

How vain and foolish, then, thought I, for timid untraveled man to try to comprehend aright this wondrous whale, by merely poring over his dead attenuated skeleton, stretched in the peaceful wood. No. Only in the heart of quickest perils; only when within the eddying of his angry flukes; only on the profound unbounded sea, can the fully invested whale be truly and livingly found out.[2]

Third, the poet can have a particular capacity to reach our value system in ways that have intensified potential to affect policy-making. A classic instance of both the Values and Policy bridges is Oliver Wendell Holmes's "Old Ironsides." When the U.S. government seriously moved toward scrapping the battle-worn and obsolete U.S.S. *Constitution*, Holmes wrote this poem, which was circulated widely in the country almost overnight. It helped mightily to save the ship from bureaucratic destruction.

Ay, tear her tattered ensign down!
       Long has it waved on high,
And many an eye has danced to see
       That banner in the sky;
Beneath it rung the battle shout,
       And burst the cannon's roar;—
The meteor of the ocean air
       Shall sweep the clouds no more!
Her deck, once red with heroes' blood,
       Where knelt the vanquished foe,
When winds were hurrying o'er the flood,
       And waves were white below,
No more shall feel the victor's tread,
       Or know the conquered knee;—
The harpies of the shore shall pluck
       The eagle of the sea!

Oh, better that her shattered hulk
    Should sink beneath the wave;
Her thunders shook the mighty deep,
    And there should be her grave;
Nail to the mast her holy flag,
    Set every threadbare sail,
And give her to the god of storms,
    The lightning and the gale![3]

Fourth, the poet can appeal to our capacity for imagination, stimulate us to exercise that capacity, and thereby broaden our intellectual and aesthetic vision, as in Henry David Thoreau's poem "Inspiration":

I hear beyond the range of sound,
I see beyond the range of sight,
New earths and skies and seas around,
And in my day the sun doth pale his light. . . .[4]

An attempt to discuss poetry with reference to public sector leadership is not without hazards. This chapter draws upon poets not necessarily regardable as "experts" on leadership. The oversimplification and exaggeration inhering in much strong poetry may mislead and not merely enlighten. Also, poets one selects may often speak "through a glass darkly"; using poetry can be a highly subjective process. In employing poetic insights, one may misunderstand and misinterpret the poets' intent. These and other potential problems are troubling indeed when someone outside the field of literature undertakes this kind of analytical essay. Nevertheless, the potential gains of relating poetry to governmental leadership make the risks worthwhile.

Abraham Lincoln seems fitting for an essay on poetry and governmental leadership, for a variety of reasons. First, he is widely considered among Americans to have been one of our greatest presidents. One might reasonably hope thus to learn much about public leadership from examining his case. Second, he was himself a great poet. This point will be amply substantiated in a moment. Third, he probably has been written about by more major poets than any other American. Many of his personal characteristics have a natural poetic appeal, lending themselves to legend, song, and historical interpretation of the nineteenth century American character. Fourth, if this were not enough, he was a central figure in the greatest domestic drama of American history, the Civil War. Because of the circumstances in which he labored and the nature of his efforts, both his strengths and his weaknesses have greatly magnified consequences in the lives of people, in America and in the world. Thus, his life is quite inevitably the stuff of epic poetry.

Lincoln had to wrestle with staggeringly huge, difficult moral quandaries. For it was far from self-evidently true that states of the Union should not be allowed to go their own independent ways; far from crystal clear that the monumental loss of life the war would entail did not outweigh whatever might be gained for the nation and its future from forcibly overcoming secession. What was the nature of the Union? Intertwined was the enormous issue of slavery. This rending moral controversy involved conflict over the question of slavery's extension to territories, the nature and limits of "property rights" and "individualism," "popular sovereignty" for societies preferring to permit slavery, the question of abolition of what many in the North especially regarded as a terrible evil, and the meanings given to the concept of equality. No work of fiction could have described for an imaginary society a more intense, dramatic, and mammoth crisis, more freighted with long-term significance for nation and world, than Lincoln had to confront when he became president.[5]

Last, in what must be fairly rare in history, poetic expression itself was employed by this leader in critical circumstances as a basic tool of communication with the American people and even the people of Europe, as an important ingredient in the management of the war, and in the effort to resolve the great political issues of the war.

LINCOLN AS GREAT POET

Several poems by Lincoln appear in the *Collected Works of Abraham Lincoln*, including, perhaps most notably, "My Childhood-Home I See Again" (1846) and "The Bear Hunt" (1846). He labored many years to build a powerful capacity for language, including in this process significant attention to Shakespeare and the Bible.[6] Much of what he said as a leader in certain fundamental messages was very poetic, even though not formally cast as poetry. His words therein were making, not merely describing, American history, in a triple sense: they were helping Americans to reinterpret their nation's history and political principles, to modify some key personal values, and to change the national polity in certain fundamental respects. Thus, in effect, Lincoln as poet invokes all five of this book's bridges between art and public life. The appealing and enduring quality of his poetic words comes from their literary strength, from their expression of his real character and convictions, from their revelation of the nature of his efforts to move a society, and from some appreciation of their impact in contributing to changing the future of the nation and the world.

This chapter can present only a few of many possible examples of the poetical power that Lincoln exercised in a leadership capacity. In the farewell address at Springfield, Lincoln expresses his profound religious faith and love for people. In so doing, he brings us to the Leadership Bridge in a manner seldom attained in the English language.

My friends: No one, not in my situation, can appreciate my feeling of sadness at this parting. To this place, and the kindness of these people, I owe everything. Here I have lived a quarter of a century, and have passed from a young to an old man. Here my children have been born, and one is buried. I now leave, not knowing when or whether ever I may return, with a task before me greater than that which rested upon Washington. Without the assistance of that Divine Being who ever attended him, I cannot succeed. With that assistance, I cannot fail. Trusting in Him who can go with me, and remain with you, and be everywhere for good, let us confidently hope that all will yet be well. To His care commending you, as I hope in your prayers you will commend me, I bid you an affectionate farewell.[7]

The first inaugural address was also poetic. Virtually all of this speech was an effort to preserve the Union peacefully. At the end, he starkly poses the implications of secession, then invokes common ties of Americans, which eventually would help knit America back together.

In your hands, my dissatisfied fellow-countrymen, and not in mine, is the momentous issue of civil war. The government will not assail you. You can have no conflict without being yourselves the aggressors. You have no oath registered in heaven to destroy the government, while I shall have the most solemn one to "preserve, protect, and defend it."

I am loath to close. We are not enemies, but friends. We must not be enemies. Though passion may have strained, it must not break our bonds of affection. The mystic chords of memory, stretching from every battle-field and patriot grave to every living heart and hearthstone all over this broad land, will yet swell the chorus of the Union when again touched, as surely they will be, by the better angels of our nature.[8]

In the Gettysburg Address, so familiar to many Americans, Lincoln effectively amended the American constitutional system in supremely poetic language. Drawing upon words of the Declaration of Independence, he redefined the heart of the American polity to include equality. He also cast the people of the states of the union as one people. As Gary Wills put it:

In his brief time . . . at Gettysburg . . . he called up a new nation out of the blood and trauma. . . . The Gettysburg Address has become an authoritative expression of the American spirit. . . . For most people now, the Declaration means what Lincoln told us it means. . . . By accepting the Gettysburg Address, and its concept of a single people dedicated to a proposition, we have been changed.[9]

One of Lincoln's highest poetical achievements is the second inaugural address. It is astonishing in the degree of its detachment, as though in some senses Lincoln had stepped outside of time and space to look at the cause he led and the opposing side with the perception of an Old Testament prophet. The moral condemnation of slavery is strongly asserted, but with a humble acknowledgment of human limitations in discerning the will of Providence, a recognition of both sides' need for forgiveness, and a spirit of reconciliation and healing. The second inaugural address speaks to future leaders of armed conflict as much as it spoke to Lincoln's own time. It is a clear example of Lincoln as both a leader in his own right and an inspiration to aspiring political figures.

On the occasion corresponding to this four years ago, all thoughts were anxiously directed to an impending civil war. All dreaded it—all sought to avert it. While the inaugural address was being delivered from this place, devoted altogether to saving the Union without war, insurgent agents were in the city seeking to destroy it without war—seeking to dissolve the Union, and divide effects, by negotiation. Both parties deprecated war; but one of them would make war rather than let the nation survive; and the other would accept war rather than let it perish. And the war came.

One-eighth of the whole population were colored slaves, not distributed generally over the Union, but localized in the Southern part of it. These slaves constituted a peculiar and powerful interest. All knew that this interest was, somehow, the cause of the war. To strengthen, perpetuate, and extend this interest was the object for which the insurgents would rend the Union, even by war; while the government claimed no right to do more than to restrict the territorial enlargement of it.

Neither party expected for the war the magnitude or the duration which it has already attained. Neither anticipated that the cause of the conflict might cease with, or even before, the conflict itself should cease. Each looked for an easier triumph, and a result less fundamental and astounding. Both read the same Bible, and pray to the same God; and each invokes his aid against the other. It may seem strange that any men should dare to ask a just God's assistance in wringing their bread from the sweat of other men's faces; but let us judge not, that we be not judged. The prayers of both could not be answered—that of neither has been answered fully.

The Almighty has his own purposes. "Woe unto the world because of offenses! for it must needs be that offenses come; but woe to that man by whom the offense cometh." If we shall suppose that American slavery is one of those offenses which, in the providence of God, must needs come, but which, having continued through his appointed time, he now wills to remove, and that he gives to both North and South this terrible war, as the woe due to those by whom the offense came, shall we discern therein any departure from those divine attributes which the believers in a living God always ascribe to him? Fondly do we hope—fervently do we pray—that this mighty scourge of war may speedily pass away. Yet, if God wills that it continue until all the wealth piled by the bondsman's two hundred and fifty years of unrequited toil shall be sunk, and until every drop of blood drawn with the lash shall be paid by another drawn with the sword, as was said three thousand years ago, so still it must be said, "The judgments of the Lord are true and righteous altogether."

With malice toward none; with charity for all; with firmness in the right, as God gives us to see the right, let us strive on to finish the work we are in; to bind up the nation's wounds; to care for him who shall have borne the battle, and for his widow, and his orphan—to do all which may achieve and cherish a just and lasting peace among ourselves, and with all nations.[10]

POETIC INTERPRETATIONS OF LINCOLN

We turn now to an examination of Lincoln from the perspectives of other poets, in the belief that they can provide insights about him as a leader and about public leadership. For this review, all identifiable published poetry on Lincoln, as listed in the seventh and eighth editions (1982, 1986) of *Granger's Index to Poetry*, has been examined.

Lincoln's Achievements

Individuals may have leadership capacities but lack inclination or willingness to fulfill leadership roles available to them. Or they may have both personal qualifications and inclination but lack opportunity. Lincoln's case involved a remarkable conjunction of ambition for political leadership, strong personal qualifications, and a colossal role on a world stage.

The saving of the Union is celebrated in Whitman's justly famous lines:

O Captain! my Captain! our fearful trip is done,

The ship has weather'd every rock, the prize we sought
    is won,
The port is near, the bells I hear, the people all exulting,
While follow eyes the steady keel, the vessel grim and
    daring;
. . . .
The ship is anchor'd safe and sound, its voyage closed
    and done,
From fearful trip the victor comes in with object won;
    Exult, O shores, and ring, O bells!. . . . [11]

Many other poets addressed this theme as well. Hermann Hagedorn, in "Master, Make Us One," describes Lincoln as follows: "Great brother to the lofty and the low / . . . . Oh you, who knew all anguish, in whose eyes, / Pity, with tear-stained face, / Kept her long vigil o'er the severed lands / For friend and foe, for race and race. . . . "[12] In a hymn of thanks for Lincoln, Oliver Wendell Holmes prays, "In One our broken Many blend, / That none again may sever!" [13] Clearly, his life and death helped accelerate the growth of American nationalism. Commenting on Lincoln's martyrdom, Corinne Roosevelt Robinson writes, "That every sad and sacrificial tear / Waters the seed to patriot mourners dear, / That flowers in love of Country . . . "[14]

A great deal of the poetic celebration of Lincoln's achievements focuses on his emancipation of the slaves. Examples are Caroline A. Mason, "His grave a nation's heart shall be; / His monument a people free!"; Mae Winkler Goodman, "You knew that slavery held the master slave— / That freedom is man's sustenance and bread / . . ."; and John Greenleaf Whittier, "The cloudy sign, the fiery guide, / Along his pathway ran, / And Nature, through his voice, denied The ownership of man. . . ."[15]

Lincoln's twin triumphs of saving the Union and freeing the slaves were seen by many poets as towering accomplishments partly because, hounded by enormous ridicule in America and from abroad, he refused to let such treatment knock him from his course. Jane L. Hardy calls him one "Fearless and firm, with clear foreseeing mind; / Who should not flinch from calumny or scorn, / Who in the depth of night could ken the morn. . . ." Edwin Arlington Robinson declares in "The Master":

He knew that undeceiving fate
Would shame us whom he served unsought;
He knew that he must wince and wait—
The jest of those for whom he fought;. . . .

Rose Terry Cooke depicts Lincoln as one "Steadfast for truth and right, when lies and wrong / Rolled their dark waters, turbulent and strong."[16]

A great deal of the poetry emphasizes Lincoln's patient, dogged persistence despite terribly heavy burdens, under what Whitman calls "time's dark events, / Charging like ceaseless clouds across the sky. . . . " In "Lincoln," Julia Ward Howe outlines the challenge: "No throne of honors and delights; / Distrustful days and sleepless nights, / To struggle, suffer, and aspire, / Like Israel, led by cloud and fire." Stephen Vincent Benét, in *John Brown's Body*, describes Lincoln's response to the panic that arose among many Northern leaders after the Union defeat in First Bull Run:

Only Lincoln, awkwardly enduring, confused by a thousand counsels, is neither overwhelmed nor touched to folly by the madness that runs along the streets like a dog in August scared of itself, scaring everyone who crosses its path.

Defeat is a fact and victory can be a fact. If the idea is good, it will survive defeat, it may even survive the victory.

His huge, patient, laborious hands start kneading the stuff of the Union together again; he gathers up the scraps and puts them together; he sweeps the corners and the cracks and patches together the lost courage and the rags of belief.[17]

Lincoln was taxed intensely by the miscarrying of many of his plans; by the bitter fruits of what often turned out to be his misjudgments in the choice of battle leaders, who often incurred substantial defeats; and by the terrible casualty rates among the soldiers. Through most of the war, the president had to deal with the fact that both elite and mass opinion in the North was fluctuating and deeply divided over the issue of war and over the interrelated issue of slavery. Tremendous resolve was needed for him to persist. Edwin Arlington Robinson suggests, "The calm, the smouldering, and the flame / Of awful patience were his own. . . . ." James Russell Lowell salutes his "supple-tempered will / That bent like perfect steel to spring again and thrust. " John Gould Fletcher seems to link Lincoln's struggle to cope with personal depression and his having strength for continued striving in his epochal tasks.

There was a darkness in this man, an immense and hollow darkness,
Of which we may not speak, nor share with him nor enter;
A darkness through which strong roots stretched downwards into the
   earth,
Towards old things;

Towards the herdman-kings who walked the earth and spoke
    with God,
Towards the wanderers who sought for they knew not what, and
    found their goal at last;
Towards the men who waited, only waited patiently when all seemed
    lost,
Many bitter winters of defeat;

Down to the granite of patience,
These roots swept, knotted fibrous roots, prying, piercing, seeking,
And drew from the living rock and the living waters about it,
The red sap to carry upwards to the sun. . . . [18]

Lincoln as Symbol

In our present era of preoccupation with image-building in commerce
and politics alike, we may well reflect on the symbolic power of Lincoln as
leader, and on the high degree of correlation between positive image and
reality in his case. In poetical interpretations of Lincoln as symbol, four
main themes seem to stand out.

First is his "Americanness." James Russell Lowell called Lincoln "the
first American." As the son of a pioneer family who was familiar with forest
and plain, the tools of hard labor, personal hardship, and struggle, he
symbolized many aspects of frontier society. Edwin Markham describes
"Evil Powers" that sent "fates"

. . . To baffle and beat back the heaven-sent child.
Three were the fates—gaunt Poverty that chains,
Gray Drudgery that grinds the hope away,
And gaping Ignorance that starves the soul. . . . [19]

And there was his inner psychological struggle. Delmore Schwartz says
of Lincoln's background, "He studied law, but knew in his own soul /
Despair's anarchy, terror and error . . . "; and "Sometimes he could not go
home to face his wife, / Sometimes he wished to hurry or end his life!"
Lincoln was also "American" in being someone of a humble background
who rose to a pinnacle of achievement by his performance, despite great
obstacles, a pattern Americans tend to admire. Robert Morris calls Lincoln
"a soul that surmounted poverty's hill, / And cried back to the world, 'You
can if you will!' "[20] Poets saw Lincoln's background and appearance as

contributing to an image of genuineness, perhaps one of this country's greatest ideals. His association with the ideas of democracy and freedom is, indeed, part of his "Americanness."

Second, and related, is the poets' perception of Lincoln as symbolizing a great product and achievement of democracy. Lyman Whitney Allen called him "The chosen liege of a chosen weal / And Liberty's offering. / . . . A people's Own. " Richard Henry Stoddard described him as "One of the People! born to be / Their curious epitome; To share, yet rise above / Their shifting hate and love. . . . "21

Third is the view of Lincoln as a symbol of hope to the world's oppressed and as a shepherd of humankind. What could the democratic land report to a skeptical world? Lincoln was a powerful voice for it, as at Gettysburg. Florence Kiper Frank writes: "What answer shall we make to them that seek / The living vision on a distant shore? / What words of life? . . . / Now as then / The oppressed shall hear him and be not afraid." Lucy Larcom declares, "Lo, the patriot martyr / Taketh his journey grand! / Travels into the ages, / Bearing a hope how dear! / Into life's unknown vistas, / Liberty's great pioneer. . . . " John James Piatt places Lincoln among the "Bringers of Light and Pilots in the dark, / Bearers of Crosses, Servants of the World."22

Fourth is the view that sees Lincoln as a providential gift from God to humanity in America's compelling hour of need. This theme, which restrictions of space prevent me from illustrating, draws many biblical parallels. Some poets present Lincoln as an Old Testament prophet. Others see similarities between Lincoln's martyrdom and continuing influence and Jesus' crucifixion and resurrection.

Lincoln's Character

Much praise from poets goes to Lincoln's character, to matters that were essentially not skills, techniques, strategies, theories, or even accomplishments, but elemental goodness. One cannot imagine Lincoln as leader apart from these qualities, or separate the reverence in which he is so widely held from his character. Basically, poetic emphasis seems to be on the features of honesty, humility, kindness, compassion, love, and unselfishness.

Stephen Vincent Benét sees Lincoln's integrity as "Honesty rare as a man without self-pity, / Kindness as large and plain as a prairie wind." Delmore Schwartz declares: "When he was young, when he was middle-aged, / How just and true was he. . . . !" Gwendolyn Brooks pleads of Lincoln, "Teach barterers the money of your star!" With respect to humility,

Lowell sees him as a man "dreading praise, not blame. . . . " Maurice
Thompson declares that he had "No breath of pride, / No pompous
striving for the pose of fame. . . . "23

Many examples of poetic commentary on Lincoln's kindness and compassion exist. Florence Earle Coates remarks, "God's pity looked on me
from Lincoln's sorrowing eyes." William Cullen Bryant writes:

> O, slow to smite and swift to spare,
>   Gentle and merciful and just!
> Who, in the fear of God, didst bear
>   The sword of power—a nation's trust.

Herman Melville describes the cruel irony of Lincoln's martyrdom on
Good Friday:

> When they killed him in his pity,
> When they killed him in his prime
> Of clemency and calm—
> When with yearning he was filled
> To redeem the evil-willed,
> And, though conqueror, be kind. . . .

Edgar Lee Masters associates with Lincoln and poignant experiences he
underwent "the forgiveness of millions toward millions. . . . "24

As interpreted by various poets, Lincoln greatly extended his capacity
to lead because of his love for the people. As George Henry Boker put it:

> He led his people with a tender hand,
> And won by love a sway beyond command,
> Summoned by lot to mitigate a time
> Frenzied by rage, unscrupulous with crime. . . .

Julia Ward Howe similarly says:

> With deliverance freighted
>   Was this passive hand,
> And this heart, high-fated,
>   Would with love command. . . .

In short, Lincoln's unselfishness is seen by many poets as a full giving of his
life for the sake of the nation. He did not let considerations of his own ego,
credit, power, comfort, convenience, or material reward stand in the road

of his doing what seemed best for the nation. Samuel Valentine Cole asserts of Lincoln, "He lost himself in the larger self / Of his country and all mankind."[25]

Lincoln as Administrator

In addition to symbolic aspects of his person and his role, and his enormous character, Lincoln's leadership drew on particular administrative skills.

Much poetry lauds Lincoln's skill as communicator and helps clarify that skill's elements. In the words of Richard H. Stoddard, "Direct of speech, and cunning with the pen. / Chosen for large designs, he had the art / Of winning with his humor, and he went / Straight to his mark, which was the human heart." Maurice Thompson writes, "His humor, born of virile opulence, / Stung like a pungent sap or wild-fruit zest." James Russell Lowell describes his ability to reach people: "His was no lonely mountain peak of mind / . . . ; Broad prairie rather, genial, level-lined, / Fruitful and friendly for all human kind." Many poets ascribe to him an extraordinary advantage in expression: a divine call, a Providential responsibility. To illustrate, Edwin Markham proclaims God "needed for his purposes a voice, / A voice to be a clarion on the wind, / Crying the word of freedom to dead hearts."[26]

Part of Lincoln's leadership power as viewed by poets lay in his ability to identify with the people of the society, and to understand many of their concerns, needs, and desires. But this was much more than merely expertise in sensing political winds and groundswells. His ability to lead America had roots in his profound faith in and commitment to democracy. W. F. Collins describes this characteristic:

> A man who drew his strength from all,
>   Because of all a part;
> He led with wisdom, for he knew
>   The common heart.
> Its hopes, its fears his eye discerned,
>   And reading, he could share.
> Its griefs were his, its burdens were
>   For him to bear
>
> . . . .
> In patient confidence he wrought,
>   The people's will his guide
>
> . . . .

> The people's man, familiar friend,
>> Shown by the sculptor's art
> As one who trusted, one who knew
>> The common heart.

Henry Howard Brownell asserts that Lincoln "even in death couldst give / A token for Freedom's strife— / A proof how republics live, / And not by a single life, / But the Right Divine of man, / And the many, trained to be free. . . . "[27]

Although profoundly brave, Lincoln made cautious judgments, kept cool under public pressure, and knew how to be flexible to cope with necessities of circumstance while tenaciously holding to basic aims. Stoddard explains: "No hasty fool, of stubborn will, / But prudent, cautious, pliant, still; / Who since his work was good, / Would do it, as he could." Another trait was drive. This helped spark him to pursue his tasks. James Whitcomb Riley refers to Lincoln as having "A fateful pulse that, like a roll / Of drums, made high above his rest / A tumult in his soul."[28]

Lincoln's objectivity about administrative matters, which enabled him to make decisions on the basis of governmental need and not his own ego, is treated by Benét. His transcendence over the personal self places Lincoln at the pinnacle of leadership virtue. Early in his administration, Lincoln is pondering the feelings of some members of his cabinet.

> Look at his Cabinet here. There were Seward and Chase,
> Both of them good men, couldn't afford to lose them,
> But Chase hates Seward like poison and Seward hates Chase
> And both of 'em think they ought to be President
> Instead of me. When Seward wrote me that letter
> The other day, he practically told me so.
> I suppose a man who was touchy about his pride
> Would send them both to the dickens when he found out,
> But I can't do that as long as they do their work.[29]

Lincoln is seen in many of the poems as one who could think in large terms in space and time, a leader with vision who could grasp the implications America's struggle had for the world. Thus Carl Sandburg asks: "Lincoln? did he gather / the feel of the American dream / and see its kindred over the earth?"[30]

Lincoln's Continuing Relevance

Lincoln's presence survives in us individually and in our national psyche in countless ways. For the student of leadership, his story can provide much that is absorbing, amazing, instructive, and heartening about what leadership at its best in a democracy can be. Lincoln's life speaks to our time and to the human future, the poets tell us.

Being awestruck, perhaps, by Lincoln's accomplishments, his character, and the treasure of his words, poets seldom have dealt much with his limitations and failures. Benét and Schwartz are major exceptions. The ambiguity of his postwar aims meant little guidance was afforded to his successor, Andrew Johnson.[31] The long, hard road that American blacks had before them in the struggle for equal rights and opportunity, the abuses that would occur within American capitalism, and other major national problems of the future were not averted by Lincoln's work. Poets have broadly recognized that in many ways Lincoln was a beginning, that much of what he sought must be the object of continuous struggle. Thomas Curtis Clark observes, "well his work was done— / Who willed us greater tasks, when set his sun." He remains for us what Gwendolyn Brooks calls "Our successful moral. / The good man." The poets help us see his "pathos and humanity" as well as his exemplary work.[32]

THE MAN OF THE PEOPLE

Because of the need to relate fragments of poetry about Lincoln to subtopics and their analysis, this chapter has sacrificed much of poetry's aesthetic strength. I close with one of the best poems, in its entirety. By invitation, Edwin Markham read "Lincoln, the Man of the People" at the dedication of the Lincoln Memorial in 1922. Many ideas referred to above are woven into this poem, in words that demonstrate the intellectual and aesthetic power fine poetry can bring to the analysis of public leadership and its relationship to values and policy.

> When the Norn Mother saw the Whirlwind Hour
> Greatening and darkening as it hurried on,
> She left the Heaven of Heroes and came down
> To make a man to meet the mortal need.
> She took the tried clay of the common road—
> Clay warm yet with a genial heat of earth,
> Dasht through it all a strain of prophecy;
> Tempered the heap with thrill of human tears;

Then mixt a laughter with the serious stuff.
Into the shape she breathed a flame to light
That tender, tragic, ever-changing face;
And laid on him a sense of the Mystic Powers,
Moving—all husht—behind the mortal veil.
Here was a man to hold against the world,
A man to match the mountains and the sea.
The color of the ground was in him, the red earth;
The smack and tang of elemental things;
The rectitude and patience of the cliff;
The good-will of the rain that loves all leaves;
The friendly welcome of the wayside well;
The courage of the bird that dares the sea;
The gladness of the wind that shakes the corn;
The pity of the snow that hides all scars;
The secrecy of streams that make their way
Under the mountain to the rifted rock;
The tolerance and equity of light
That gives as freely to the shrinking flower
As to the great oak flaring to the wind—
To the grave's low hill as to the Matterhorn
That shoulders out the sky. Sprung from the West,
He drank the valorous youth of a new world.
The strength of virgin forests braced his mind,
The hush of spacious prairies stilled his soul.
His words were oaks in acorns; and his thoughts
Were roots that firmly gript the granite truth.
Up from log cabin to the Capitol,
One fire was on his spirit, one resolve—
To send the keen ax to the root of wrong,
Clearing a free way for the feet of God,
The eyes of conscience testing every stroke,
To make his deed the measure of a man.
He built the rail-pile as he built the State,
Pouring his splendid strength through every blow:
The grip that swung the ax in Illinois
Was on the pen that set a people free.
So came the Captain with the mighty heart.
And when the judgment thunders split the house,
Wrenching the rafters from their ancient rest,
He held the ridgepole up, and spiked again
The rafters of the Home. He held his place—
Held the long purpose like a growing tree—

Held on through blame and faltered not at praise.
And when he fell in whirlwind, he went down
As when a lordly cedar, green with boughs,
Goes down with a great shout upon the hills,
And leaves a lonesome place against the sky.[33]

NOTES

1. *The Oxford Book of American Verse*, ed. F. O. Matthiessen (New York: Oxford University Press, 1950), 70–71.

2. Herman Melville, *Moby Dick* (New York: W. W. Norton, 1967), 378.

3. *The Poetical Works of Oliver Wendell Holmes*, Household Edition (Boston: Houghton, Mifflin, 1900), 1.

4. *Collected Poems of Henry Thoreau*, ed. Carl Bode (Baltimore: The Johns Hopkins University Press, 1965), 230–33.

5. See Stephen B. Oates, *With Malice Toward None: The Life of Abraham Lincoln* (New York: Harper & Row, 1977); and J. David Greenstone, *The Lincoln Persuasion: Remaking American Liberalism* (Princeton: Princeton University Press, 1993).

6. Allan Nevins, "Lincoln, War Song, and War Poetry," ed. Goddard Lieberson, *The Union* (New York: Columbia Records, n.d.), 57.

7. In *The Lincoln Reader*, ed. Paul M. Angle (New Brunswick: Rutgers University Press, 1947), 309.

8. In *The Lincoln Reader*, 335–36.

9. "The Words That Remade America: Lincoln at Gettysburg," *Atlantic Monthly* 269 (June 1992): 57, 79. See also Wills's *Lincoln at Gettysburg: The Words That Remade America* (New York: Simon and Schuster, 1992).

10. In *The Lincoln Reader*, 491–93.

11. *Leaves of Grass*, ed. Charles Collen (New York: Thomas Y. Crowell, 1933), 196.

12. *Poems for Special Days and Occasions*, comp. Thomas Curtis Clark (Freeport, NY: Books for Libraries Press, 1970), 21. Reprinted with permission of Ayer Company Publishers, Inc.

13. *Lincoln's Birthday*, ed. Robert Haven Schauffler (New York: Dodd, Mead, 1946), 151–52.

14. *Our Holidays in Poetry*, comp. Mildred P. Harrington and Josephine H. Thomas (New York: H. W. Wilson, 1929), 23. Lines from "Lincoln" are reprinted from *The Call of Brotherhood and Other Poems* by Corinne Roosevelt Robinson (New York: Charles Scribner's Sons, 1912).

15. Caroline A. Mason, "President Lincoln's Grave," in *Our Holidays in Poetry*, 38–39; Mae Winkler Goodman, "Your Glory, Lincoln," in *Poems for the Great Days*, comp. Thomas Curtis Clark and Robert Earle Clark (Plainview, NY: Books for Libraries Press, 1973), 35–36. Reprinted with permission of Ayer

Company Publishers, Inc.; John Greenleaf Whittier, "The Emancipation Group," in *Poems for the Great Days*, 31.

16. Jane L. Hardy, "Lincoln," in *Our Holidays in Poetry*, 21; *Selected Poems of Edwin Arlington Robinson*, ed. Morton D. Zabel (New York: Collier Books, 1965), 65; Rose Terry Cooke, "Abraham Lincoln," in *Lincoln's Birthday*, 143.

17. "Hush'd Be the Camps To-day," in *Leaves of Grass*, 197; Julia Ward Howe, "Lincoln," in *Great Americans as Seen by the Poets*, ed. Burton Egbert Stevenson (Philadelphia: J. B. Lippincott, 1933), 71; Benét quote from *John Brown's Body* by Stephen Vincent Benét, p. 28. Copyright 1927, 1928 by Stephen Vincent Benét, copyright © 1954, 1955 by Rosemary Carr Benét, reprinted by permission of Henry Holt and Company, Inc.

18. "The Master," in *Selected Poems of Edwin Arlington Robinson*, 66; James Russell Lowell, "Ode Recited at the Harvard Commemoration," in *The Poetical Works of James Russell Lowell*, Cambridge Edition, ed. Marjorie R. Kaufman (Boston: Houghton Mifflin, 1978), 344; "Lincoln," in *Selected Poems of John Gould Fletcher*, ed. Lucas Carpenter and Leighton Rudolph (Fayetteville: The University of Arkansas Press, 1988), 183, reprinted by permission of the University of Arkansas Press.

19. Lowell, "Ode," in *Poetical Works*, 344; seven lines from "Young Lincoln" from *Poems of Edwin Markham*, selected and arranged by Charles L. Wallis, 83–84, copyright 1950 by Virgil Markham, copyright renewed, reprinted by permission of HarperCollins Publishers, Inc.

20. Delmore Schwartz, "Lincoln," in *Selected Poems (1938–1958), Summer Knowledge*, 236–37, copyright © 1959 by Delmore Schwartz. Reprinted by permission of New Directions Publishing Corporation; Robert Morris, "The Cabin Where Lincoln Was Born," in *Great Americans as Seen by the Poets*, 54.

21. Lyman Whitney Allen, "The People's King," in *Poems for the Great Days*, 27, reprinted with permission of Ayer Company Publishers, Inc.; Richard Henry Stoddard, "An Horatian Ode," in *Lincoln's Birthday*, 199.

22. Florence Kiper Frank, "Lincoln," in *Poems for the Great Days*, 31, reprinted with permission of Ayer Company Publishers, Inc.; Lucy Larcom, "Tolling," in *Great Americans as Seen by the Poets*, 76–77; John James Piatt, "The Dear President," in *Poems of American History*, ed. Burton Egbert Stevenson (Boston: Houghton Mifflin, 1936), 539–40.

23. Benét, *John Brown's Body*, 60; Schwartz, *Summer Knowledge*, 237; Gwendolyn Brooks, "In the Time of Detachment, in the Time of Cold 1965," in Brooks et al., *A Portion of That Field: The Centennial of the Burial of Lincoln* (Urbana: University of Illinois Press, 1967), 1–2; Lowell, "Ode," in *Poetical Works*, 344; Maurice Thompson, "At Lincoln's Grave," in *Great Americans as Seen by the Poets*, 79–81.

24. Florence Earle Coates, "His Face," in *Our Holidays in Poetry*, 14–15; William Cullen Bryant, "To the Memory of Abraham Lincoln (1865)," in *Our Holidays in Poetry*, 41; Herman Melville, "The Martyr," in *A Treasury of Great*

Poems, English and American, rev. ed., ed. Louis Untermeyer (New York: Simon and Schuster, 1955), 918–19; Edgar Lee Masters, "Anne Rutledge," in *Spoon River Anthology* (New York: Collier Books, 1962), 229.

25. George Henry Boker, "Lincoln," in *Our Holidays in Poetry*, 18; "Julia Ward Howe's Elegy," in *The Lincoln Tribute Book: Appreciations by Statesmen, Men of Letters, and Poets at Home and Abroad*, ed. Horatio S. Krans (New York: Knicker-bocker Press, 1909), 121–22; Samuel Valentine Cole, "Abraham Lincoln," in *Our Holidays in Poetry*, 3–5.

26. Richard H. Stoddard, "Abraham Lincoln," in *Our Holidays in Poetry*, 5–6; Maurice Thompson, "At Lincoln's Grave," in *Great Americans as Seen by the Poets*, 79–81; James Russell Lowell, "Ode," in *Poetical Works*, 344; Edwin Markham, "Young Lincoln," in *Poems of Edwin Markham*, 83–84.

27. The poem "The Lincoln Statue (Gutzon Borglum, Sculptor)" by W. F. Collins was included in *Our Holidays in Poetry*, 25, which was published in 1929 by the H. W. Wilson Company; Henry Howard Brownell, "Abraham Lincoln," in *Lincoln's Birthday*, 178.

28. Stoddard, "An Horatian Ode," in *Lincoln's Birthday*, 199; Riley, "Lin-coln," in *The Complete Poetical Works of James Whitcomb Riley* (New York: Garden City Publishing Co., 1937), 331–32.

29. *John Brown's Body*, 60.

30. Excerpt from *The People, Yes*, Section 57, by Carl Sandburg, copyright 1936 by Harcourt Brace & Company and renewed 1964 by Carl Sandburg, reprinted by permission of the publisher.

31. See Richard Ellis and Aaron Wildavsky, " 'Greatness' Revisited: Evaluat-ing the Performance of Early American Presidents in Terms of Cultural Dilem-mas," *Presidential Studies Quarterly* 21 (Winter 1991): 15, 30.

32. The poem "Abraham Lincoln, the Master," by Thomas Curtis Clark was included in *Our Holidays in Poetry*, 6–7, which was published in 1929 by the H. W. Wilson Company; Brooks, "In the Time of Detachment," in *A Portion of That Field*, 1–2.

33. "Lincoln, Man of the People," in *Poems of Edwin Markham*, 81–83.

Lessons in Leadership from
Lonesome Dove

Patricia R. Russell and Dillard B. Tinsley

A CATTLE DRIVE AS ENTREPRENEURSHIP

A popular Western novel of the American frontier seems an unlikely place to find lessons in leadership. The typical Western is an escapist form of literature; its readers seem lured to avoidance of complexities in a fictional world where problems are easily solved by a brave horseman with a gun. The setting is an American version of the pastoral world, which further removes it from modern realities. Yet in *Lonesome Dove* (1985), novelist Larry McMurtry provides an exciting Western narrative that includes fictional portraits of contrasting leadership styles. Practical lessons can be drawn for modern leaders, for in the novel, one form of leadership is shown to be ultimately self-defeating, and another moves leader and organization together positively into the future.[1]

Lonesome Dove centers around a cattle drive from Texas to Montana in the late nineteenth century. Most of the action occurs as the herd moves north. The drive is initiated and carried out under the leadership of Woodrow F. Call, called "Captain" because of many years of service as an officer in the Texas Rangers. Captain Call's strength of will organizes an extensive array of characters and manages many of the events as he pushes on to accomplish his personal and organizational goals. Call establishes his cattle business in Montana, but he soon abandons it to transport the body of Gus McCrae back to Lonesome Dove. In many ways Call is the classic entrepreneur.

In dramatic contrast to Call, McMurtry presents a secondary character, Clara Allen, owner and manager of a horse ranch in Nebraska. Call's herd passes through Nebraska on its way to Montana, and he stops to buy horses at Clara's ranch. Clara is also a major love interest of Augustus McCrae, Call's longtime friend and partner in the cattle drive. Call again visits Clara on his return to Texas with the body of Gus. Clara Allen exhibits the kind of long-term commitment and cooperative managerial style that reflects a mature entrepreneurship from which public administrators may learn. Readers can study Call's and Clara's contrasting leadership styles, which have implications for public administrators in the real world today.

THE ENTREPRENEURIAL CONCEPT

Although support for modern public administrators to become more entrepreneurial appears in current literature of the field, the concept of "public entrepreneurship" is controversial. However, successes do exist, and entrepreneurship's promise must be explored, especially in view of trends to a more turbulent environment for public administration created by increased diversity of personnel and complexity of challenges.[2] The lessons should be considered by anyone of the discretionist school of public administration, which "views independent action by administrators as essential where the political system has broken down such that politicians no longer reflect the true will of the people or the best interests of the community as a whole."[3]

Entrepreneurs establish and build organizations. Once established, organizations need strong leadership for continued success.[4] Public administrators can choose appropriate entrepreneurship techniques from business, then use personal experience and insights to avoid abuses. Definitions of the concept generally include (1) recognition of a desired future state characterized by growth or change and (2) the self-perceived power and ability to realize the goals necessary to achieve that future state.[5] Entrepreneurs are innovative, willing to take risks, aggressive, willing to work long hours, self-confident, highly competitive, superior in conceptual ability, educated, and healthy.[6] In an environment filled with opportunity, "they see clearly what others don't see at all."[7] Manfred Kets de Vries notes their high energy, imagination, and dislike of routine work. But a dark side to entrepreneurship can exist as well, which is the lesson for us from *Lonesome Dove*.[8]

CALL'S ENTREPRENEURIAL LEADERSHIP

Literature has long recognized the heroic individual whose strength of will prevails in overcoming the challenges of life in order to change the world. Woodrow Call's positive characteristics include the ability to impose his will upon others and get them to work together in pursuit of his dream. He compels his men to meet high performance standards. Augustus McCrae is convinced that the men want Call to be their leader because he has confidence in his ability, while others doubt themselves. Call makes some mistakes as a Texas Ranger and as leader of the cattle drive, and some men die, but he does not allow himself to dwell on his mistakes. He believes that he has done well, given the constraints of the frontier environment in which he is forced to operate (356).

Call's purpose is to get the job done. He had been extremely effective as a Ranger when the people of Texas needed protection from hostile Indians. McCrae believes that being a Ranger was a task that suited his friend. Indeed, Call still tries to keep his Indian-fighting skills sharp. He regularly goes off alone to listen to the sounds of the land that may provide clues needed by an Indian fighter. Call is not a patient man, but he takes time to plan his operations carefully. He also recognizes that things usually do not go as planned, so that flexibility and adaptability are needed. He does a great deal of self-appraisal; therefore, he has a clear sense of his own abilities and of his limits. He also understands that chance plays an important role in the success or failure of enterprises, whether they be battles or cattle drives (117).

After years of running a little cattle company in the isolated settlement of Lonesome Dove, on the Mexican border of Texas, Call starts thinking of a cattle drive that will break him away from his routine. He has been thinking of a drive for over a year when Jake Spoon arrives at Lonesome Dove with praise of Montana as cattle country. Call understands Jake's character flaws, but he also believes that Jake can recognize good land for cattle. Call reasons that getting to Montana first will give the Hat Creek Cattle Company the pick of the land in this still open territory, where fortunes can be made (80). Unlike Jake, Call possesses the vision of a possible future, the leadership qualities, and the financing to organize and sustain the drive; unlike Augustus, he has the desire, perhaps even the need, to break away from the boredom of routine. Call sees an entrepreneurial opportunity where others do not.

Although Call takes risks, he does not believe in taking unnecessary risks. When the Hat Creek outfit is stealing cattle in Mexico, Gus wants to "slip by" the Mexicans' camp, but Call orders a detour, saying, "It's foolish to take chances" (110). The narrator tells us that Captain Call "thrived" on crisis (318). Faced with eighty waterless miles in Wyoming, Call takes a considered risk in going forward. Although he realizes that it is probably not rational to try to drive the cattle so far without water available, he chooses to take a high but calculated risk, and to take it immediately, without allowing time for fear to discourage him (705). This is clearly an entrepreneurial way of thinking.

Call shows high energy and organizational skills in setting up his cattle drive. He leads rustling raids for horses and cattle in Mexico. He acquires the men needed for the job, and he draws on his vigor and health as the only man who works double shifts in preparing the herd for the drive (179). Careful planning lays a foundation for the enterprise that his entrepreneurial nature carries through. Call is able to perceive a desired future state to be reached by growth or change, and he has the self-perceived power to reach his goals. He is the strong leader who can create a successful organization.

Woodrow Call is a traditional, authoritative leader in accord with the military model. He can skillfully evaluate and command men. For example, he knows that the African-American Josh Deets is the only man on the drive who is much help as a planner, and he implicitly gives Deets authority over white men (123). He recognizes Dish as the most competent cowhand, wishing that all the cowboys were as skilled (58). Also, Call's personality allows him to put himself into orders in a way that causes men to comply. "Call was barely middle-sized—but when you walked up and looked him in the eye it didn't seem that way" (8).

Call is essentially a loner, with quite limited concern for others. He does not hand out kind words. He takes it for granted that others live for work just as he does, and that they will perform to their best ability as a matter of personal pride. He respects the abilities of his men but is rather puzzled that they don't do more for themselves. He grieves over the hanging of Jake Spoon and is unable to reconcile himself to the facts that Jake was not personally strong enough to avoid crime and that he, Call, could not save Jake from himself. Gus has no such regrets. He recognizes that those who fail to live up to the code that passes for the law in the West are responsible for their own actions and must be punished according to the code.

Jake Spoon's case proves Gus wrong in his conviction that Call has no sympathy for human weakness (421). However, Call is primarily a fighting man. He sometimes attacks the enemy in defiance of the odds. Gus says, "He might plan elaborately before a battle, but once it is joined his one desire is to close with the enemy and destroy him" (440). Gus might be correct about Call's carrying a fight to the death (as with the scout, Dixon); but Call does carefully evaluate what he can do, might do, and cannot do.

THE "DARK SIDE" OF CALL

Woodrow Call has many of the positive traits of the entrepreneur, but he also displays the "dark side." Kets de Vries notes that integrating an entrepreneur into an organization may be difficult because of certain characteristics of that type of personality, such as (1) need for control, (2) sense of distrust of the world around them, and (3) "concern to be heard and recognized, to be seen as heros. Some entrepreneurs continually need to show others that . . . they cannot be ignored."9 These aspects of the "dark side" are particularly relevant to Call, and they should be noted by readers concerned with public administration who may fall prey to similar "dark sides" of themselves, to the detriment of their organizations and of the public welfare.

Captain Call ferociously attacks Dixon, an army scout who quirts the young cowhand, Newt. This attack relates to the need to be recognized and to amount to something. On the plains, before the encounter in town, Dixon had spoken contemptuously to Call. Gus asserts that Call had once killed another man who had scorned him. Call demands the respect he believes he has earned, and he explains his attack on Dixon by saying, "I hate a man who talks rude . . . I won't tolerate it" (665).

Captain Call reveals his distrust of the world in his continued habit of going off alone at night, away from his men, trying to retain his Indian-fighting skills, and seeking to maintain an edge even though the country seems safe (27, 28). He even chooses his horse because the "Hell Bitch" is dangerous, which serves to keep him alert (168). Some elements of distrust are shown by Call's constant need to hurry and to avoid commitment to others.

The most tragic aspect of Call's personality is his need for control. He controls his men and the circumstances into which he leads them as much as possible. The only area of life in which his control tragically fails is in his relationships with women. He is critical of men involved with whores; but he feels drawn to the whore Maggie, who has a lonely look and would not be a danger to anyone. Call loses control when Maggie enters his life, because Maggie becomes pregnant. He hides the fact that he is Newt's father, he never marries Maggie, and he never mentions her name. When Maggie dies, Call loses forever the chance to atone for his actions. He cannot bring himself to acknowledge the fact that Newt is his son, because that would mean acknowledging that he had failed to live up to his personal code of always maintaining control.

To deal with his failure, Call tries to avoid all mention of women and to avoid them whenever possible. But the painful memories always return, and he is tormented by his awareness that he is not in fact the model of self-discipline others think he is. Call sees himself as a fraud, he wonders if his life has meaning, and he tries to compensate for his sense of inadequacy by accepting more and more responsibility and by working harder than anyone else in his business enterprises.

The characteristics de Vries ascribes to the "dark side" of the entrepreneurial character provide insight into the dangers that may befall public administrators. Many public administrators enter government service with a strong desire to do good and to be recognized as leaders. If their genuine motivation to make a difference becomes subordinated to their need for recognition or other goals, trouble may follow. For example, the need for public agencies to be accountable to legislative bodies has sometimes caused administrators to focus on control. Rigid and overly regulated behaviors can permeate control-oriented bureaucracies, and real service to the public deteriorates.

Captain Call dooms his own happiness by allowing the dark side of his entrepreneurial personality to dominate his behavior, causing himself and his son lifelong emotional and psychological pain. Indeed, he does not even seem to recognize the problems with his behavior. Anyone with an entrepreneurial approach to organizations must come to terms with the passages in the novel that use Call to show that life is much more than merely work and discipline. Development of one's entrepreneurial personality should be weighed against the effects of doing so on other people and on personal relationships. Wise public administrators know that career accomplishments and control of others have little value for a mind in turmoil. Thus, when Jimmy Carter assumed the presidency, one of his first actions was to send a memo to his top appointees reminding them of their obligations to their families and warning them against the temptation to become overly committed to their administrative responsibilities. As governor of Georgia, Carter had recognized the tendency in public servants to work too long, thereby damaging personal relationships.

Call's epic journey to bury his friend Augustus McCrae is a type of entrepreneurial behavior, although it is not profitable in business terms and is damaging in personal terms. The journey reflects Call's motivation, his determination to do his duty, no matter how foolish it is or how inconsiderate of the needs of others. Novels have an advantage over management textbooks; psychological problems like Call's would not usually be dramatized in a textbook, but fiction can probe the full spectrum of human behavior. As noted, Call has a compulsion to get things done. Gus says he does not know where Call got his concept of duty, but that Call likes "to think everybody does their duty, especially him" (746). He is incapable of recognizing the reality that no man can live for duty alone, not even Woodrow Call. The tragic aspect of Call's entrepreneurial personality is that he will sacrifice everything to his prime purpose, to his concept of doing his duty as leader. Consequently, at the end of the novel he is alone, without wife or child, admitting to a reporter for a Denver paper that his whole project has been futile for him. His entrepreneurial vision has cost the lives of most of the people who could have been close to him: Maggie, Gus, Deets, Jake Spoon. He still refuses to acknowledge his only son. McMurtry reinforces the self-destructive nature of Call's vision by surrounding his character with images of death and sterility: poisonous snakes, sandstorms, a plague of grasshoppers, Gus's corpse, the town of Lonesome Dove itself. All the fertile places are left behind by Call.

MCMURTRY'S ENTREPRENEURIAL MODEL: CLARA ALLEN

Clara Allen's entrepreneurial style clearly contrasts with that of Captain Call. Her business competence is evident early in the novel, when Gus recounts the story of the deaths of her parents in an Indian raid and of Clara's return to Austin to run their store. Gus acknowledges that Clara's strong personality controlled the relationship between the two of them, and July Johnson, too, submits to her strong will.

Clara Allen recognizes the future state that she desires to make into reality. Because she is a nineteenth-century American woman, her goals involve a husband and family as well as a financial enterprise that will support them. She is courted by many men but chooses a Kentucky horse trader whom others see as dull and unpromising. Despite many difficulties, together they establish a successful horse farm on the Platte River. Clara chooses her husband as Call chooses his wranglers—for his utility in helping her reach her goals. Moreover, she has entrepreneurial drive; she persists in her enterprise despite the deaths of her three sons and her husband. Intermediate goals achieved include building a frame house to replace the sod one in which her sons died, purchasing a piano for her daughters, and maintaining sole control over her capital, the money she gained from the sale of her parents' business. Like Call, Clara usually manages to do what she wants to do.

Clara takes risks to achieve her ends. Marrying a man less gifted than herself, she defies him when it is necessary. She lives with the constant threats of hard Nebraska winters, Indian attacks, illness, and death. With one hired hand, Cholo, she continues to run the ranch during the illness of her husband and after his death. She takes on the traditionally male tasks of gelding and trading horses; her skill at the latter is evident in her uncompromising dealings with a frustrated Captain Call, who is unused to having someone else control the terms in his business dealings. Clara also takes emotional risks, as when she adopts the abandoned infant she calls Martin and later when she persuades the child's father, July Johnson, to become part of the family. The physical risks Clara Allen takes are analogous to those of Call, but she willingly takes the emotional risks he shuns.

Lonesome Dove's contrasting characters, Clara Allen and Woodrow Call, show that real success is emotional as well as physical and economic. Iva Wilson generalizes that there is a contrast between conventionally male and female leadership styles in relation to modern organizations, asserting that "Women are encouraged to be sensitive, while men are encouraged to be aggressive and determined. . . . Sensitivity in business situations is often considered a weakness, but in fact it is the *combination* of sensitivity, aggressiveness and determination that makes the best managers."10

Public administration, as a reflection of the broader society, is becoming increasingly collegial and less authoritarian. The spirit of cooperation and the sharing of power that have traditionally characterized women's approaches to problem solving are not necessarily gender-related, and they have become appropriate managerial adaptations to conditions in our changing social and work environments.

Clara Allen's leadership style is collegial rather than authoritative. Because she is female and could not have belonged to the Texas Rangers, the hierarchical command structure of that organization is not available for her to emulate. She must induce men voluntarily to support her enterprise without diminishing their sense of self-worth. There is no question about her exercise of personal power, but she chooses to use it in ways that will maximize the success of the organization rather than to earn recognition for herself. She integrates others into her organization by sharing power; she is not ruled by a desire to control every element of her enterprise.

Clara recognizes the warped motivation, the desire for total control, that leads Call to return Gus's body to Lonesome Dove. Clara wants to bury Gus close to her home, to be a comfort to her and to Lorena, another woman who had loved Gus and whom Clara has taken into her household. Call chooses what he sees as his duty to follow Gus's last request, and carries his body to Texas, where it will comfort no one. Clara is understandably bitter about what she sees as the selfishness of Call's decision, a decison that reflects his lack of concern for others and his need for control.

LESSONS FROM FICTION

What is one's duty? Can anyone always do it? How does devotion to duty affect others? Is there something higher than duty? Can one balance duty to one's organization with concern for others as human beings who have social and psychological needs? Can or should one admit failure to do one's duty? These are some of the questions that arise from *Lonesome Dove*. As an entrepreneur, Call is seen as a man of vision. He does succeed in getting his herd to Montana and establishing a ranch there. Anyone considering such an entrepreneurial approach to life, however, must include an evaluation of the human costs of Captain Call's vision.

Clara Allen serves as both a critic of Call's vision of life and as an alternative model to it. To reinforce the reader's sense of her positive entrepreneurship, the novelist surrounds her with images of fertility: a grove of trees in Texas, the rich grasslands on the North Platte, picnics and cakes, her two daughters, her adopted infant son, her home. These positive images provide an opportunity to experience the illuminating effects that positive leaders can have on those who look to them for guidance.

The insights from this novel are relevant to entrepreneurial behavior— and to patterns of life for public administrators today. Fictional works like *Lonesome Dove* offer explorations of the possibilities in dominant individuals whose wills impose change on the world. These are lessons in fictional portraits of leaders that can apply to actual administrative behavior. Beyond this, the novel allows a reader to explore the possible transformations that could have occurred in two fictional entrepreneurial personalities, along with their possible ramifications, given different critical decisions being made. Such exploration should lead each of us to consider how our own personalities might be changed positively in the direction of more effective and fuller lives, both as professional administrators and as human beings.

NOTES

1. Larry McMurtry, *Lonesome Dove* (New York: Simon and Schuster, 1985). Page numbers cited in text are from this source.

2. David Osborne and Ted Gaebler, *Reinventing Government* (Reading, Mass.: Addison-Wesley, 1992); Larry D. Terry, "Why We Should Abandon the Misconceived Quest to Reconcile Public Entrepreneurship with Democracy," *Public Administration Review* 53 (Summer 1993): 393–95. Blue Wooldridge and Jennifer Wester, "The Turbulent Environment of Public Personnel Administration: Responding to the Changing Workplace of the Twenty-first Century," *Public Personnel Management* 20 (Summer 1991): 207–24.

3. Richard C. Box, "The Administrator as a Trustee of the Public Interest," *Administration and Society* 24 (November 1992): 323–45; Gary L. Wamsley, Robert N. Bacher, Charles T. Goodsell, Philip S. Kronenberg, John A. Rohr, Camilla M. Stivers, Orion F. White, and James F. Wolf, *Refounding Public Administration* (Newbury Park, Calif.: Sage, 1990).

4. Harold C. Livesay, "Entrepreneurial Dominance in Businesses Large and Small, Past and Present," *Business History Review* 63 (Spring 1989): 1–21; Carl J. Bellone and George Frederick Goerl, "In Defense of Civic-Regarding Entrepreneurship or Helping Wolves to Promote Good Citizenship," *Public Administration Review* 53 (July/August 1993): 396–98.

5. Howard H. Stevenson and David E. Gumpert, "The Heart of Entrepreneurship," *Harvard Business Review* 63 (Spring 1985): 84–94.

6. Robert L. Anderson and John S. Dunkleberg, *Entrepreneurship: Starting a New Business* (New York: Harper & Row, 1990).

7. Daryl G. Mitton, "The Compleat Entrepreneur," *Entrepreneurship: Theory and Practice* 13 (Spring 1989): 12.

8. Manfred F. R. Kets de Vries, "The Dark Side of Entrepreneurship," *Harvard Business Review* 52 (Spring 1985): 160–67.

9. Ibid., 163.

10. Iva Wilson, as quoted by Celia Kuperszmid Lehrman, "Tell Her She Can't," *EF* (March/April 1990): 42.

Part V

Contributions to Policy-Making and Teaching from the Arts

12

Public Policy and Popular Imagination

Howard E. McCurdy

FROM ART TO CULTURE TO POLICY

What public managers do is shaped to a considerable extent by art. The policies they administer often germinate in the popular culture that art helps to sustain. Art influences public policy by enlisting support for new directions, inspiring governments to undertake new activities, and creating many of the constraints under which managers labor. Our understanding of the relationship between art and government is broadened considerably by crossing the Policy Bridge and gaining insights into the role that popular culture plays in framing public policy.

Ideas precede action. Rational arguments for one undertaking or another exist in pockets of society long before such ideas gain sufficient support to become official government policy. They gain public support as they penetrate popular culture. Art plays a critical role in this process. Literature, painting, movies, and television all work to create a receptive audience for new ideas. Art reaches a mass audience and touches emotions in ways that debates among policy specialists do not. Art also helps to create the expectations that actual programs must satisfy.

Four examples from the history of public policy in the United States illustrate this process. The abolition of slavery, the regulation of food and drugs, the conservation movement, and the exploration of space were all inspired to a considerable extent by works of art. What began as ideas among small groups of believers became public policy as those ideas entered popular culture. The cause of abolition was furthered by a single novel, as was the movement to regulate food and drugs. The conservation movement required a complete reversal in popular attitudes, a dramatic shift encouraged largely by nineteenth-century works of art. In the case of space exploration, art weakened support for the endeavor by raising expectations that public managers could not meet. It is very hard to maintain political support, a key ingredient of program success, when government policies violate images in the public mind. In this sense, art helps to create the boundaries within which public programs operate.

THE ABOLITIONIST MOVEMENT

President Abraham Lincoln, upon meeting Harriet Beecher Stowe, is said to have remarked, "So you're the little lady who started the war." Stowe's *Uncle Tom's Cabin*, first published in book form in 1852, dramatically affected popular attitudes and demonstrated the ability of art to shape policy debates.

Stowe undertook to write the book as a result of the Compromise of 1850. Much of the public debate over that pre–Civil War legislation concerned the extent to which Northerners would be obliged to return runaway slaves to the South. The Southern point of view proceeded from the premise that slaves were property and protected as such under the U.S. Constitution, a doctrine expounded more completely in the Supreme Court's *Dred Scott* decision of 1857. To her "perfect surprise and consternation," Stowe heard people she considered to be religious and humane asserting a Christian duty to obey the Fugitive Slave Law: "These men and Christians cannot know what slavery is; if they did, such a question could never be open for discussion."[1]

Stowe was familiar with the institution of slavery as a result of living for eighteen years in Cincinnati. Fugitive slaves often fled through the Cincinnati area into the free state of Ohio. Stowe's sister-in-law, Isabella Beecher, urged her to "write something that will make this whole nation feel what an accursed thing slavery is."[2]

Uncle Tom's Cabin accomplished exactly that. The story, first serialized in weekly installments in the *National Era*, personalized the debate through the characters of Eliza, Uncle Tom, and Simon Legree. It attracted millions of readers, became part of American popular culture, and put a human face on a policy debate in ways that gripped the emotions of the nation.

People who might fail to remember the legal details of the Compromise of 1850 could hardly forget the image of Eliza carrying her child Harry in her arms, skipping across ice flows in the Ohio River, "which lay, like

Jordan, between her and the Canaan of liberty on the other side." Eliza undertook her escape after learning that the indebted owner of the Kentucky plantation on which she was held planned to take young Harry from her and sell the child to a New Orleans slave dealer. With the slave dealer in immediate pursuit, Eliza, "nerved with strength such as God gives only to the desperate," jumped from the Kentucky shore onto the moving ice.

With wild cries and desperate energy she leaped to another and still another cake. . . . She saw nothing, felt nothing, till dimly, as in a dream, she saw the Ohio side, and a man helping her up the bank. "Yer a brave gal, now, whoever ye ar!" said the man, with an oath.[3]

In making the literary case against slavery, Stowe appealed to two deeply held nineteenth-century values: mother love and Christian duty. In her concluding chapter, Stowe called upon the mothers of America, "who have learned, by the cradles of your own children, to love and feel for all mankind," to give sympathy to slaves whose families were destroyed by the internal slave trade. Every nineteenth-century mother had watched a child suffer through terrible childhood diseases, and many, like Stowe herself, had watched one die. Resurrecting that unforgettable pain, Stowe pleaded with her readers to "pity those mothers that are constantly made childless by the American slave-trade!"[4]

In weekly services across the nation, Christians prayed for the day of redemption. Stowe turned this biblical devotion into the moral tone of the novel. She warned devout Christians that "every nation that carries in its bosom great and unredressed injustice" possesses the seeds of its own destruction, a moral lesson repeated by Abraham Lincoln in his second inaugural address. "Christians," Stowe reminded them, "every time that you pray that the kingdom of Christ may come, can you forget that prophecy associates in dread fellowship, the *day of vengeance* with the year of his redeemed." The Christian church, she warned, "has a heavy account to answer" by permitting its Southern branches to perpetuate injustice and cruelty. The Union would not be "saved" so long as it accommodated itself to this source of moral decay, Stowe asserted in the last sentence of her book. Employing the Christian meaning of salvation, she appealed to her readers to save the nation through "repentance, justice and mercy."[5]

Stowe's moral and religious pleading seems ponderous by the standards of twentieth-century literature. At a time when serial literature served as a primary source of family entertainment, however, publication of the well-paced *Uncle Tom's Cabin* did more than any other event to define public perceptions of slavery. Even Southern critics acknowledged the power of the book. The work, admitted one Southern reviewer, "has found its way to every section of the country . . . filling the minds of all who know nothing of slavery with hatred for that institution."6

THE REGULATION OF FOOD AND DRUGS

The novel *Uncle Tom's Cabin* shows how art can shape public perceptions about governmental issues. Upton Sinclair's *The Jungle* (1906) provides a classic example of how art can be translated directly into public policy.

Sinclair began publishing the novel in serial form in a socialist weekly, whose publishers had bankrolled the author's research with the hope of creating public sympathy for the plight of stockyard workers. The book deals primarily with the broken lives of immigrants whose labor supported the Chicago stockyards. The hero of the novel, Jurgis Rudkus, suffers unimaginable tragedies resulting from the filth and injury to be found in turn-of-the-century immigrant neighborhoods.

Readers were not greatly moved by Sinclair's depiction of human misfortunes. They were, however, outraged by the background information he presented on the meatpacking industry. A substantial amount of the meat and meat by-products consumed by Americans at the turn of the century emerged from Midwest packing plants. Hardly a dozen pages in the book dealt with details such as the folklore of workers who disappeared from slippery planks into boiling vats, to emerge somewhat later as Durham's Pure Beef Lard. It was these details that gripped the public's attention when the whole novel emerged in January 1906, however, and made the unknown twenty-seven-year-old author an instant celebrity. "I aimed at the public's heart," Sinclair later confessed, "and by accident I hit it in the stomach."7

For more than a decade reform groups had sought to place the meatpacking industry under federal regulation. Industry groups resisted these efforts, preferring the loose system of local supervision that ignored diseased cattle and hogs. Following the publication of Sinclair's novel, industry leaders prepared for a new round of resistance. They set out to refute Sinclair's allegations and portray his book as the result of a disordered mind. The charges contained in Sinclair's novel were front-page news across America, however, and were generally confirmed by progressive reformers. The form of Sinclair's allegations, moreover, being presented in a well-written novel to meat-consuming Americans, captivated the public more readily than meat packers' reassurances in forums like the *Saturday Evening Post*.

President Theodore Roosevelt promptly invited Sinclair to the White House to discuss the book and dispatched a special government commission to Chicago to investigate his charges. The commissioners returned with a scathing report, which Roosevelt released when the meat packers refused to modify their opposition. The Neill-Reynolds report rekindled media interest in the issue. Sales of *The Jungle* rose as the market for packed meat and meat products fell. Less than six months after publication of the novel, Congress enacted the Pure Food and Drug Act and the Beef Inspection Act, establishing the modern system of federal regulation.

The novel had a direct impact on public policy. Meat packers who had successfully resisted prior efforts at reform carried out within policy circles could not overcome the firestorm of criticism unleashed by *The Jungle* among the public at large. Sinclair's novel abruptly changed public perceptions of the quality of their daily meals and forced meat packers to accept federal regulation as the only effective means of restoring public confidence in their products.

THE CONSERVATION MOVEMENT

Works of art play a critical role in shaping the public perceptions to which government policy must respond. Sometimes this requires a total alteration of public impressions. Nowhere is this more vividly illustrated than in the American conservation movement.

In spite of a few voices extolling the beauty of wilderness, most people in earlier times viewed wild areas as savage and evil. This view was in opposition to concepts of an earthly Eden, which regarded paradise not as an unspoiled wilderness but as a well-cultivated garden. Untamed wilderness was uncontrollable and frequently dangerous. Only by taming the land and its animals could the small population of humans then inhabiting the earth create an earthly sanctuary. In a cultivated garden, humans lived in harmony with nature. In a wilderness, nature consumed them. Early settlers in America largely accepted the image of nature as hideous and repugnant.

So long as Americans in general retained this savage view of nature, little support could be mustered within the society for its preservation. The use of government power to preserve wilderness areas required a major cultural shift. To build support for a system of national parks and national forests, conservationists had to change the public image of wild areas. What had traditionally been viewed as savage had to be seen in the public eye as a place of spiritual renewal. This was accomplished largely through art and literature.

The movement to create a new view of the American wilderness began in the early 1800s. In part, it was promoted by romantics who, looking back at the disappearing wilderness, lamented the loss of values special to the American experience. In his nineteenth-century romantic novels on frontier culture, written after most of the East had been tamed, James Fenimore Cooper denigrated the values of characters who saw no worth in wild areas. Slash-and-burn pioneers occupied the lowest position in the social order of Cooper's novels. The highest positions were reserved for persons like Natty Bumppo (Leatherstocking), who found moral instruction in the lessons of nature.

Among the most effective promoters of preservation in the early nineteenth century were artists who saw in the American wilderness a counterpart to European magnificence. By standards of that time, Europe was a more civilized place in which to live than the United States. It surpassed the United States in the quality of its manufactured goods. It possessed more history, grander monuments to antiquity, better music, and finer art. Faced with an impending inferiority complex, Americans searched through their distinguishing characteristics for qualities worthy of national pride. Many found that source of superiority in nature. Hence Americans began to promote the quality of their scenery. Great forests were touted as the artistic equivalent of ancient columns, and colossal mountains became a replacement for castle ruins. Wild nature became the basis for a form of spiritual nationalism.

American landscape painters promoted this notion among the public with great effectiveness. Prior to the era of glossy magazines and easy transport, most Americans experienced natural wonders through landscape art. An extremely popular form of artistic communication, especially in the cities, landscape paintings were exhibited much as movies would be shown a century later. The public embraced landscape art at the same time that frontier novels became fashionable. In 1823, Thomas Cole gave up his career as a portrait painter and began to paint landscapes. His new venture took him to the Catskill Mountains, which he represented in paintings that merged geological wonders, luminosity, and vast cloudscapes. The popular response to his art gave rise to what was known as the Hudson River School of American painting and a series of disciples who continued to produce romantic paintings of landscapes in which wonders of nature dwarfed signs of human civilization.

As slavery and the Civil War shook the eastern United States, a second generation of landscape artists portrayed the solemnity of the West. Following his first journey across the Great Plains in 1858, Albert Bierstadt launched a hugely successful career by painting such natural wonders as the Rocky Mountains and California's Yosemite Valley on large canvases. Thomas Moran attracted a similar following with his paintings of the Yellowstone Plateau, the Tetons, and the Sierra Nevadas. By the use of exaggeration and light, the landscapes of these highly romantic painters portrayed the West as a scenic sanctuary, an unspoiled paradise free from the grimy realities of the East.

In 1871 Moran accompanied the Hayden expedition to the Yellowstone Plateau. His artistic record of the journey helped build congressional support for preservation of the region. The following year President Grant signed legislation creating Yellowstone National Park. Congress appropriated $20,000 for Moran's paintings of the Grand Canyon of the Colorado and the Grand Canyon of the Yellowstone. These two large paintings were hung in the U.S. Capitol, formally endorsing the notion that scenic wonders provided a source of national pride and providing a monument to the influence of art on public policy.

Although the art of Bierstadt and Moran fell out of favor as the twentieth century approached, the spiritual notions that their paintings engendered remained. Such notions were perpetuated by the railroads, which used images of American natural wonders to promote the family vacation. Directors of the newly formed National Park Service joined forces with the railroads to build a clientele for the national park movement. Tourists initially traveled by railroad to the parks and stayed in hotels built by the railroad industry. By the early twentieth century, the popular image of wilderness areas had completely changed, permitting the development of an entirely new form of public policy.

SPACE EXPLORATION

Not only does art inspire public policy, as in the case of the conservation movement, it also creates the boundaries within which public policies are carried out. Public officials ignore those boundaries at their peril, as managers of the National Aeronautics and Space Administration (NASA) have painfully learned.

Lunar and planetary voyages captivated public imagination for many decades before the United States actually undertook them. In 1835 Edgar Allan Poe wrote "The Unparalleled Adventure of One Hans Pfaal," in which Poe dispatched his hero to the moon in a homemade balloon as a logical method to help him escape his creditors. That same year Richard Adams Locke perpetuated the great "Moon Hoax" in the New York *Sun*. A forerunner of modern tabloids, the *Sun* reported that astronomer Sir John Herschel had observed a large number of creatures on the lunar surface through a specially constructed telescope. In 1865 Jules Verne wrote his fictional account *From the Earth to the Moon*, with a sequel five years later in which his three-person crew circumnavigated the lunar surface. Visitors to the Pan-American Exposition in Buffalo in 1901 took a simulated trip to the moon in a winged spacecraft, a ride so popular that it inspired promoters to build the hugely successful Luna Park amusement facility in New York City. By the 1930s, fans of extraterrestrial adventure could satiate themselves through a variety of science fiction pulp magazines, not to mention the adventures of Buck Rogers and Flash Gordon in the comic strips, movies, and radio.

Beginning in the 1930s, promoters of space exploration made a concerted effort to convince the American public that these imaginary stories could become real. The American Interplanetary Society, the forerunner of the American Institute of Aeronautics and Astronautics, was founded in 1930 by science fiction fans. One of its founders, David Lasser, wrote the first serious treatment of space exploration in the English language in 1931. Lasser was the editor of *Amazing Stories*, a leading science fiction pulp. Thin lines separated science fiction and science fact.

By the 1950s space boosters had managed to create substantial interest in the possibility of space flight. The starkly realistic paintings of astronomical artists like Chesley Bonestell showed viewers what a trip to the moon might actually look like. In March 1952 *Collier's* magazine began an eight-part series with a group of articles titled "Man Will Conquer Space Soon." In 1955 Walt Disney aired the first of three programs on space flight on his highly popular "Disneyland" television series. The second program, which also aired in 1955, described the technical requirements for a voyage to the moon. Millions of Americans watched the shows.

Following the orbital flight of Yuri Gagarin in early 1961, President John F. Kennedy searched for a spectacular mission that would capture the imagination of the world. "Tell me how to catch up," he urged his space advisers. "Is there any other space program which promises dramatic results in which we could win?"[8]

By selecting the goal of a voyage to the moon and back, Kennedy appealed to a deeply held mystique. By 1961 space boosters had managed to convince Americans that a voyage to the moon was both possible and desirable. Project Apollo enjoyed widespread support in part because the preparations so closely fulfilled public expectations. Through fictional media like the 1950 movie *Destination Moon* and space art, members of the public had been given an increasingly realistic view of a lunar expedition. NASA's efforts did not disappoint them. The high point in public support for the space program occurred on Christmas Eve, 1968, when NASA astronauts first circumnavigated the moon. The pictures they brought back from that voyage (they orbited the moon but did not land on it) looked remarkably like an artistic depiction of the venture published twenty years earlier by Chesley Bonestell in *The Conquest of Space*.

Widespread support did not adhere to the next three human space flight adventures. In 1972 NASA received authority to develop the space shuttle, the first manned spacecraft capable of flying back from orbit. In one respect, the design of the space shuttle fulfilled an important public expectation. It put wings back on American spacecraft, ridding NASA of what author Tom Wolfe had characterized as the "human cannonball" approach to spaceflight.[9] Artists and publicists had established the requirement for wings on rocketships long before any began to fly.

In imaginative literature, moreover, modern spacecraft are relatively easy to fly. From Han Solo's *Millennium Falcon* created for the movie *Star Wars* to Captain Kirk's *Starship Enterprise* designed for the "Star Trek" television series, the spacecraft of the public mind operate as effortlessly as modern aircraft. NASA officials encouraged this expectation in their effort to win approval for the shuttle program. The space shuttle, they promised, would make spaceflight safe, easy, and economical. It would become so routine that anyone could fly into space with a modest amount of training. Just as NASA sought to fulfill public images about the shape of a rocket ship, so it sought to encourage public expectations about making space-flight accessible to the average person. Those expectations were shattered in 1986, when the space shuttle *Challenger* exploded 73 seconds into its flight. NASA had selected a schoolteacher, Christa McAuliffe, to join the *Challenger* crew to fulfill the promise that civilians outside government could fly in space.

Unfulfilled expectations also afflicted NASA's effort to design a politically acceptable space station, a project for which it won presidential approval in 1984. Nurtured on the romance of frontier forts, many Americans accepted space stations as the stepping-stones to outer space. As part of the effort to promote space exploration, the March 1952 issue of *Collier's* magazine featured an illustrated story that pictured a large, rotating facility in orbit about the Earth. The *Collier's* article helped to solidify the image of space stations in the public mind. Stanley Kubrick reinforced this image in 1968 when he released *2001: A Space Odyssey*. Kubrick's space station consisted of a rotating wheel measuring some 900 feet across and holding an international crew of engineers, scientists, and civil servants.

NASA officials encouraged the belief that they could build a facility that matched artistic expectations when, in 1969, they issued plans for a 50-to-100-person space base. As they moved closer to an actual space station, however, their designs departed more and more from original expectations. Their configurations were not round, did not rotate, and would not hold a large crew. "2001 It's Not," headlined a popular science magazine.[10]

Both the space station and space shuttle programs had difficulty maintaining political support. Within Washington, D.C., both programs were viewed as less than full-blown policy successes. The difficulties encountered by both flowed from many factors, including challenging technologies and a growing budget deficit. In part, however, both the space shuttle and NASA's proposed space station suffered because the actual programs differed so significantly from the images established in the public mind.

A similar problem affected NASA's historical desire to send humans to Mars. The planet Mars had long fascinated both artists and visionaries. At the turn of the century, astronomer Percival Lowell, thinking he had detected vegetation strips on the Martian surface through his telescope, suggested that an advanced race of Martians had constructed canals to carry water from polar regions to warmer equatorial lands. Seizing upon the public interest in Mars, H. G. Wells presented his highly acclaimed novel *War of the Worlds*, which made an indelible mark on American popular culture with its newscast-style radio broadcast in October 1938.

NASA's first close-up pictures from Mars hardly satisfied public expectations. The planet appeared lifeless, desolate, and cold. Temperatures recorded by the *Viking* spacecraft on the surface of the Red Planet dropped to a chilly -191° F. in winter. Worse still for advocates of exploration, the planet looked like the moon! *Mariner IV*, which provided the first close-up pictures during its 1965 flyby, disappointed hopes that earthlings might discover canals on the planet's surface.

To combat the impression of a dead planet, NASA stopped issuing photographs that made Mars look like the moon. Instead, the space agency featured photographs and paintings that promoted the planet's geological wonders, such as Olympus Mons (at 15 miles in height possibly the tallest mountain in the solar system) and the huge system of Martian canyons. NASA even helped sponsor conferences on "terraforming" Mars—promoting the expectation that modern technology could unlock water deposits and create an Earth-like atmosphere.

These efforts did little to sustain political support for a human venture to Mars. In spite of the 1989 endorsement by President George Bush, the so-called Space Exploration Initiative received a cool reception on Capitol Hill. Congress refused to appropriate even the modest funds necessary to start studying the technology needed for a mission to Mars, much less finance the actual expedition. Many factors contributed to the congressional repudiation, but the fact that the reality of Mars differed so extensively from artistic expectations did not help the cause.

DREAMS AND DIFFICULTIES

People will pay to see their dreams realized, but only if the government satisfies the images contained in the public mind. When a government program departs significantly from the image that the public has of it, or produces a view of nature with which the public disagrees, its sets itself up for difficulties that few officials can work their way through.

Art plays a significant role in creating public expectations. It does that through its power to affect popular culture. As a motivating force, art can inspire government officials to engage in new endeavors by creating popular support for them. It can alter public perceptions in ways that break down old barriers and make new activities acceptable. Its influence, however, is not wholly enabling. Art can also act as a powerful force restricting the scope of public activities. Just as it excites some policies, it discourages others. The expectations created by art in the public mind act both as a source of empowerment and as a boundary on the activities of public managers. In short, the Policy Bridge enables policy analysts and administrators to broaden their perspective to include visions previously unseen and to rein in their impulses to engage in hopeless endeavors.

NOTES

1. Harriet Beecher Stowe, *Uncle Tom's Cabin* (Boston: Houghton Mifflin, 1851), 493 (chap. XLV).

2. Moira Davidson Reynolds, *Uncle Tom's Cabin and Mid-Nineteenth Century United States* (Jefferson, NC: McFarland & Company, 1985), 7.

3. *Uncle Tom's Cabin*, 58, 66–67 (chap. VII).

4. Ibid., 494–95 (chap. XLV).

5. Ibid., 499–500 (chap. XLV).

6. *Uncle Tom's Cabin and Mid-Nineteenth Century United States*, 12.

7. Upton Sinclair, *The Jungle* (New York: New American Library, 1905), 349.

8. Hugh Sidey, *John F. Kennedy, President* (New York: Atheneum, 1963), 122; John F. Kennedy, memorandum for the vice president, April 20, 1961, NASA History Office archives.

9. Tom Wolfe, "Columbia's Landing Closes a Circle," *National Geographic* 160 (October 1981): 475.

10. M. Mitchell Waldrop, "Space City: 2001 It's Not," *Science* 83 (October 1983), 60–67.

13

Teaching Social Equity in a Diverse Society: *The Merchant of Venice*

Elsie B. Adams, Frank Marini, and Darrell L. Pugh

SOCIAL EQUITY AND WILLIAM SHAKESPEARE

Teaching provides one means of bridging the gap between the arts and public administration theory and practice. One way of making this connection in the classroom is through the use of literature, which—because of its appeal to the imagination as well as to reason—can illuminate and inspire the practice and study of public administration. Literature offers not only an opportunity for analysis of problems but also the possibility for vicarious experience of the situations and individuals that produce problems. It is a medium by which students of public administration can explore values in depth, gain greater appreciation for them, and supplement their understanding—without the fear of making mistakes that comes with real-life choices.[1]

In this chapter, we are interested in how literature can enhance an understanding of the concept of social equity. This concept, expressed in one or another way, has always been important for public administration. And the centrality of the relevant concerns has been explicitly emphasized with the term "social equity" since the 1970s. It is likely, moreover, that with the passage of time, social equity will be an even more important concept for the field, with issues of diversity increasingly coming to the forefront (as the role of women continues to change, as traditional minorities continue to be a central concern, as new immigration patterns add new complexities of cultural and religious diversity, and as issues such as gay rights and greater parity for the physically, mentally, and learning disadvantaged are added to traditional concerns of minority rights).

Sidestepping some definitional confusion over the term in the field, we here consider social equity as administration with an eye to treating all individuals fairly according to their merits and to seeing that they receive what they deserve. This meaning accords with the traditional understanding of equity dating back to Aristotle.

This meaning also accords, in our legal tradition, with the development of equity law. Equity law is a branch of English jurisprudence, dating to the sixteenth century, that sought to mitigate the deficiencies in English common law. It evolved from the rather abstract application of principles of justice to petitions presented to the monarch in plea to redress wrongs for which the common law provided no remedy. Thus equity law historically dealt with the matter of treating a given plaintiff/appellant differently from others under a given law because such variation from the normal expectations of the law seemed justified as a matter of justice, fairness, and appropriateness.[2]

It is interest in these latter qualities—justice, fairness, and appropriateness—that governs the concept of equity as we are using it. The questions that lie at the heart of our discussion have to do with how a given society defines these qualities and how well that society governs itself according to them.

We have selected William Shakespeare's *The Merchant of Venice* as a play that addresses directly—on many fronts—a concern for equity and its relationship to law and to a society that professes a belief in a stable and predictable administration of law and fairness. The climactic episode in the play is a trial in which a bankrupt debtor (Antonio, the merchant of the title) is called to account by his creditor and expected to pay with a literal pound of his flesh. The trial scene—which is complicated by the fact that the creditor is a Jew in a predominantly Christian (and hostile) society and that the judge is a woman (disguised as a man) at a time when women had no civil rights—offers multiple opportunities for examination of issues relating to justice and to fairness. In the play there is no simple or clear solution to the claims of the law (called "justice" in the play) in conflict with concepts of fairness or equity (called "mercy" in the play). Furthermore, the play highlights the problems attendant on a concept of equity that exists alongside discrimination on the basis of national origin, race, gender, or religion. In the society depicted in *The Merchant of Venice*, what seems to count most is who you are—insider or outsider, male or female, Christian or Jew, Venetian or foreigner.

THE PLAY RECALLED

The Merchant of Venice is one of Shakespeare's romantic comedies, written toward the end of the sixteenth century.[3] The plot interweaves two old stories: one involves a business loan with a flesh bond as surety; the other involves a marriage lottery in which the successful suitor is determined by his choosing the correct casket out of three possibilities. In Shakespeare's version of the first story, Antonio, a successful merchant who is temporarily out of funds, borrows money for his impecunious friend Bassanio from the Jewish moneylender Shylock. At Shylock's apparently jesting suggestion, Antonio—who has no anxieties about being able to pay the debt—pledges as bond a pound of his flesh. As fate would have it, Antonio's ships do not come in, and Antonio is called to court by Shylock to pay the flesh bond—in effect, to give up his life. With this story Shakespeare merges the marriage lottery story, in which Antonio's bosom friend Bassanio is the successful suitor, winning both the fair Portia and her wealth when he chooses the casket made of lead (instead of the "losing" caskets of gold and silver). During the trial scene the two plots further fuse as Portia, disguised as a learned doctor of law, argues and wins the case for Antonio and utterly defeats the vengeful Shylock.

At the trial the play takes a somber, potentially tragic, turn—but tragedy is averted (if one can overlook the fate of Shylock). In the final act of the play, Bassanio and his friend Gratiano (who is married to Portia's maid) are called to account by their wives for giving away their marriage rings, tokens of their marital vows. As a matter of fact, the new husbands have given the rings as presents to the learned doctor and his clerk for saving Antonio's life at the trial. The joke is—as the audience knows and the erring husbands do not—that the doctor and clerk were actually Portia and her maid in disguise. Finally the disguises are revealed; the lovers are restored to each other; and all seems to end happily.

But there is a dark side to this Shakespearean comedy. Deception, betrayal, and threat accompany the fun and romance. We are left with a feeling of malaise at the end of Act IV as the Jew is stripped of his wealth and made to convert to Christianity under threat of death, and at the end of Act V as the two husbands renew their vows of marital fidelity under threat of cuckoldry. And throughout the play we see a society that dispenses unequal and inequitable treatment to its various members: in Shakespeare's Venice it helps to be an insider—to be "one of us" (male, Christian, Venetian).

THE ISSUE OF RACIAL AND ETHNIC PREJUDICE IN THE PLAY

One of the major dimensions around which the issue of equity can be interpreted in *The Merchant of Venice* is that of ethnicity. Characters in the play who are not Venetian are regarded in law as aliens (i.e., individuals who are neither citizens nor nationals of the state in which they reside). However, these characters are accorded certain rights: first, any bonds or agreements entered into between Venetian citizens and aliens are fully recognized; second, foreigners are given full access to Venetian courts.[4] It is the existence of these two rights that ultimately leads to the trial scene, where the alien Shylock demands that the court uphold the contract that Antonio has made with him.

At the trial, though his life is forfeit, Antonio holds that the course of law cannot be denied even for strangers because the state is dependent on the trade and commerce that they bring to Venice. He argues:

> The Duke cannot deny the course of law;
> For the commodity that strangers have
> With us in Venice, if it be denied,
> Will much impeach the justice of the state,
> Since that the trade and profit of the city
> Consisteth of all nations. (III.iii.26–31)

The argument, significantly, is not that the law should be upheld because it is right to do so, but that the law should be upheld for "the trade and profit of the city." As we look carefully at the play, we see that such mercenary concerns motivate other principal characters: just as Shylock and Antonio profit from business ventures, Bassanio profits from his marriage venture. In fact, it would be fair to say that Shakespeare's Venice thrives on venture capitalism, on "trade and profit," whether it be in international trade or in the marriage market.[5]

However, despite the fact that Venetian trade requires some legal status to be accorded those who are not Venetian, there is ample evidence in the play that, among Venetians, aliens are viewed as both socially and morally inferior, and that this attitude affects the determination of justice for the play's alien characters. For example, Shylock is hated and condemned by Venetian society for his profit in moneylending. And this attitude of suspicion and contempt extends to all who are foreign born.

Early in the play (I.ii), Portia's treatment of her suitors from various countries makes manifest the attitude of the dominant culture toward aliens. With her maid, Portia criticizes suitors from southern Italy, Spain, France, England, Scotland, and Germany by making use of negative national stereotypes. Italians are characterized as uncouth, Spaniards as melancholic, the French as lacking any character, the English as unlearned and tasteless, the Scots as stingy, and the Germans as vile drunkards. Only one suitor receives the approval of the two Venetian women: "*a Venetian, a scholar and a soldier*" [emphasis ours], that is, Bassanio, who is declared "the best deserving a fair lady" and "worthy of . . . praise" (I.ii.91–97). In this scene Portia—with her anti-foreign, racist prejudices—functions as her culture's representative, preferring one of her own sort to share her wealth and love and to reinforce the values of her class and culture. It is no accident that the Venetian Bassanio is the successful suitor of Portia.[6]

When in this same scene Portia learns of the approach of the Prince of Morocco, a Moor, she serves up her harshest rebuke: "If he have the condition [character] of a saint, and the complexion of a devil [devils were traditionally depicted as black], I had rather he should shrive me than wive me [I would rather have him serve as my confessor than as my husband]" (I.ii.106–7). Later, as the Moor prepares to make his choice among the caskets, he confronts Portia directly about her reaction to his race only to have her lie to him: "Yourself, renowned prince, then stood as fair / As any comer I have looked on yet / For my affection" (II.i.20–21). When the Moor chooses incorrectly and fails to win Portia's hand, Portia ends the scene with a racist dismissal: "A gentle riddance! Draw the curtains, go. / Let all of his complexion choose me so" (II.vii.77–78).

Throughout the play—whether the choice be of lovers suitable for the Christian woman or of merchants suitable for Venetian commerce—we see a basic "us–them" attitude on the part of the Venetian citizens. Just as Portia has prejudged her Venetian suitor and found him worthy while she condemns foreign suitors, so the society praises highly the merit of Antonio and his Christian cohorts and condemns the Jewish businessmen who are part of the same mercantile effort.

THE ISSUE OF RELIGIOUS BIGOTRY

In addition to prejudice based on race and national origin, Shakespeare's Venetians exhibit a profound religious bigotry, so pronounced that some modern spectators regard the play as intensely anti-Semitic. Another way of viewing the play, however, is as a kind of exposé of a bigoted society—not an anti-Semitic play but a play *about* anti-Semitism. We embrace this second view.

Shylock, the Jew who is the center of attention in the play and who serves as foil to Antonio, is despised and reviled by the good citizens of Venice. This in part has to do with his role as moneylender. The medieval Christian church had condemned usury; this left Jews to perform the vital financial function of moneylending for the citizenry—a service for which they were hated.[7] But the hatred also has to do with Shylock's race and religion: as M. M. Mahood points out in his introduction to the play, "The Jew . . . was the scapegoat of Christendom and the usurer the scapegoat of a nascent capitalism."[8] The hatred is reflected by both the high and the low in Shakespeare's Venice: from the magistrate in charge of the city, who defines Shylock as "an inhuman wretch, / Uncapable of pity" (IV.i.4–5), to the gentlemen of Venice with their unthinking ridicule of Shylock and their virulent anti-Semitic epithets, to the servant who teases Shylock's daughter for converting to Christianity and thereby increasing the price of pork.

The ostensible hero of the play, Antonio the merchant, also participates in the anti-Semitism rampant in the play. Shylock complains, when Antonio is seeking a loan, that "You call me misbeliever, cut-throat dog, / And spit upon my Jewish gaberdine, / And all for use of that which is mine own" (I.iii.103–5). Antonio answers,

> I am as like to call thee so again,
> To spit on thee again, to spurn thee too.
> If thou wilt lend this money, lend it not
> As to thy friends,
>
> . . . .
> But lend it rather to thine enemy. (I. iii. 122–27)

To a modern audience, the abuse of Shylock is shocking: he is treated by Antonio and other Venetians as less than human, labeled "dog" or "devil," and frequently called not by name but simply "Jew."[9]

Shakespeare himself would probably have known no practicing Jews, for they had been banished from England since 1290, when Edward I (with the advent of Italian banking) expelled all Jews except those who converted to Christianity. To create Shylock, Shakespeare drew on a literary stereotype of a monstrous, money-grubbing Jew. What is remarkable is the degree to which Shakespeare humanizes the stereotype, giving to Shylock one of the most eloquent statements of our common humanity in all literature. Shylock hates Antonio to the point of desiring his death, offering the following motivation for his attitude: "He hath disgraced me, and hindered me half a million, laughed at my losses, mocked at my gains, scorned my nation, thwarted my bargains, cooled my friends, heated mine enemies, and what's his reason? I am a Jew" (III.i.43–45). Then follows the famous speech ("Hath not a Jew eyes?" etc.), that insists that all people, regardless of religious or racial differences, have essentially the same needs, feelings, reactions. The speech ends with the observation that the Jew learns revenge from the Christian; Shylock insists that his desire for revenge is a response learned from Christian example: "The villainy you teach me I will execute" (III.i.46–56). At this point in the play, Shylock has numerous reasons for hating Antonio and his society: Shylock has been humiliated and treated with contempt, segregated into a ghetto, and made to wear a badge signifying his Jewishness. His daughter, Jessica, has eloped with a Christian and is squandering the family fortune.

Furthermore, Antonio is a business rival. Interestingly, both Shylock and Antonio make money through risk-taking ventures. Whereas Shylock lends money at interest, Antonio invests in goods that he ships and sells in foreign markets. Both businessmen seem to a modern audience more alike than unlike; yet one is reviled and the other revered, solely on the basis of differences in ethnicity and religion.[10]

THE ISSUE OF SEXISM

Just as the play focuses our attention on inequities caused by such factors as race, national origin, and religion, it also makes a sharp distinction between the status of women and the status of men. The society depicted is an extremely sexist one. A woman cannot choose her own husband and is considered subservient to both father and husband.[11] Yet we see in this, as in so many of Shakespeare's plays, intelligent, strong-willed women who pretend innocence and ignorance and resort to disguise, manipulation, and threat as strategies for self-protection.

At the beginning of the play Portia complains to her maid about the terms of her father's will, which arranged for Portia to marry the man who selects the right casket: "I may neither choose who I would, nor refuse who I dislike, so is the will of a living daughter curbed by the will of a dead father" (I.ii.19–22). In the patriarchal society, Portia is honor bound to obey her father's will; yet, like many other Shakespearean heroines, she succeeds in marrying the man of her own choice—partly through her subtle manipulation of the contest.[12]

Just as her father controlled (or tried to control) his daughter's choice of husband, so the husband is entitled to control both his wife and her property. The minute Portia marries Bassanio, she submits herself and all

she owns to him. Billing herself as "an unlessoned girl, unschooled, unprac-
tised," she gives everything to her new husband:

> But now I was the lord
> Of this fair mansion, master of my servants,
> Queen o'er myself; and even now, but now,
> This house, these servants, and this same myself
> Are yours, my lord's. (III.ii.167–71)

That Portia is only assuming—perhaps out of modesty, perhaps out of
necessity—the role of "an unlessoned girl" is clear shortly afterward. While
Bassanio rushes off (with Portia's money) to rescue his bankrupt friend,
Portia and her maid disguise themselves as men and go to join Bassanio
and the others in court. There Portia poses as a young learned doctor of
Rome. The fact that Portia, in male clothing, has sufficient ability to argue
and judge a court case successfully belies her modest pose at home. She may
be "unlessoned" and "unschooled" (women were not offered formal education), but she is not, as she says, a simple "girl" who might be able to learn.
She is already learned, and wise beyond her years.[13] By juxtaposing the
"unlessoned girl" with the learned judge, Shakespeare makes a potent
comment on the nature of a society that would keep intelligent, resourceful
women in subservient roles. Their only recourse is pretense, and only in
male disguise are they seen as equal.

Another evil of the sexist society is seen in the use of threat as a means
of control in marriage. When Bassanio gives away Portia's ring, which he
swore to keep until his death, Portia uses one of the few weapons that she
has: "I'll have that doctor [to whom Bassanio gave the ring] for my bedfellow"
(V.i.232). The threat of infidelity (and/or an exercise of shrewishness) may
have been the only means for women without power to strike back at erring
husbands. Of course, in *The Merchant of Venice* Portia is herself the doctor
who (in male disguise) received the ring, so her threat can be taken, by the
audience at least, as a pleasant joke. Bassanio is not so amused: he is made
to understand that oath-breaking works both ways for Portia. She agrees
to stay faithful to her word (i.e., her marriage vows) only if he does the
same.

THE TRIAL: NEITHER JUSTICE NOR MERCY

All these subjects, depicting a society that allows ethnicity, national
origin, religion, and sex to determine its definitions of fairness and justice,

culminate in the famous trial scene of Act IV. In teaching *The Merchant of Venice*, it is a good idea to assign students parts in this scene to read aloud in class—interrupting the reading to question or explicate key points. In this way students can follow—almost line by line—the complex unfolding of legal and ethical problems as they develop and are resolved.

The scene begins as the Duke of Venice and his attendant judges enter, along with the accused, Antonio, and his Venetian friends. Before the plaintiff, Shylock, enters the courtroom, the Duke expresses pity for Antonio and declares:

> Thou art come to answer
> A stony adversary, an inhuman wretch,
> Uncapable of pity, void and empty
> From any dram of mercy. (IV.i.3–6)

The trial has not even begun, and the magistrate has prejudged the case, finding Antonio the pitiable victim of an "inhuman" accuser. When Shylock later refuses to budge from his decision to demand the fatal penalty in spite of the Duke's pleas for mercy on Antonio's behalf, the Duke considers dismissing the court unless he receives advice and assistance from a learned doctor whom he has summoned (IV.i.104–7). As the head of the court and of the city, the Duke seems to be a curiously ineffectual administrator: he encourages an atmosphere in which the fiercely anti-Semitic abuse of Shylock finds a welcome; he seems to carry expert consultation to an extreme, eventually turning everything over to Portia; and finally he acquiesces in allowing one party to the dispute (Antonio) to set conditions and penalties (even emendations of the Duke's own judgment) for the other party.

Throughout the trial Shylock remains obdurate in his demand that the letter of the law be enforced. He reminds the court more than once that the credibility of Venice as an international center of trade rests on upholding the law. He also draws a parallel between his having bought the pound of Antonio's flesh and the Venetians owning and using purchased slaves (IV.i. 90–100). His point here is that in the devaluing of human life—looking on it as part of a business transaction—the Venetians are no different from him. But Shylock has clearly lost sight of his business objectives in his demand for revenge on Antonio; he is offered repayment of the debt up to three times his investment, and he declines to accept it. He is a man consumed by the desire for revenge. Though his constant appeal is to the law and to "justice" as represented by the law, his deepest motive is a profound and abiding hatred for Antonio.

Into the atmosphere of hatred and prejudice steps the learned young doctor from Rome, Dr. Balthazar (Portia), who has been sent by the Duke's consultant to help judge the case. Her first action is to plead with Shylock to allow mercy to temper justice. Just as he has refused the Duke's similar pleas for mercy, Shylock again insists on the letter of the law.

At this point, Bassanio advocates—in what might be something like the usual equity argument in English law—that the law be set aside. He urges Portia (as judge), "To do a great right, do a little wrong" (IV.i.212). Here, as elsewhere in the play, we see Bassanio in an extremely unattractive light. He is the kind of person who squanders one fortune and then asks for a loan to gain another, who gambles with his friend's money (and life) in securing that loan, who later is generous with his wife's money in offering to rescue his friend, and who—at the trial—offers to sacrifice not only himself but also his wife to save Antonio. It is no surprise, then, to hear him propose bending the rules and breaking the law as a way of fixing a bad situation.

Portia, however, is unwilling to set aside the law—citing, as others have, the danger to the state in allowing such a precedent. Instead she allows Shylock to come right to the brink of taking Antonio's life. The appearance of the knife for cutting the pound of flesh and of the scales to weigh it signals the point of greatest dramatic tension in the play. Only when Shylock advances toward the bared breast of Antonio, ready for sacrifice, does Portia intervene.

Then begin a series of interpretations of the law that stun Shylock (and the audience as well). Portia stops the killing with three pronouncements, each of which differs from the other and each of which inflicts a heavy penalty on Shylock. First, she grants the pound of flesh but forbids the shedding of one drop of blood, asserting that "if thou dost shed / One drop of Christian blood, thy lands and goods / Are by the laws of Venice confiscate" (IV.i.305–7). When Shylock offers, in that case, to take the money that is owed him, Portia insists that "justice" is all that is owing to him. She then adds another wrinkle to the fabric of law that she is weaving: if one gram (one "scruple") more or less than one pound is taken, then the penalty is not only confiscation of Shylock's goods but also the taking of his life. It should be noted that in each of these interpretations of the law, Portia is relying on what the contract does *not* state. As Frank Whigham notes, she is ad-libbing a "creative interpretation" of the law, finding "the necessary escape clause in the white spaces between the lines, where no strict construction is possible."[14] Her argument is this: the contract says a pound of flesh; this means *exactly* one pound, no more nor less; furthermore, since there is no reference to the shedding of blood, a penalty is forthcoming for this violation as well. Though Portia makes allusion to the law, to those of us interested in the question of legal and ethical fairness, it seems suspiciously as though Portia is largely improvising as she proceeds.

As Shylock recognizes defeat and states his intention to leave the court, Portia pulls out her last devastating stop:

> Tarry, Jew:
> The law hath yet another hold on you.
> It is enacted in the laws of Venice,
> If it be proved against an alien
> That by direct or indirect attempts
> He seek the life of any citizen,
> The party 'gainst the which he doth contrive
> Shall seize one half his goods, the other half
> Comes to the privy coffer of the state,
> And the offender's life lies in the mercy
> Of the Duke only, 'gainst all other voice [i.e., without appeal]. (IV.i.34–52)

Here it can perhaps be argued that Shylock only gets what is coming to him. After all, he was given ample opportunity to take his money and drop the charges against Antonio. He was repeatedly enjoined to show mercy, and he stubbornly refused. So Portia may only be giving him what he asked for: the letter of the law—one pound and no more or less; no shedding of blood, since it is not "so nominated in the bond" (to use Shylock's earlier phrase). The anti-alien law takes us by surprise, as we discover "that factional bias is built in even in law, that Shylock was excluded by definition as alien to begin with."[15]

What follows is, according to the court, an example of Venetian Christian "mercy." The Duke spares Shylock's life but threatens to take away his means of livelihood, since the law permits the state to take half of Shylock's wealth and Antonio to take the other half. Antonio then asks the state to forgo its half and give Antonio "the other half in use, to render it / Upon his [Shylock's] death unto the gentleman / That lately stole his daughter" (IV.i.379–81). Furthermore, Antonio requires that Shylock convert to Christianity. The Duke insists that Shylock agree to these terms, "or else I do recant / The pardon that I late pronounced here" (IV.ii.387–88). In short, in dizzying succession, Shylock is coerced into giving up his money, his estate, and—finally—his religion, and, as a further humiliation, is made to will that, on his death, his estate go to Jessica's Christian husband.

TEACHING THE PLAY

What, finally, can we take away from our study of *The Merchant of Venice*? In teaching the play, what issues can be raised, what problems presented, what conclusions drawn? First of all, we observe that if we are interested in creating policies for a just society—where justice is distributed even-handedly, and where adjustments are made as necessary to assure that all receive fair treatment—we must be on guard against the temptation to favor those who are most like us and to discriminate against others. Shakespeare's play powerfully illustrates the fact that a society may, while striving to enforce laws impartially for both insiders and outsiders and while giving lip service to this ideal, accord quite disparate treatment based on race, national origin, religion, or gender. For example, in the marketplace, the Venetian whose fortune is made in international trade is respected and even loved by his fellows, whereas the Jew who helps to support the financial enterprise through capital loans is hated and reviled. A woman's integrity as a person is accorded little value in the society of Shakespeare's play. She is given little or no choice as to disposition of either her self or her goods; she is controlled by her father until she marries, and then she is controlled by her husband. In order to assert her worth or to gain a degree of autonomy, she must resort to subterfuge, deception, or shrewishness. Likewise, strangers do not enjoy a valued position in this repressive culture. Socially and legally, people from other countries or of other races are viewed with contempt or suspicion. Portia finds only her Venetian suitor "worthy." And the Venetian law cited by Portia against Shylock specifically distinguishes between aliens and citizens.

The Merchant of Venice teaches us both that rigid literalism in interpreting rules can be unjust and that, if we abandon the law in our attempts to find equitable adjustments, we encounter considerable risk. In the name of mercy the Venetian court does a good deal of damage while moving into a realm so amorphous that rulings and decisions seem arbitrary and random. For example, at the end Portia seems to be making rulings almost extemporaneously, exacting different—and stiffer—penalties as she proceeds. The Duke pardons Shylock, granting him his life so "That thou shalt see the difference of our spirit" (IV.i.364), that is, presumably showing Shylock a mercy that Shylock had denied to Antonio. Then, a few minutes later, the Duke threatens to "recant / The pardon" unless Shylock accedes to

Antonio's demands. How Antonio came to be authorized to exact penalties—specifically, that Shylock will his estate to Jessica's husband and that Shylock convert to Christianity—is not clear, unless we are to assume that there is yet another Venetian law that says the citizen whose life is threatened by an alien may exact whatever penalties he wishes. It seems safer to assume that Antonio, like Portia and the Duke, is improvising a kind of Venetian "justice." Shylock's downfall is dramatically powerful but—when it is examined from either a legal or a moral/ethical point of view—it is also frightening. We seem to be in a world where no fixed or certain rules apply. Personal impulse—on Portia's part or the Duke's or Antonio's—seems to govern.

Finally, we are impressed in our study of *The Merchant of Venice* with the fact that a 400-year-old play contains so many issues that are alive and pressing today. It offers us a glimpse of a sexist, racist, ethnocentric, bigoted society that is nevertheless striving for a kind of equal protection under the law and equitable ("merciful") treatment of individuals. As we observe in what respects that society succeeded and how much it failed, we find ideas that may assist us in assessing our own objectives, successes, and failures as we attempt to define or refine or exercise our own idea of social equity.

NOTES

1. For a more extensive discussion of the use of literature in teaching public administration, see Frank Marini, "Literature and Public Administration Ethics," *American Review of Public Administration* 22 (June 1992): 111–25.

2. Richard A. Posner, *Law and Literature: A Misunderstood Relation* (Cambridge, Mass.: Harvard University Press, 1988), 96, provides a good working definition of equity: "the prudent recognition that strict rules of law, however necessary to a well-ordered society, must be applied with sensitivity and tact so that the spirit of the law is not sacrificed unnecessarily to the letter. . . . [T]he rules are tempered in application in order to bring them into closer harmony with their underlying principles, or, to put the same point differently, in order to make a better fit between the rules and the conduct sought to be regulated by them." For a discussion of Shakespeare's possible influence on equity law, see W. Nicholas Knight, "Equity, *The Merchant of Venice* and William Lambarde," *Shakespeare Survey* 17 (1974): 93–104.

3. Internal and external textual evidence suggests that 1597 would be a good guess as to the year of the play's composition. Because of the extensive editorial apparatus and scholarly glosses, we have used in the classroom and in this chapter the New Cambridge Shakespeare edition of the play, edited by M. M. Mahood (Cambridge: Cambridge University Press, 1987). The citations in the text corre-

spond to this edition. For teaching purposes a number of inexpensive paperback editions are available, as is a videotape of the 1981 BBC production.

4. Mahood's "Introduction" to the New Cambridge Shakespeare edition, 15.

5. Ralph Berry, *Shakespeare's Comedies: Explorations in Form* (Princeton: Princeton University Press, 1972), 113–44.

6. Frank Whigham, "Ideology and Class Conduct in *The Merchant of Venice*," *Renaissance Drama* n.s. 10 (1979): 93–115.

7. Montagu Frank Modder, *The Jew in the Literature of England* (New York: Meridian Books; Philadelphia: Jewish Publication Society, 1960 [first published in 1939]), 2–7.

8. Mahood's "Introduction," 21.

9. In teaching the play, it is instructive to remind students that anti-Semitism is not dead. According to the results of a survey released in November 1992 by the Anti-Defamation League, one in five Americans holds views that are unquestionably anti-Semitic (reported in *San Diego Union*, November 16, 1992, pp. 1, 5).

10. *Shakespeare's Comedies*, 133. For an interesting reading of Shylock and Antonio as psychological counterparts (contending that both are outsiders, as Jew and closet homosexual, respectively), see Seymour Kleinberg, "The Merchant of Venice: The Homosexual as Anti-Semite in Nascent Capitalism," *Journal of Homosexuality* 9 (1983): 113–26.

11. Karen Newman discusses the status of Renaissance women in "Portia's Ring: Unruly Women and Structures of Exchange in *The Merchant of Venice*," *Shakespeare Quarterly* 38 (Spring 1987): 19–33.

12. When it is Bassanio's turn to choose, Portia orders music, an amenity that did not accompany other suitors' choices. The lyrics of the song sung while Bassanio makes his choice warn against trusting the appearance of a thing (that which is "engend'red in the eye"), as over against the reality behind it. Furthermore, the first lines of the song rhyme with "lead" and furnish a valuable clue to the nature of the winning casket (the one made of lead and not those of gold or silver). One could argue that though the contest promises equal treatment of all suitors, Portia does all that she can to rig the outcome to favor her choice, the Venetian candidate.

13. Newman points out that Portia becomes "the unruly woman" of folklore, that is, "a woman who steps outside her role and function as subservient, a woman who dresses like a man, who embarks upon behavior ill-suited to her 'weaker' intellect, a woman who argues the law." "Portia's Ring," 28. See also Lisa Jardine, "Cultural Confusion and Shakespeare's Learned Heroines," *Shakespeare Quarterly* 38 (Spring 1987): 1–18.

14. "Ideology and Class Conduct," p. 110.

15. Ibid.

Part VI

The Significance of Made Connections

Epilogue: Toward Enriched Administration

Nancy Murray

A PAINTED VISION REVISITED

Now, dear reader, you have experienced our allegorical landscapes and have figuratively walked on both sides of the river. The lush and verdant land offers its gifts to you in a spirit of hope and inspiration. The festival of ideas to which you were invited is not over. Rather, it has barely begun! We ask you to remain for the excitement ahead.

Join with us as we envision a government in which ideas and ideals are united in meaningful action. Help us resurrect the wisdom found in the words of ancient writers like Thucydides, Herodotus, Homer, and Plutarch. Let us follow the example of heroes like Odysseus, who took charge of their own destinies and relied upon the quality of their minds to attain "virtu" and serve the polis in appropriate ways. During the waning days of the twentieth century, let us adopt one of the great historical themes of the Renaissance: the joining of vision with action. Our modern tendency to replace vision with action causes many unfortunate situations in both public and private life.[1]

As stated in Chapter 1, conceptual bridges connecting public adminis-tration with the arts provide an opportunity to infuse practical administra-tive processes with vision and creative imagination. Using the metaphor of light, the arts can illuminate how an individual public administrator perceives the role he or she plays in government. For example, the Wheel of Fortune of our book's frontispiece can be perceived as consistent with the ancient Taoist philosophy which teaches that wisdom lies in seeking that which is constant among the "changing phenomena" that compose the world in which we live. The simple recognition that "being is a form of doing" can alter an individual's perception of reality and elevate him or her to a level of thinking that embraces universal truths.[2]

The still figure at the center who is turning the Wheel is aware of the deep significance of simplicity and quiet in the face of continual turmoil. The ability to see value in what is small and to hold on to what is constant leads to genuine power and is the highest form of action. Aristotle taught that perfect action "does not spring from wisdom in general, nor even from the highest kind of wisdom; but, if at all, from a special practical wisdom, which is at bottom a knowledge of man."[3]

Many would argue that the business of life is to master this knowledge, whether one is a public administrator or not. Perhaps the reason the arts in general persist from century to century and generation to generation is because they fulfill a deep-seated need in us to understand ourselves and others. The painter's palette, the writer's ideas, the poet's words, the musicians' notes are meaningless in themselves. It is when they are in concert with one another that they inspire the unconscious mind of the viewer, the reader, the concertgoer. Stephen Kuder reminds us that the words of the poet John Donne can inspire leaders to climb the "cragged and steep" hill upon which truth stands, and grasp the essence of leadership that lies beyond rational thought.

When public administrators avail themselves of the wisdom the arts impart, they are more able to make connections between the actions that define what life is and the vision of what it can become.

BRIDGES TO AN ELEVATED MIND

Like the image standing slightly behind the central figure in the Wheel of Fortune, public administrators who have achieved self-knowledge are able to exercise restraint. They do not scramble for places of honor or engage in activity for the sole purpose of appearing busy and important. They are not easily provoked into reacting to trivial matters and can display an open and honest demeanor when relating to colleagues, politicians, and citizens. Their actions are measured, and they possess a certain grace under pressure. Aristotle might call such impressive public servants "magnanimous" or "ornaments of the virtues."[4]

The premise of our Theory Bridge is that public administrators can discover how to elevate their thinking so that they can see beyond the narrow confines of everyday occurrences and appreciate the essential meaning of their work. In this way, as Charles Goodsell states, the "art" of public administration can bring "intrinsic satisfaction." They have become aware of another level of functioning and are closer to one of the ideals we are promoting in this book, the public administrator as artisan. The increasing awareness that the arts can bring also allows for what Goodsell calls "the thrill of mastery."

We believe the satisfaction that comes from mastery of tasks is a natural yearning that inhabits every individual. This need can be fulfilled when a person is able to see the value and the beauty in all work, from the apparently important to the seemingly insignificant. If beauty contains elements of truth, as Murray states in Chapter 3, then distinctions often made between different tasks are illusory and ought to be abandoned. Such a view requires a reevaluation of how we perceive the work that is done in public agencies.

We propose that elevation of the minds of public administrators can begin with the development of an appreciation of artisanship within the field. Accompanying this shift in thinking might be an emphasis on the pursuit of the arts in general. We also propose that more attention be given to Eastern philosophy so that its ancient beliefs in intuitive values can be incorporated into the theoretical framework of our Western doctrines. Chapter 3 reminds us of the place of honor accorded the "finer pastimes" by both Confucius and Aristotle—a union of the best of Western and Eastern thinking.

A powerful example of the influence art can have on the public consciousness is provided by Howard McCurdy, who in Chapter 12 deals with the Policy Bridge. McCurdy reviews the early days of the conservation movement, when nineteenth-century landscape painters captured the magnificence of the American wilderness. The message contained in their paintings was so inspiring that it gave rise to a form of "spiritual nationalism." The public was so impressed with the innate beauty of the American wilderness that it vowed to protect the natural environment for generations to come.

Modern films provide a bridge that makes connections between the values citizens perceive and the actual values inherent in public bureaucracy. Marc Holzer and Linda Slater make the point that films exert a tremendous power over their audience, to the extent that reality is filtered by the lens of the camera. Morton Kroll argues that the "administrator-viewer" of a film who is able to integrate its cultural, social, and political nuances will experience an intellectual and emotional awakening. The values portrayed in this medium can influence, either positively or negatively, the way in which the average citizen and the public administrator view one another.

Elsie Adams and Frank Marini raise intriguing questions concerning bureaucratic theory and values that continue to challenge scholars in the field of public administration. Connections they make across the Theory and Values bridges challenge the reader to transcend negative images of bureaucratic functioning. They wisely suggest that we develop more ele-vated models of individual behavior and social organization, and cast aside our present flawed alternatives.

The reality that administrators create is, in part, dependent upon the way in which they perceive themselves and the events in which they are involved. If the arts in general and films in particular can be used as instruments that contribute to the perceptions and beliefs of individual human beings, then the vision they project holds substantial influence over the actions people take. The tendency, today, to replace vision with action can be overcome by an elevation of the minds of individual decision makers when they attend to the best that the arts can offer.

When public administrators experience the illumination and the inspi-ration that emanate from the visual arts, literature, or great music, they are close to the top of Donne's "huge hill" upon which truth stands. This elevation of mind initiates the transformation wherein action bows to vision.

BRIDGES TO ENRICHMENT

The Leadership Bridge moves to the forefront in Part IV of the book. Michael Carey brings to our attention some insightful ideas expressed by the poet Percy Bysshe Shelley and the religious leader John Henry New-man. Shelley argues that the purpose of art is to transform through enlightenment, while Newman prizes the enlargement of mind that results from a learning experience. Newman argues that truly educated individuals are able to move beyond the limits of self-interest and to develop a more centered way of perceiving the world and their role in it. The Wheel of Fortune can be used to interpret how individuals can alter their perceptions of both the world and themselves, and thus seek high-mindedness. Indi-viduals make a choice about whether they will position themselves on the rim or at the center of the Wheel. Opportunity for growth and higher consciousness is present at all positions represented in the Wheel of Fortune.

Those individuals of high consciousness who have chosen to serve the public through elected office or as political appointees are aware of the inherent dangers along the perimeter of the Wheel. They constantly remind themselves of the perils of ego gratification and of the fickle nature of the crown. They are, more than likely, familiar with the feelings expressed by Queen Elizabeth that Catherine Gira told us about: the crown is not as pleasing to wear as it is to see.

Career civil servants who have matured to a high level of consciousness are aware that the profession they have chosen does not lend itself to a scramble for the visible power that is attained at the top of the Wheel. They accept that their contribution lies in the exercise of subtle power as they assist in the actual turning of the Wheel. The self-delusion and self-isolation of Richard II, as related by Gira, inspires us by obverse example away from hollow individuals worshiping a hollow crown. The nature of much of the work of high-level career bureaucrats is such that they nonetheless run the risk of believing they are omnipotent. They, like elected officials, can yearn to ride the Wheel upward in fulfillment of unchecked ambition.

There is perhaps no more highly admired public official in American history than Abraham Lincoln. He stands as an example of good government for both elected politicians and career civil servants. Dalmas Nelson provides a moving tribute to the qualities of leadership that sustained Lincoln's presidency. Nelson attributes Lincoln's greatness, in part at least, to his ability to express political principles and personal values in language that illuminated issues and inspired the country. Nelson reminds us that Lincoln was able to reach the people directly by touching the human heart.

Qualities emanating from unassuming emotional and psychological postures are evident in the best of our public administrators. Unafraid to listen to their inner voices, these individuals can make decisions based on both rational thought and intuitive judgment. They are capable of suppressing their own egos in order to serve the broader interests of the public trust. They are cognizant of the long-lasting effects of their work and are aware that power accrues to them simply because of their grasp of policy issues, their understanding of governmental processes, and their ability to implement mandated legislation. They also recognize that elected officials depend upon the professional civil service to guide them in the making of public policy. Public administration, as the bedrock of good government, requires that practitioners be of the highest caliber society can produce.

This book attempts to use the arts as a means for developing higher levels of consciousness among public administrators so that more of them can benefit from inner enrichment. When individuals are inspired by a work of art, they experience both an emotional and a psychological uplift. It is in this process of growth that change occurs. Patricia Russell and Dillard Tinsley warn us of the turmoil that can follow when a leader fails to develop personal bonds with others. Had Captain Call seen the deeper implications of his one-sided obsessions, his life might have improved significantly.

This insight can provide an important lesson to newly elected politicians and their administrative appointees. The experience of power is often so intoxicating that appointees become compulsive about their actions and impose unreasonable demands upon themselves and others. Such a situation requires a high degree of maturity among those career public administrators charged with advising high officials. They must appear to be committed to the policies of the administration while simultaneously living a balanced life. This is difficult to accomplish when their private lives are not respected by the appointed officials to whom they report.

Elsie Adams, Frank Marini, and Darrell Pugh's chapter, concerning the Teaching Bridge, educates us about the role literature can play in the development of individuals by making the provocative observation that, through the vicarious experiences of literary characters, public administrators can learn and grow. They argue further that the difficult passage from blind acceptance of the familiar to fair and equitable treatment of everyone can be more easily traversed through the experience of literature. We recoil from the biased remarks and unfair treatment that are accorded Shylock and vow never to stereotype human beings.

When public administrators experience an enrichment of character, it is usually because of revelations from a higher order of reality. This kind of transformative experience can result from exposure to philosophy, religion, spirituality, or, as this book contends, the arts. When a person raises the level of his or her consciousness, the effect can be impressive because each of us exerts a powerful influence on others. The entire organization benefits as a consequence. Enrichment of character, like impoverishment of character, is never an isolated event affecting one person alone.

A NEW LOOK AT THEORETICAL CONNECTIONS

It is fitting at the conclusion of this book to return to the Theory Bridge in order to complete our appraisal of how the arts can be used to enrich the assumptions underlying the study of public administration. Through the stimulating lives of heroic characters and the resilience of the human spirit exemplified in literature, the study and practice of public administration are both illuminated and inspired. Goodsell mentions Ordway Tead's belief that public administration transcends its practical nature to embrace the attributes associated with a "fine art." He also refers to Kenneth Eble's argument that since administration is involved with the intricacies of fulfilling vision through people, it requires the wisdom of great art.

It is our view that public administration, as a field of study and practice, has attributes of both science and art. The technological needs of public administration are well recognized and, to a large extent, have been met. Considerable effort has been expended in developing theoretical foundations in the rationalist and technological aspects of public administration. Contributions to the field from theoretical constructs in the arts have been sketchy at best. We believe that the theoretical base of public administration should continue to build upon scientific assumptions. At the same time, we propose that the theoretical base needs to be broadened to include aesthetic assumptions as well.

Let us go back in time to see if we can enhance our understanding of the nature of public administration. If we can make the connection between its scientific and artistic aspects, we will better appreciate the call for new theoretical concepts. Since we are proposing a kind of rebirth in the field, the Renaissance seems a likely time period for us to visit.

We recall an event said to have occurred in the life of Leonardo da Vinci (1452–1519). This towering individual was, by all accounts, a man of diverse and considerable talents: painter, sculptor, architect, musician, mathematician, and writer. Most scholars would also attest to his stature as a scientist. Science, as Leonardo saw it, resulted from a combination of experience and reason. He is credited with the words "Remember, when discoursing with water, to address first experience and then reason." He was also, however, wise enough to realize that individual experience is an inadequate measure of reality. He consequently read voraciously in order to supplement his practical knowledge and achieve "experience by proxy."[5]

Leonardo was known for his tendency to jot down notes on matters he considered important. We can conclude from one of these notations that a heated argument once took place among humanists in the court of the duke of Milan. The dispute concerned the status of painting in the liberal arts. Some disputants, who tended to be writers rather than painters, believed that knowledge acquired by painters, coming as it does from experience, is merely mechanical. Conversely, they argued that knowledge acquired by writers, coming as it does from thought, is scientific. Inasmuch as the writers opined that the mechanical expression of direct experience was inferior to the written expression of thoughts present in the mind, they proposed to exclude painting from the liberal arts.[6]

Leonardo was incensed at what he considered to be the ignorance of the pro-writing contingent. He argued that just because painting requires keen observation and the development of manual skills rather than words to achieve its purpose, it should not be accorded inferior status as an art form. He accused the writers of failing to value experience emanating from the senses and of underestimating the importance of mechanical dexterity. To the charge that fields of knowledge founded upon experience must be considered mechanical because they require manual skill in order to be expressed, he responded: "All arts that pass through the hands of scribes are in the same position, for they are a kind of drawing which is a branch of painting."[7]

A comparison of how painters, writers, and public administrators obtain and use the knowledge they need to fulfill their purposes reveals an interesting connection between public administration and both of these art forms. Painters and public administrators alike have a need to achieve mastery in the practice of their respective crafts. To this end, both rely upon their senses to acquire the knowledge they need. Through sight, touch, and hearing, painters are able to capture, in their imaginations, the essence of a waterfall, and through their mechanical skills, transfer that experience to canvas. Likewise, through sight, touch, and hearing, hospital administrators are able to capture in their imaginations the essence of a superior health care facility, and through their mechanical skills transform that vision to reality.

Writers and public administrators alike acquire the knowledge they need to practice their crafts through mental activity. Both process what they have learned, in formal education and experience, through the creative processes of their minds. For example, writers spend substantial amounts of time in silent reflection before they are able to write. Likewise, commissioners and heads of governmental agencies deliberate long and hard over major policy or organizational changes and the ramifications of such steps.

We are suggesting that the arts can contribute to an enhancement of the administrative order for the good of all. We are not concerned about just making the field more interesting or having bureaucrats "feel good inside," although these can be welcome by-products. Our intent is to enrich administrative theory to allow bureaucrats to experience the human condition more deeply, so that they can experience administrative life more deeply.

The first line in Thomas Moore's 1992 book is relevant to our proposal: "The great malady of the twentieth century, implicated in all our troubles and affecting us individually and socially, is 'loss of soul.' "[8] Public administrators, as the professional guardians of the national administrative trust, deserve guidance on the very personal journey toward regaining their souls. When the boundaries of administrative theory are expanded to include the arts, individuals will be free to see the spark of the artist that resides in each of them. Just as Moore regards the arts as a principal medium in which to perform personal "soul work," so by means of the arts public administrators have an opportunity to contemplate their souls—allowing vision to accompany action once again.

A THIRD NORM

We are committed in this book, and in our academic lives in general, to promoting a belief in the basic practicality of public administration. Those values of the field instrumental to achievement of higher policy ends, such as efficiency, economy, dependability, and effectiveness, have been given due attention by academics and practitioners. Moralistic values of the field, such as those which prescribe lawful, ethical, equitable, responsive, and participative behavior, are increasingly addressed in the academic literature and seriously discussed within the practitioner community.

We are not promoting the arts for the purpose of improving these two categories of administrative norm, as crucial as they may be.[9] Our purpose in compiling this book and suggesting a broadening of the theoretical base of the field is, rather, to increase awareness of a third category of administrative norm, qualitative enrichment of the experiences of bureaucrats as administrative actors and as participants in administrative life. This "quality of administrative life" issue in its deepest sense has been largely ignored by students, scholars, and practitioners in public administration.

Further, we are committed to the proposition that the current tendency of the arts to tear down public administration as a profession can be reversed. The arts can act as a constructive vehicle, not only for enriching the lives and work of public administrators by means of our bridges but also for elevating the perception of the general public toward government work so that the "huge hill" of truth concerning the rather impressive attainments of American public administration can be surmounted.

Unlike instrumental and moralistic reforms of the public sector, whose purposes are firmly anchored in the external society's demands, the arts can connect with values integrally associated with the administrative experience itself. We distinguish between two levels of public administration here. The most fundamental level is that of individual administrators whose internal voices must be heard so that they can lead more enriched lives, both as private persons and as persons working in an official capacity. This "soul work" is accomplished by such steps as imparting a sense of artisanship and by adapting the concept of the Tao to their daily work lives. The consequence is a more genuinely experienced professional life.

The arts also possess the potential to infuse administrators with a deeper understanding of the social bureaucratic world in which they work. This connection carries them to a more profoundly experienced professional life. Through inspiration, the arts can provide administrators with intuitive knowledge in performing as leaders. It allows them to relate more fully to fellow employees, people they serve, and the broader community and polity in whose administrative activities all citizens, including themselves, participate. The arts can enrich these collectivities by exciting the public imagination to redefine the public interest in areas of ongoing policy concern and to enter into new joint ventures of idealism and enterprise. The arts, by sensitizing the old and socializing the young to the mores of the democratic administrative experience, help the entire society discern a more illuminated and inspired reality.

NOTES

1. See on this point Ronald Berman, *Twentieth Century Interpretations of Henry V: A Collection of Critical Essays* (Englewood Cliffs, N.J.: Prentice-Hall, 1968), 9, 10.

2. Note James K. Feibelman, *Understanding Oriental Philosophy* (New York: Horizon Press, 1976), 148–49.

3. John Leofric Stocks, *Aristotelianism* (New York: Cooper Square Publishers, 1963), 97.

4. Ibid., 94–95.

5. Will Durant, *The Story of Civilization: Part V, The Renaissance* (New York: Simon and Schuster, 1953), 221–22.

6. *Main Currents of Western Thought*, ed. Franklin Le Van Baumer (New Haven: Yale University Press, 1978), 139.

7. Ibid.

8. Thomas Moore, *Care of the Soul* (New York: HarperCollins, 1992), vi.

9. Exhibiting art in an office may enhance employee morale, for example, and having welfare clients stage street theater could stimulate greater citizen participation.

Selected Bibliography

Bennis, Warren. *On Becoming a Leader*. Reading, Mass.: Addison-Wesley, 1989.

Brueggemann, Walter. *The Prophetic Imagination*. Philadelphia: Fortress, 1978.

Burns, James MacGregor. *Leadership*. New York: Harper, 1978.

Eble, Kenneth E. *The Art of Administration*. San Francisco: Jossey-Bass, 1978.

Egger, Rowland. "The Administrative Novel," *American Political Science Review* 53 (June 1959): 448–55.

Eliade, Mircea. *Images and Symbols: Studies in Religious Symbolism*. New York: Sheed and Ward, 1969.

Friedsam, H. J. "Bureaucrats as Heroes." *Social Forces* 32 (March 1954): 269–74.

Frye, Northrop. *The Educated Imagination*. Bloomington: Indiana University Press, 1964.

Gotshalk, D. W. *Art and the Social Order*. New York: Dover, 1962.

Holzer, Marc, Kenneth Morris, and William Ludwin, eds. *Literature in Bureaucracy: Readings in Administrative Fiction*. Wayne, N.J.: Avery Publishing Group, 1979.

Kegan, Robert. *The Evolving Self: Problem and Process in Human Development*. Cambridge, Mass.: Harvard University Press, 1982.

Kroll, Morton. "Administrative Fiction and Credibility." *Public Administration Review* 25 (March 1965): 80–84.

McCurdy, Howard E. "Fiction, Phenomenology, and Public Administration." *Public Administration Review* 33 (January–February 1973): 52–60.

————. "How Novelists View Public Administration." In *A Centennial History of the American Administrative State*, ed. Ralph C. Chandler. New York: Free Press, 1987.

McDaniel, Thomas R. "The Search for the 'Administrative Novel.'" *Public Administration Review* 38 (November–December 1978): 545–49.

Marini, Frank. "Literature and Public Administration Ethics." *American Review of Public Administration* 22 (June 1992): 111–25.

Okakura, Kakuzo. *The Book of Tea*. Rutland, Vt: Charles E. Tuttle, 1956.

Rawson, Philip S., and Laszlo Legeza. *Tao: The Eastern Philosophy of Time and Change*. New York: Avon Books, 1973.

Santayana, George. *The Sense of Beauty*. New York: Charles Scribner and Sons, 1896.

Smullyan, Raymond M. *The Tao Is Silent*. New York: Harper & Row, 1977.

Tead, Ordway. *The Art of Administration*. New York: McGraw-Hill, 1951.

Vaill, Peter B. *Managing as a Performing Art*. San Francisco: Jossey-Bass, 1989.

Waldo, Dwight. *Perspectives on Administration*. University, Ala.: University of Alabama Press, 1956.

————. *The Novelist on Organization and Administration: An Inquiry into the Relationship Between Two Worlds*. Berkeley: University of California Press, 1968.

Wamsley, Gary L., Robert N. Bacher, Charles T. Goodsell, Philip S. Kronenberg, John A. Rohr, Camilla M. Stivers, Orion F. White, and James F. Wolf. *Refounding Public Administration*. Newbury Park, Calif.: Sage, 1990.

Wolfe, Humbert. "Some Public Servants in Fiction." *Public Administration* 2 (January 1924): 39–57.

Index

About the Editors and Contributors

ELSIE B. ADAMS is professor of English and comparative literature at San Diego State University. A specialist in late nineteenth-century British literature, she has published extensively on Bernard Shaw, Israel Zangwill, and other British writers. She coedited *Up Against the Wall, Mother . . . : On Women's Liberation* (1971).

MICHAEL R. CAREY is executive assistant to the president and associate professor of organizational leadership at Gonzaga University in Spokane, Washington. He directed Gonzaga's Organizational Leadership Program from 1987 to 1994. Besides teaching in the areas of leadership and organization theory, Dr. Carey has been a consultant for many educational, manufacturing, health care, and service organizations.

CATHERINE R. GIRA is president of Frostburg State University in Frostburg, Maryland. Prior to assuming this position in 1991, she served for nine years as provost at the University of Baltimore. Dr. Gira has been a professor of English for many years and has published widely on Shakespeare, Renaissance art and literature, and issues of higher education.

CHARLES T. GOODSELL is professor at the Center for Public Administration and Policy, Virginia Polytechnic Institute and State University, Blacksburg, Virginia. He is author of *The Case for Bureaucracy*, now in its third edition. In addition to public administration, Dr. Goodsell has published in the areas of political economy, comparative administration, and the social meanings of public architecture.

MARC HOLZER is professor of public administration at the Newark campus of Rutgers, the State University of New Jersey. He also serves as chair of the Section on Humanistic, Artistic and Reflective Expression (SHARE) of the American Society for Public Administration. In addition, Dr. Holzer is editor in chief of *Public Voices*, a new journal that publishes original fiction, reflective essays, and artistic commentary relevant to bureaucracy.

MORTON KROLL is professor emeritus of political science and public affairs at the University of Washington in Seattle. For many years he also served as university ombudsman. Dr. Kroll chaired the King County Arts Commission and served on the board of several Seattle arts organizations.

STEPHEN R. KUDER is associate professor of religious studies at Gonzaga University in Spokane, Washington. He teaches a course, "Leadership and Imagination," to students in a Master of Arts program in organizational leadership. A member of the Jesuit order for thirty-four years, Father Kuder holds a master's degree in English from Boston College and a doctorate in religion and literature from the Graduate Theological Union in Berkeley, California.

FRANK MARINI is professor of public administration and urban studies, as well as of political science, at the University of Akron in Ohio. For many years he also served as provost of this institution. Previously Dr. Marini taught at Syracuse University and directed public administration programs at the Maxwell School of Citizenship and Public Affairs. A founder of the "new public administration" movement, he edited the 1971 volume *Toward A New Public Administration: The Minnowbrook Perspective*.

HOWARD E. McCURDY is professor of public affairs at the American University in Washington, D.C. A specialist in public administration and science policy, Dr. McCurdy is author of *Inside NASA* (Baltimore: The Johns Hopkins University Press. 1993), a book on the organizational culture of the U.S. space program. He is author of a number of publications on the role of fiction in public administration, including the first text to use works of fiction as case studies.

NANCY MURRAY is associate professor in the Department of Public Administration at Pace University in White Plains, New York. She received a Ph.D. in public administration from New York University in 1986. At Pace, Dr. Murray organized a conference, held in 1991, on administrative leadership and liberal learning that attracted thinkers from throughout the country and became the origin of this book. She is currently preparing a book that relates ideas from Eastern philosophy to public administration.

DALMAS H. NELSON is professor of political science at the University of Utah, having taught there since 1975. He is author of *Administrative Agencies of the U.S.A.: Their Decisions and Authority* (1964) and coeditor of *Essays in Law and Politics by Francis Dunham Wormuth* (1978) and *Toward A Humanistic Science of Politics: Essays in Honor of Francis Dunham Wormuth* (1983). His publications also include several journal articles related to administrative law and human resource management.

DARRELL L. PUGH is professor of public administration and urban studies at San Diego State University. His research interests include the history of American public administration, and he is author of the definitive history of the American Society for Public Administration, *Looking Back, Moving Forward* (Washington: ASPA, 1988). Also concerned with professionalism in the public service, Dr. Pugh recently edited a volume of the *International Journal of Public Administration* on this topic.

PATRICIA R. RUSSELL is professor of English at Stephen F. Austin State University in Nacogdoches, Texas. She is also chair of the Department of English and Philosophy at Stephen F. Austin. Dr. Russell specializes in the literature of the English Renaissance and in literature for children, and has published in both of those areas. She conducts teacher workshops in children's literature and coaches writing for the Academic Pentathlon in Nacogdoches.

LINDA G. SLATER earned the master's degree in public administration from Rutgers University. She has put her academic training to good use as recycling coordinator and solid waste administrator for Charleston County in South Carolina, a position she has held since 1991. Ms. Slater held similar administrative posts at the county and municipal levels in New Jersey.

DILLARD B. TINSLEY is professor in the Department of Management and Marketing at Stephen F. Austin State University in Nacogdoches, Texas. He has published more than fifty articles on marketing, entrepreneurship, and small business management, in liberal arts journals as well as management publications. Dr. Tinsley served on the editorial review board for the *Journal of Small Business Management* and was a 1979 Mitchell Prize laureate.

Springer

Berlin
Heidelberg
New York
Barcelona
Budapest
Hong Kong
London
Milan
Paris
Santa Clara
Singapore
Tokyo